Babies and Young Children

Book 1   Development 0–7

Marian Beaver
Jo Brewster
Pauline Jones
Anne Keene
Sally Neaum
Jill Tallack

Basford Hall College, Nottingham

Stanley Thornes (Publishers) Ltd

First published in 1994 by
Stanley Thornes (Publishers) Ltd
Ellenborough House
Wellington Street
Cheltenham
Glos. GL50 1YW

96 97 98 99 00 / 10 9 8 7 6 5 4 3

A catalogue record for this book is available from The British Library.

ISBN 0 7487 1785 4

Typeset by GCS
Printed and bound in Great Britain at The Bath Press, Avon.

CONTENTS

Key features of the book

Acknowledgements

KEY FEATURES OF THE BOOK

This book is divided into chapters covering the physical development, cognitive and language development and emotional and social development of children aged 0-7 years. The book is divided into chapters to make it easy to read. It is important to realise that children's actual development cannot be divided up in this way. All the areas of development dealt with in this book are interdependent.

Each chapter begins with a list of the information that you can find in that chapter.

Throughout the book there are exercises for you to do. They are headed *Check*, *Think* or *Do*.

Check: these sections contain questions for you to answer. The answers will be found in the chapter that you have just read.

Think: these sections contain questions and tasks which ask you to think carefully about what you have read and to apply your knowledge to different situations.

Do: these sections contain practical tasks for you to do.

When you do these exercises make sure that you keep a record of the work. It may be useful for evidence of underpinning knowledge for NVQ qualifications.

There is a list of key words at the end of each chapter. You need to know what they mean. Where you are unsure of their meaning you need to go back through the chapter and find out.

ACKNOWLEDGEMENTS

The authors and publishers would like to thank the following people and organisations for permission to reproduce photographs and other material.

Dr S Lingam for the chart on page 83
Royston Westgarth/BDA (page 198)
Guardian Newspapers Ltd (page 232)
Mrs Jean Reed (page 237)
Maggie Murray/Format for the cover photograph.

Every attempt has been made to contact copyright holders and we apologise if any have been overlooked.

SECTION 1
Physical development

PHYSICAL GROWTH

Physical growth

Physical growth is the increase in size which takes place as the child develops.

The adult human is composed of many cells, but begins life as a single cell, the fertilised egg. The fertilised egg then divides into two cells then into four, eight, sixteen and so on. This process of cell division is the basis for human growth.

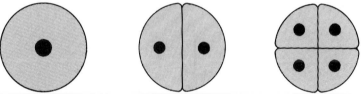

One cell divides into two...   the two cells divide again...   and so on

At first the new cells are smaller than the original parent cell but they soon grow to full size. For this to happen they must have food to provide the material for growth. Eventually these cells will turn into different types of cell; for example some cells will become muscle cells, some brain cells, some nerve cells. The process by which cells become specialised like this is called *differentiation* and it plays a vital part in forming the adult human.

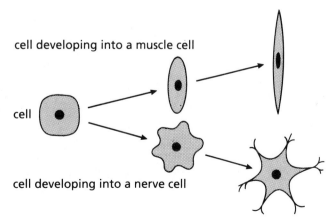

cell developing into a muscle cell

cell

cell developing into a nerve cell

In a growing child cell division takes place in all parts of the body and the child gets steadily larger. Some parts of the body grow more quickly than others. This process alters the proportions of the body as the child gets bigger. The head grows quickly in the early stages of development and then slows down, whereas the legs and arms grow slowly at first and speed up later.

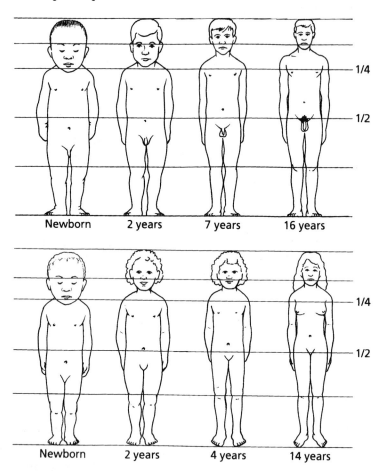

Changing body proportions

The growth of different parts of the body at different rates is closely linked to development:
- the head grows quickly in fetal life because the brain is developing rapidly
- the neck lengthens and strengthens after birth to support the head and enable it to turn; this takes place as the baby develops the ability to see things further away
- the chest becomes broader and stronger as the lungs develop and the child becomes more active in sitting and standing
- the arms lengthen and the hands increase in size and strength as the child develops the ability to manipulate objects
- the legs and feet increase in size and strength as the need to balance, walk, run, jump, and climb develops.

THE HEAD

The growth of the head is affected by the structures within it, such as the eyes, teeth, nose, sinuses and brain. As the head grows the baby chubbiness disappears and the face lengthens to give a more angular appearance. These changes are also linked with the ability to chew food and develop speech.

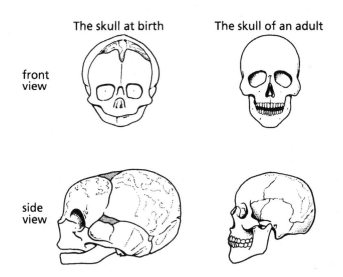

The developing skull

THE HANDS

The hands at birth are chubby and the bones in the ends of the fingers are tiny seeds of cartilage. As the bones grow harder and lengthen, the layer of protective fat disappears and the hands develop more strength for lifting and manipulating objects.

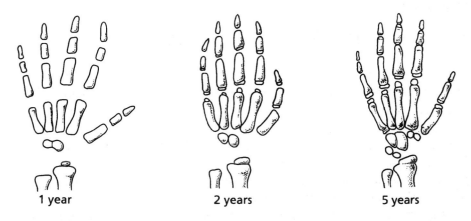

The developing bones of the hand

Bone development

The skeleton provides the body with:
- support, for example, the neck supports the head
- protection, for example, the skull protects the brain.

Bone development begins in fetal life when some of the body cells specialise and form bone cells. There are different types of bones:
- long bones, for example the bones of the legs and arms
- flat bones, for example the bones of the skull
- irregular bones, for example the bones of the spine
- sesamoid bones, for example the bones of the kneecap.

Developed bones are hard and strong so that they can do the job of supporting the body and protecting its organs. Bones begin, however, as softer materials:
- cartilage from which bone cells form long bones
- membrane from which bone cells form flat bones.

In fetal life much of the skeleton is composed of cartilage and membrane. The process of changing from the soft cartilage and membrane to the hard bone is called *ossification*.

LONG BONES

The long bones of growing children are made up of cartilage and ossified (hardened) bone. This because the cartilage part of the bone can grow, while the ossified part gives the bone its strength. Ossification is a very gradual process and takes 18 to 20 years to complete.

Long bones begin in fetal life as a rod of cartilage

Centres of ossification appear in the middle and each end of the long bone

As the long bones grow, the area of ossified bone increases, leaving a narrow neck of cartilage at each end of the bone, allowing continued growth

A fully ossified bone when growth is completed, by 18–20 years; a fully ossified bone will not grow any more

FLAT BONES

The bones of the baby's skull are flat bones; the bones are made up of membrane, cartilage and ossified bone. The brain grows very rapidly while the baby is developing before birth. To enable this to happen there are gaps between the bones of the skull called *fontanelles* The fontanelles also allow the shape of the baby's head to alter during labour (this is called *moulding*) so that the birth of the head is easier. There are two fontanelles which you need to know:

- the *anterior* fontanelle, at the front of the head
- the *posterior* fontanelle, at the back of the head.

Both fontanelles are covered by tough membrane which protects the brain. The anterior fontanelle is quite noticeable at birth but gradually becomes smaller as the bones of the skull grow together and ossification takes place. It is usually closed by the time the baby is 18 months old. The posterior fontanelle is much smaller and closes up soon after birth.

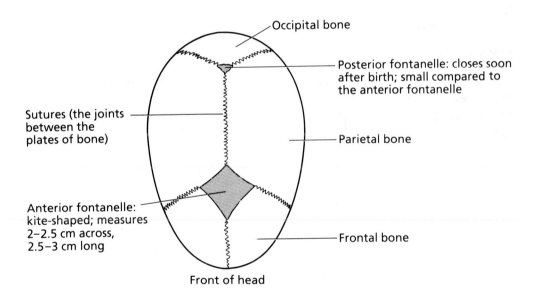

The top of the head of a newborn baby

Now you know that children's bones are not fully ossified there are important things to remember when you are caring for them.

- Handle babies and small children carefully. Support a small baby's head and support babies when they are learning to sit and walk.
- Remember that as the bones ossify they will gradually grow strong enough to take the baby's full weight.
- Make sure that shoes and clothes allow room for fingers, toes and limbs to grow and move; the cartilage part of the bone is soft and will easily be deformed by poorly fitting socks, shoes and clothes.

- Provide children with a diet which will support bone growth.
- See that children have the opportunity to take suitable exercise and have adequate rest.

These points are vital if the bones are to grow properly.

CHECK!

Check your knowledge by doing this exercise on body proportions and bone growth.
1 What proportion of the newborn's total length is the head?
2 What proportion of the total length of the adult is taken up by the legs?
3 Why does this change in proportions happen?
4 What is the process of the hardening of the bones called?
5 What is the essential function of cartilage?
6 What is the essential function of hardened bone?
7 By what age are the long bones fully hardened?

Measuring physical growth

CENTILE CHARTS

Physical growth in children can be measured in different ways. It is important to remember that there can be a wide variation in measurements and that such variations are quite normal. Average measurements are often useful as they provide a guide for assessors when measuring children. The best way to record a child's growth is to use a *centile* (or *percentile*) *chart*. More information and the advantages of using centile charts in all areas of child development will be found in Chapter 5. In the area of physical development there are centile charts for:
- weight
- height
- head circumference.

Study the charts below and the explanation which follows to make sure that you know how to interpret the information centile charts provide.

The following explanation refers to the top chart on page 7, for girls. The bold line marked 50 represents the average measurements. Other dotted lines show a range of measurements above and below the average.

For example, the dotted line marked 97 (the 97th centile) shows weights of girls who are heaviest within their age group. If a girl aged 6 months weighs 9 kg her weight will be plotted on the dotted line marked 97. This means that 97 per cent of girls will weigh less than she does and 3 per cent will weigh more.

The dotted line marked 3 (the 3rd centile) shows the weights of girls who are lightest in their age group. If a girl aged 6 months weighs 6 kg then her weight will be plotted on the dotted line marked 3. This means that 97 per cent of girls will weigh more than she does and 3 per cent will weigh less.

Recording a child's measurements regularly on the correct centile chart will produce

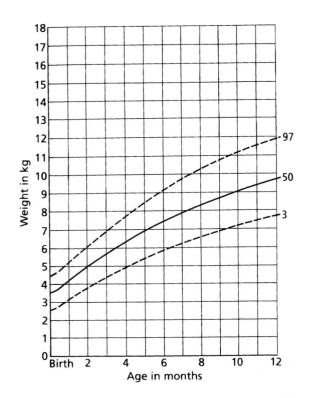

A centile chart for weighing girls

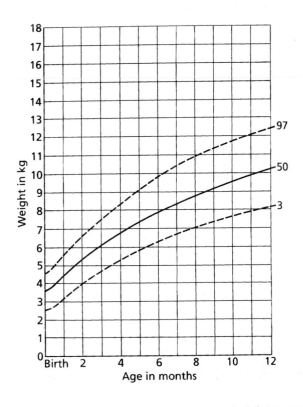

A centile chart for weighing boys

a new line on the chart. The new line will show the progress of this particular child.

CHECK!

1 What measurements can be recorded on a centile chart?
2 Which centile lines on the charts represent average measurements?
3 Are there different charts for girls and boys?
4 If you plot the weight of a child and it falls on the 97th centile, what is the relationship of this child's weight to other children of the same age and sex?

THINK!

Why is using a centile chart to record measurements more valuable than making a list of those measurements?

DO!

1 You now know that there are centile charts for recording weight, height and head circumference. There are also separate charts for girls and boys. Use the centile charts to find out the average weights of a) a girl and b) a boy at:
   i) birth
   ii) 5 months
   iii) 12 months.
2 Look at this list of weights. They are for a girl:
   birth weight   3.5 kg
   1 month   4.0 kg
   2 months   4.5 kg
   4 months   5.0 kg
   6 months   6.0 kg.
   The weights are increasing. Now plot them onto the correct centile chart. Note your results and say what you think is happening to the child's weight.
3 Use centile charts to record the measurements of a child you are studying over a period of time. You can link this task with the child study in Chapter 3, page 50.

Factors affecting physical growth

Children are individuals and the way they grow will vary. There are many influences on the way in which a child grows, but these factors can be broadly divided into three main groups:

■ *antenatal* factors: occurring before birth

- *perinatal* factors: occurring during the birth (discussed in Chapter 6)
- *postnatal* factors: occurring after the birth.

The following information provides a summary of antenatal and postnatal factors. A more detailed discussion of these will be found with perinatal factors in Chapter 6.

ANTENATAL FACTORS

The following factors can all have a profound influence on the growth of the unborn baby. The harmful influence of many of them can be minimised by good preconceptual and antenatal care.

Heredity

A child inherits genes from both parents and these will decide, for example, the maximum height to which a child will grow and the shape and size of the body. A more detailed explanation of heredity is given in Chapter 6, *Factors affecting physical development*.

Multiple pregnancies

Two or more babies growing in the uterus at the same time may mean that one or more will be lighter than the average birth weight. Modern diagnosis with ultrasound scan will enable twin or multiple pregnancies to be discovered much earlier. This means that with careful management of the pregnancy the babies will have a much better chance of growing well in the uterus.

Illness of the mother

Women who are known to have a medical condition such as, for example, diabetes will need extra care and careful monitoring during their pregnancy, as such a condition may affect the growth of the fetus (the unborn baby). Illnesses in pregnancy may mean that the mother's diet is not sufficient to sustain fetal growth. Good care at this time will enable early detection of illness, and the adverse effects on the fetus of the mother's illness or a medical condition can be kept to a minimum and the mother can experience a normal pregnancy.

Diet in pregnancy

The growth of the fetus is closely linked to the amount and quality of the food the mother is eating. There are many reasons why diet during pregnancy may be deficient. Good antenatal care will provide women with the information which will help them to understand how important a good quality diet is to the growth of the fetus. Good food can be expensive and people on low incomes may find providing a high quality diet difficult. They may need extra help and advice from their midwife or health visitor.

Smoking in pregnancy

Smoking in pregnancy by the mother or those around her slows down the growth of the fetus. Giving up smoking is strongly encouraged. If at all possible this decision should be made by both partners before they decide to conceive.

POSTNATAL FACTORS

Diet

The right amount of food containing the correct nutrients is essential for growth. Breast milk will provide all the right nutrients for the growing baby. Once a baby is weaned onto solid food, a good diet will enable satisfactory growth and muscle development to take place. Adults need to provide, and encourage children to select and eat, a healthy balanced diet. Poverty or famine will mean that food is in short supply or is not supplying the right balance of nutrients. This will restrict normal healthy growth.

Exercise

Exercise helps muscle and bone development. The adult needs to provide safe opportunities for the child to take suitable exercise. It is important to make sure that the exercise takes account of the child's stage of bone development (see *Bone development*, page 4). Children who cannot exercise by themselves because they are ill, or have restricted movement because of a disability, will need an adult carer to help them exercise their bodies. *Physiotherapists* are the professionals who will help the adult to understand how to do this effectively.

Illness

Severe illness may slow the rate of growth but this is usually temporary and children soon catch up.

Smoking

Smoking in a child's environment may slow the rate of growth.

Hormones

Hormones are chemicals made by the endocrine glands: the testes, ovaries and pituitary glands produce hormones which influence growth. Hormones affect the body shape. As puberty approaches the sex hormones cause the typical feminine and masculine outlines to develop.

Seasons

Growth is faster in the spring, slower in the autumn.

Environment

Our environment is our total surroundings. Growth depends on the provision of a healthy hygienic environment, but it also depends on the child feeling secure, loved and wanted. For more detail on the influence of the environment, see Chapter 10, *Introduction to social and emotional development*.

Variations in growth rate

Growth is a continuous process, but there are spurts in the rate of growth. Growth is individual and is controlled by genetic information. Children will achieve different heights, weights and proportions as they move towards maturity. Growth and physical development are very closely linked. As children grow, develop their bones and muscles and learn to balance and co-ordinate their bodies, they will move through the stages of acquiring physical skills. They will do this at their own pace. A baby of 3 months will not be able to sit or walk because the bones and muscles are not sufficiently developed to support the weight of the body – the proportions of the body are still top heavy and the legs need to grow longer and stronger to take the child's full weight. Physical skills, like sitting and standing, will not be achieved until the body reaches the stage in growth required to support the skill.

Key terms
You need to know what these words and phrases mean. Go back through the chapter to find out.

Differentiation	Moulding
Cartilage	Percentile
Ossification	Percentile chart
Fontanelle	Centile

2 DEVELOPMENT FROM CONCEPTION TO BIRTH

This chapter includes:
- **The male and female reproductive organs**
- **The menstrual cycle**
- **Conception**
- **Implantation**
- **Fetal growth and development**
- **The importance of preconceptual and antenatal care.**

The male and female reproductive organs

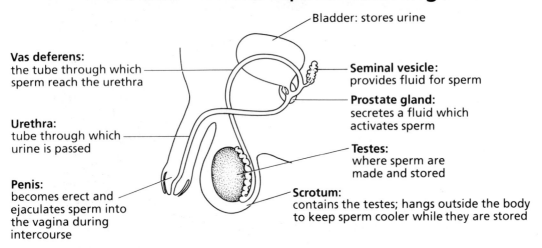

Bladder: stores urine

Vas deferens: the tube through which sperm reach the urethra

Seminal vesicle: provides fluid for sperm

Prostate gland: secretes a fluid which activates sperm

Urethra: tube through which urine is passed

Testes: where sperm are made and stored

Penis: becomes erect and ejaculates sperm into the vagina during intercourse

Scrotum: contains the testes; hangs outside the body to keep sperm cooler while they are stored

The male reproductive organs

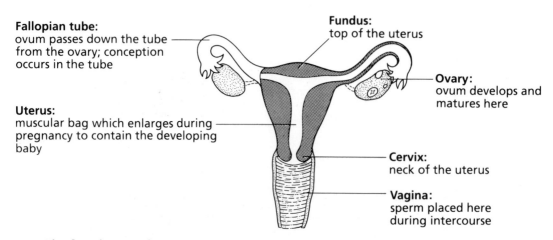

Fallopian tube: ovum passes down the tube from the ovary; conception occurs in the tube

Fundus: top of the uterus

Ovary: ovum develops and matures here

Uterus: muscular bag which enlarges during pregnancy to contain the developing baby

Cervix: neck of the uterus

Vagina: sperm placed here during intercourse

The female reproductive organs

The menstrual cycle

The menstrual cycle concerns the production of a ripe ovum by the ovary and the preparation of the uterus to receive it. If the ovum is fertilised after it has been released from the ovary then conception takes place. The menstrual cycle usually takes about 28 days to complete, but this will vary from woman to woman. The menstrual cycle is controlled by two *hormones* (chemical messengers) called *oestrogen* and *progesterone* which are produced by the ovary. The first part of the cycle (*proliferation*) is stimulated by oestrogen: the *endometrium* (the lining of the womb) is reconstructed. The second part of the cycle (*secretion*) is stimulated by progesterone and the endometrium becomes thickened and highly vascularised (supplied with blood vessels) in order to nourish the fertilised ovum. In the premenstrual phase (*regression*) the endometrium stops growing 5–6 days before menstruation.

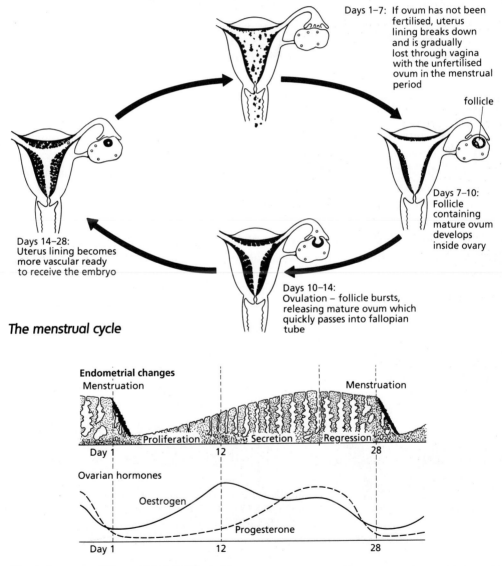

Days 1–7: If ovum has not been fertilised, uterus lining breaks down and is gradually lost through vagina with the unfertilised ovum in the menstrual period

follicle

Days 7–10: Follicle containing mature ovum develops inside ovary

Days 14–28: Uterus lining becomes more vascular ready to receive the embryo

Days 10–14: Ovulation – follicle bursts, releasing mature ovum which quickly passes into fallopian tube

The menstrual cycle

Endometrial changes
Menstruation
Menstruation
Proliferation
Secretion
Regression
Day 1
12
28

Ovarian hormones
Oestrogen
Progesterone
Day 1
12
28

The influence of the ovarian hormones

Conception

At around day 12 of the menstrual cycle a woman's ovaries release one ripe *ovum* (egg). The ovum quickly passes into the fallopian tube. During intercourse mature sperm from the male are deposited at the *cervix* (the neck of the womb) in the female. The sperm are contained in a fluid called *semen*. If intercourse takes place around the time the ovum is released the first active sperm to reach the ovum in the fallopian tube will penetrate the outer shell and fertilise the ovum. *Conception* will have taken place. As soon as this happens the outer shell of the ovum becomes resistant to any other sperm so that only one sperm is allowed to fertilise the ovum. When the ovum and sperm unite at fertilisation, genetic information from both partners combines to create a new individual (see Chapter 6, *Factors affecting physical development*). The fertilised ovum immediately begins to divide, first into two cells then into four. It continues to divide in this way as it passes down the fallopian tube to arrive in the uterus. The uterus lining has been preparing to receive it. The ball of cells settles into the uterine lining. This is called implantation and happens at around day 21 of the menstrual cycle.

Implantation

Once it has implanted into the lining of the uterus the fertilised ovum continues to divide and develop. The number of cells increases and an *embryo* forms. Besides producing the embryo the fertilised ovum also gives rise to the placenta (afterbirth), umbilical cord and amnion (the membranes which make the sac which contains the developing baby). These structures are developed for the support of the baby and they leave the uterus with the baby at birth.

- The developing baby until eight weeks after conception is called the *embryo*.
- The developing baby from eight weeks after conception until the birth is called the *fetus*.

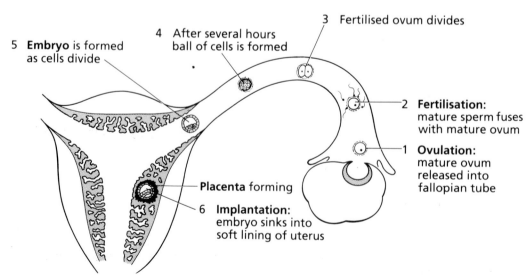

The stages leading to implantation

THE PLACENTA

The life support system of the embryo and the fetus is the placenta. The placenta has finger like projections called *villi*. The villi fit closely into the uterine wall. The placenta is joined to the embryo by the umbilical cord. Inside the cord is an artery and a vein. The artery takes the blood supply from the embryo into the placenta and the vein returns the blood to the embryo.

In the placenta are capillaries filled with the embryo's blood. In the wall of the uterus are large spaces filled with the mother's blood. The embryo's blood and the mother's blood do not mix. They are separated by the wall of the placenta, but they are brought very close together. The wall of the placenta is very thin. This allows oxygen and nutrients to pass from the mother to the fetus and waste products to be passed back to the mother for disposal.

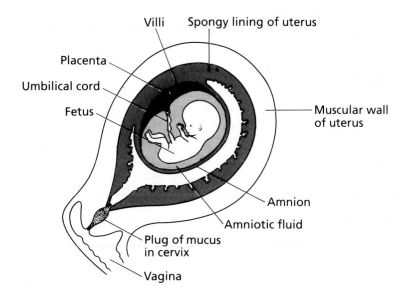

The developing embryo/fetus

CHECK!

1 Give the name of the narrow opening between the uterus and the vagina.
2 Where is the prostate gland?
3 Explain how ovulation occurs.
4 Where are sperm made?
5 What is semen?
6 Which two hormones are produced by the ovary?
7 Where does fertilisation take place?
8 What is the term used to describe the developing baby until eight weeks after conception?
9 What is the term used to describe the developing baby from eight weeks after conception until birth?

Fetal growth and development

The growth and development of the embryo and fetus take place over the 40 weeks of pregnancy. The time table of growth and development for all babies follows the same pattern. Any harmful influences during this time can result in abnormalities in growth or development. These are antenatal factors affecting growth and development and are explained in detail in Chapter 6, *Factors affecting physical development*.

4–5 WEEKS AFTER CONCEPTION

Five weeks after conception is when most pregnant women are beginning to think that they are pregnant. Yet already the nervous system in the embryo is beginning to develop. Cells fold up to make a hollow tube. This is called the neural tube. It will become the baby's brain and spinal cord, so the tube has a head end and a tail end. At the same time the heart is forming and the embryo already has some of its own blood vessels. A string of these blood vessels connect the mother and the embryo and will become the umbilical cord.

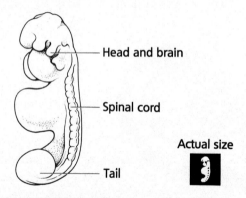

The embryo 5 weeks after conception

6–7 WEEKS AFTER CONCEPTION

The heart is beginning to beat and can be seen beating on an ultrasound scan. Small swellings called limb buds show where the arms and legs are growing. At seven weeks the embryo is about 8 mm long.

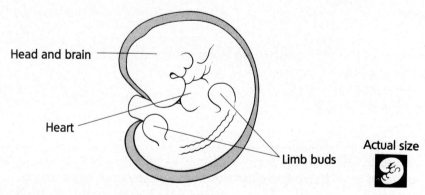

The embryo 6–7 weeks after conception

8–9 WEEKS AFTER CONCEPTION

The developing baby is now called the fetus. The face is slowly forming. The eyes are more obvious and there is a mouth with a tongue. The major internal organs (the heart, brain, lungs, kidneys, liver and intestines) are all developing. At nine weeks the fetus is about 17 mm long from head to bottom.

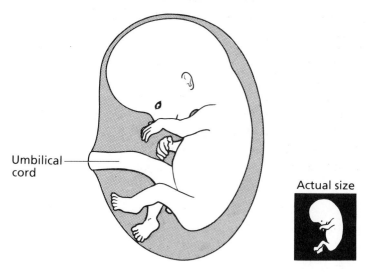

Umbilical cord

Actual size

The fetus 8–9 weeks after conception

10–14 WEEKS AFTER CONCEPTION

Twelve weeks after conception the fetus is fully formed. From now on it has to grow and mature. The fetus is already moving but the movements cannot be felt by the mother. By about 14 weeks the heart beat is very strong and can be heard using an ultrasound detector. The heart rate is very fast – about 140 beats per minute. At 14 weeks the fetus is about 56 mm long from head to bottom.

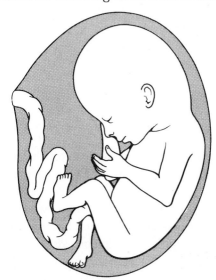

The fetus 10–14 weeks after conception

15–22 WEEKS AFTER CONCEPTION

The fetus is now growing quickly. The body has grown bigger so that the head and body are more in proportion. The face looks much more human and the hair is beginning to grow as well as the eyebrows and eyelashes. Fingers and toenails are now growing. The lines on the skin are now formed and the fetus has its own finger prints. At about 22 weeks the fetus becomes covered in fine downy hair called *lanugo*. At about 18–22 weeks movements are first felt by the mother. If this is a second baby movements are often felt earlier, at about 14–16 weeks after conception. At 22 weeks the fetus is about 160 mm long from head to bottom.

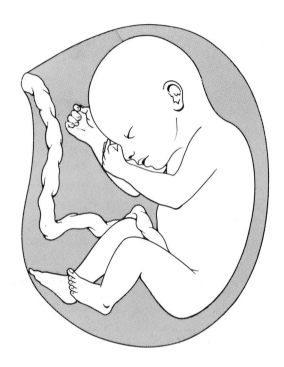

The fetus 15–22 weeks after conception

23–30 WEEKS AFTER CONCEPTION

The fetus is now able to move around and responds to touch and sound. The mother may be aware that the fetus has its own times for being quiet and being active.

The fetus is covered in a white creamy substance called *vernix*, which is thought to protect the skin as the fetus floats in the amniotic fluid. At about 26 weeks the eyes open. At 28 weeks the fetus is viable, which means that it is now thought to have a good chance of surviving if born. Many babies born before 28 weeks do survive, but often have problems with their breathing. Specialised care in special care baby units (SCBU) helps more babies born early to survive. At 30 weeks the fetus is about 240 mm long from head to bottom.

31–40 WEEKS AFTER CONCEPTION

During the last few weeks the fetus grows and puts on weight. The skin which was quite wrinkled is now smoother and the vernix and lanugo begin to disappear. It is important that the fetus moves into the head-down position, which is the safest position for the birth. The fetus at 31–40 weeks is illustrated overleaf.

The importance of preconceptual and antenatal care

The health of the mother and that of the developing fetus are very closely linked. To give the fetus the best chance of developing and growing normally a good system of antenatal care is needed. Preconceptual advice and care may also be available.

PRECONCEPTUAL CARE

Preconception is the term used to describe the time between a couple deciding they would like to have a baby and when the baby is conceived. This is the time when future parents can make sure they are in the best of health so that their child has the greatest chance of growing and developing normally. In some places it may be possible to attend preconceptual clinics for help and advice. These clinics may be part of the local maternity services or part of the general practitioner service.

ANTENATAL CARE

Throughout pregnancy regular check-ups at hospital, antenatal clinic, by a general practitioner or a combination of these carers, will make sure that the mother and the developing fetus are both fit and well. The health of the mother can be maintained or improved. Checks can be made on the growth and development of the fetus and any problems, large or small, can be identified early. Pregnancy and delivery can be planned by the parents to suit their needs. The prime aim of antenatal care is to help the mother successfully deliver a live healthy infant.

CHECK!

1 What will the neural tube eventually become?
2 Name the fluid in which the fetus floats.
3 How long is the fetus at nine weeks?
4 When is the fetus fully formed?
5 What is lanugo?
6 When does the mother first feel the fetus move?
7 When does the fetus respond to sound?
8 What is vernix?
9 When do the eyes of the fetus open?
10 What is the best position for the fetus to be in ready for the birth?

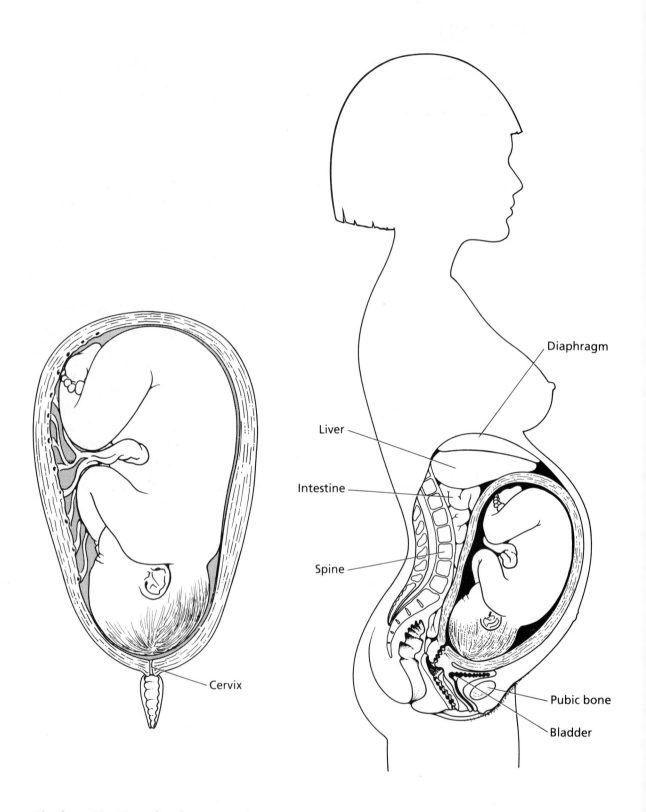

Diaphragm

Liver

Intestine

Spine

Pubic bone

Bladder

Cervix

The fetus 31–40 weeks after conception

THINK!

1 Try to think of all the things, positive and negative, that might affect the baby during pregnancy.
2 Think of things that the parents need to be aware of to make sure that their baby has a good chance of growing and developing well.

DO!

1 Write about a page on the development of the young human up to birth. Include the following words in your account: embryo, fetus, differentiate, uterus, implantation.
2 Try to watch a video about fetal development; there are many to choose from. Ask your tutor or health visitor for advice about this.

Key terms
You need to know what these words and phrases mean. Go back through the chapter and find out.

Oestrogen	Implantation
Progesterone	Embryo
Vascular	Fetus
Menstrual cycle	Villi
Ovum	Preconceptual care
Sperm	Antenatal care
Conception	Viable

3 PHYSICAL DEVELOPMENT

> **This chapter includes:**
> - An introduction to physical (gross and fine motor) development
> - Physical development (1) from birth to 18 months; (2) from 2 to 7 years of age.

An introduction to physical development

Physical means anything to do with the body and can be used in a wide range of contexts, from how people look physically to how they move physically.

Development means a change in performance and is usually associated with progression, becoming more complicated or skilful. It could also be defined as an increase in complexity.

With these two definitions you can see that the phrase *physical development* means the way that the body increases in skill and becomes more complex in its performance. This will involve movement. The progress of muscular movement is called *motor development*.

DEVELOPMENTAL NORMS

There is a recognised pattern of physical development which it is expected that children will follow. These are known as the developmental *norms*. *Norm* should not be confused with *normal*, a word which is not encouraged when describing physical development because there is such a wide range of *normal* (i.e. acceptable or satisfactory) development. It is dangerous to assume that children are *abnormal* if they do not all progress in exactly the same manner. Variations will always exist, since each child is an individual developing in their own unique way.

A likely expectation is that babies will be mobile (rolling, crawling, creeping, bottom-shuffling or walking) by the time they reach their first birthday – but a baby may have been concentrating on acquiring fine motor, social or language skills and may have advanced beyond the average in one or more of these developmental areas. In gross motor development she may not have progressed beyond sitting, but has been absorbing huge amounts of information from the world around her. Examining only her lack of mobility could make the examiner assume that her development was delayed, but the overall picture is of a child who has not yet seen the need for mobility but can do many other things in advance of her age.

Nevertheless, knowledge of these patterns of expected development does help us to look at the child as a whole, and to measure their progress as an individual and as a member of the human species.

HUMAN ATTRIBUTES

The human animal, (we are all animals) has several biological attributes, different from most other animals, which make it easy to separate the different areas of development:

- the ability to stand on two legs and walk, which leaves the hands free for more complicated tasks
- the use of the hands and flexible fingers in co-ordination with the eyes
- possession of a spoken language, and the ability to translate non-verbal messages, allowing communication between people
- the evolution of complicated social structures for the benefit and protection of all individuals.

The first two characteristics are relevant to the study of physical development because they concern movement, so it is necessary to look at them separately and in more detail.

GROSS MOTOR SKILLS

The ability of the human animal to use two legs and walk involves the whole body. These whole body movements are described as *gross motor* skills. Sometimes they are

Crawling

Sitting from lying down

Bear-walking

Walking with two hands held

Walking with one hand held

Walking alone

Example of gross motor skills involved in the development of walking

referred to as *posture and large movements*. These terms have the same meaning and cover the stages a child goes through in developing control of the body:

- learning to support the head
- rolling over
- sitting
- crawling
- pulling to stand
- walking
- running
- climbing the stairs
- hopping
- playing football
- skipping
- riding a tricycle and a bicycle
- standing on one leg
- swimming
- climbing.

There are many more examples of gross motor skills; they all require strength, stamina and suppleness to increase co-ordination, balance and judgement.

FINE MOTOR SKILLS

The second human characteristic is the use of the hands in co-ordination with the eyes. This allows human beings to perform very delicate procedures with their fingers, with the eyes influencing the precise movements of the fingers.

These manipulative aspects of physical development are called *fine motor* skills, and include aspects of vision and fine and delicate movements.

The role of those who monitor the physical development of children is to know whether a child can easily perform a certain skill or whether it is a new skill for them and they require further practice.

CHECK!

1 What does *motor development* mean?
2 Why should you beware of using the word 'normal' in describing development ?
3 What are the four characteristics which make humans different from most other animals?

THINK!

1 Think of all the things you have used your hands for today.
2 Think of the different movements involved in a simple physical activity such as climbing the stairs.

Finger play

Attempting to grasp objects

Holding and
exploring objects

Palmar grasp using
whole hand

More delicate palmar grasp
involving the thumb

Primitive pincer grasp

Exploring with the
index finger

Delicate/mature
pincer grasp

Development of manipulation

DO!

Try to do up some buttons, eat your lunch, fit shapes in a shape-sorter, thread a needle, tie up shoelaces with your eyes shut or with a blindfold on. You will realise how important this hand/eye co-ordination is. Watch a child using fine motor skills, for example a baby using a spoon, a child tying a shoelace or any other activity requiring hand/eye co-ordination. Look for concentration, perseverance, frustration. How can you help them in this area of development?

Physical development (1) from birth to 18 months

TERMINOLOGY USED IN STUDYING PHYSICAL DEVELOPMENT

The following terms are in common use in assessing physical development and it is important that you are familiar with them and understand what they mean.

- Prone: lying face down
- Supine: lying on the back
- Ventral suspension: held in the air, face down
- Head lag: the head falls back when pulled to sit
- Reflex: involuntary response to a stimulus
- Neonate: a newborn baby
- Stimulus: something that arouses a reaction
- Posture: position of parts of the body
- Symmetrical: balanced movements both sides of body
- Asymmetrical: jerky, unco-ordinated movements

NEONATE

The newborn baby in the first month of life is often called the *neonate,* which means 'newly born'. New babies have an attitude of *flexion,* which means that they are curled up, with arms and legs bent inwards towards the body. They will maintain this fetal position (the position they were in inside the womb), but will gradually extend (straighten) the arms and legs. A baby which was in the breech position may lie with the legs straight up, one each side of the face, if this was the position in the womb.

Descriptions of the typical postures of neonates are given below.

Prone

- The baby lies with the head turned to one side-resting on the cheek.
- The body is in a frog-like posture with the bottom up and the knees curled up under the tummy.

- The arms are bent at the elbows and tucked under the chest with fists clenched.

Supine

- The baby lies with the head to one side.
- The knees are bent towards the body, with the soles of the feet touching.
- The arms are bent inwards towards the body.
- Jerky, random kicking movements can be seen.

Ventral suspension

- The head and the legs fall below the level of the back, so the baby makes a complete downwards curve.

Sitting

- When the baby is pulled upwards into a sitting position there is complete head lag. The head falls backwards as the body comes up and then flops forwards onto the chest.
- If the baby is held in a sitting position, the back is completely curved and the head is on the chest.

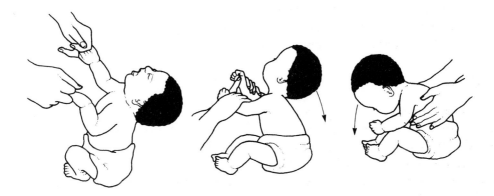

Fine motor skills

- The fists are clenched
- The baby can focus 15–25 cm and stares at brightly coloured mobiles within visual range.
- The baby concentrates on the carer's face when feeding.

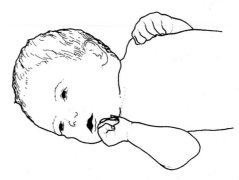

Primitive reflexes

A reflex is an automatic, involuntary movement made in response to a specific stimulus. Testing the presence of reflexes in babies, children and adults can help doctors to assess the health of the central nervous system. Everyone should have a range of 'protective reflexes', like blinking, coughing and sneezing, but new babies have a range of other survival reflexes, called the *primitive reflexes*, which are only present during the first few months of life, after which they are replaced by actions which the baby chooses to do – voluntary actions. The primitive reflexes are a reminder of how the human race has evolved over millions of years.

The presence or absence of these reflexes in a new baby can measure the maturity of the baby. For instance a baby born prematurely may not have developed full reflex action, but examination should only be performed by a qualified doctor, midwife or health visitor who is trained in this area.

If these reflexes continue for longer than the first few months of life it can mean that the child has some form of developmental delay and should be examined by a paediatrician. The best time to observe and test these reflexes is when the baby is awake but not hungry. A crying baby who is hungry, uncomfortable or unhappy or a baby who is tired or drowsy will not perform well.

Reflex	Stimulus	Response
Rooting	Brushing the cheek with a finger or nipple	The baby turns to the side of stimulus
Sucking	Placing nipple or teat into the mouth	The baby sucks
Grasping	Placing object into baby's palm	The fingers close tightly around the object

Primitive reflexes *continued opposite*

Primitive reflexes *continued*

Reflex	Stimulus	Response
Placing	Brushing top of foot against table top	The baby lifts its foot and places it on a hard surface
Walking	Held standing, feet touching a hard surface	The baby moves its legs forward alternately and walks
Moro (startle)	Insecure handling or sudden loud noise	The baby throws head and the fingers fan out; the arms then return to the embrace posture and the baby cries

1 MONTH

Gross motor development

Prone

- The baby lies with its head to one side but can now lift its head to change position.
- The legs are bent, no longer tucked under the body.
- The arms are bent away from the body, the hands usually closed.

Supine

- The head is on one side.
- The arm and leg on the side the head is facing will stretch out.
- Both arms may be bent, with legs bent at the knees, the soles of the feet facing each other.

Ventral suspension

- The head is on the same level as the back and the legs are coming up towards the level of the back.

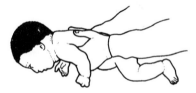

Sitting

- If the baby is pulled to sit the head will lag, falling backwards, but will remain steady for a moment as sitting position is achieved, then it will bob forwards again.

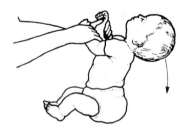
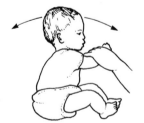

- The back is a complete curve when the baby is held in sitting position.
  Note The head should be supported at all times.

Fine motor development

- The baby turns its head towards the light and stares at bright shiny objects.

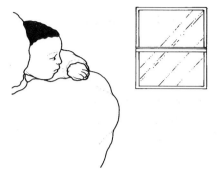

- The baby is fascinated by bright shiny objects and follows moving objects within 5–10 cm from the face.

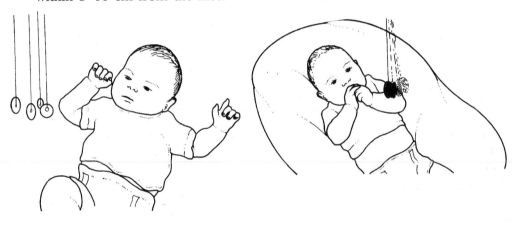

- The baby gazes attentively at carer's face whilst being fed, spoken to or during any caring routines.

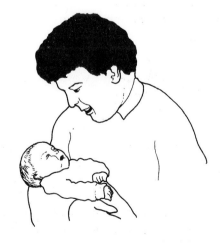

- The hands are usually closed. All the primitive reflexes are still present.

3 MONTHS

Gross motor development

Prone

- The baby can now lift up the head and chest supported on the elbows, forearms and hands.

- The baby may scratch at the floor and bob head in a rocking movement.

- The bottom is flat now, with the legs straighter and kicking alternately.

Supine

- The baby usually lies with the head in a central position.

- There are smooth, continuous movements of the arms and legs.
- The legs can kick strongly, sometimes alternating and sometimes together.

- The baby waves the arms and brings hands together over the body.

Ventral suspension
- The head is now held up above the level of the back, and the legs are also on the same level.

Sitting
- When the baby is pulled to sit the head should come forwards steadily with the back.

- The head may fall forwards after a short time in the sitting position.
- There should be little or no head lag.

- When held in a sitting position the back should be straight, except for a curve in the base of the spine – the lumbar region.

Standing
- The baby will sag at the knees when held in a standing position.
- The placing and walking reflexes should have disappeared.

Fine motor development

- The baby is now very alert and aware of what is going on around.

- The baby moves its head to look around, and follows adult movements.

- Finger-play – the baby has discovered its hands and moves them around in front of its face, watching the movements and the patterns they make in the light.

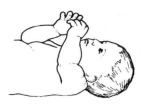

- The baby holds a rattle or similar object for a short time if placed in the hand. Frequently hits itself in the face before dropping it!

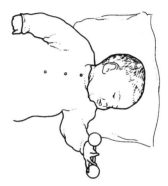

- The baby recognises the bottle or the breast and waves the arms around in excitement.

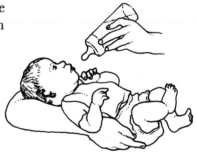

6 MONTHS

Gross motor development

Prone
- The baby can now lift the head and chest well clear of the floor by supporting on outstretched arms. The hands are flat on the floor.

- The baby can roll over from front to back.

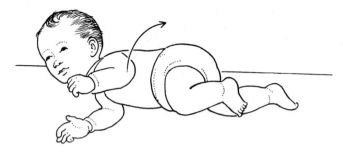

- She may pull the knees up in an attempt to crawl, but will slide backwards.

Supine
- The baby will lift her head to look at her feet.

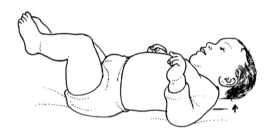

- She may lift her arms, requesting to be lifted.

- She may lift up her legs, grasp one or both and attempt to put them in her mouth, often successfully.

- She will kick strongly, enjoying the exercise.
- She may roll over from back to front.

Sitting

■ If pulled to sit the baby can now grab the adult's hands and pull herself into a sitting position; the head is now fully controlled with strong neck muscles.

■ She can sit for long periods with support, the back is straight.

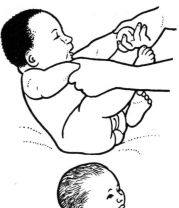

■ She may sit for short periods without support, but will topple over easily. She cannot yet put an arm out to break the fall.

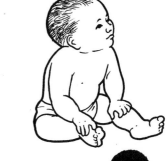

Standing

■ If the baby is held standing she will enjoy weight bearing and bouncing up and down.

■ The baby may also demonstrate the downward parachute reflex: when held in the air and whooshed down feet first, the legs will straighten and separate and the toes will fan out.

Fine motor development

■ The baby is bright and alert, looking around constantly to absorb all the visual information on offer.

- She is fascinated by small toys within reaching distance, grabbing them with the whole hand, using a palmar grasp.

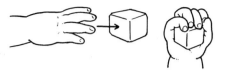

- She transfers toys from hand to hand.

- She puts them in the mouth to explore them.

- If a toy is dropped the baby will watch where it falls, if it is within sight.
- If a toy falls out of sight the baby does not look for it. At this age the world ends where she can see it!

9 MONTHS

Gross motor development

Prone
- The baby may be able to support his body on knees and outstretched arms.
- He may rock backwards and forwards and try to crawl.
- Moving backwards in the crawling position precipitates forward movement.

Supine
- The baby rolls from back to front and may crawl away, roll around the floor or squirm on his back.

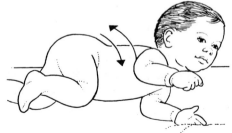

Sitting

- The baby is now a secure and stable sitter — he may sit unsupported for 15 minutes or more.

- He can keep his balance when turning to reach toys from the side.

- He leans forward to retrieve toys, returning to an upright sitting position.

- He puts out his arm(s) to prevent falling.

- Some babies may begin to bottom-shuffle, moving around the floor in the upright, sitting position using the legs to propel them.

Standing

- The baby can pull himself to a standing position, supporting first on the knees.
- When supported by an adult he will step forward on alternate feet.
- He supports his body in the standing position by holding on to a firm object.
- He may begin to side-step around furniture.

- He cannot yet lower himself to the floor and falls backwards onto his bottom.
- He may begin to crawl upstairs but cannot get down safely.

- The forward parachute reflex: when the baby is held firmly during a controlled forwards fall (head first), the arms will shoot out and straighten and the fingers will fan out.

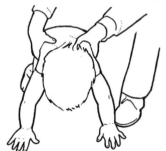

Fine motor development

- Visually alert and curious, the baby is exploring objects before picking them up.
- He grasps objects, usually with one hand, inspects with the eyes and transfers to the other hand.

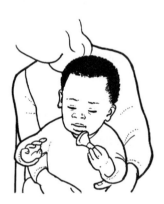

- He may hold one object in each hand and bang them together.

- He uses the index finger to poke and point; this finger starts to straighten and play a greater role.

- He uses the inferior pincer grasp with index finger and thumb.

- He drops objects or bangs them onto a hard surface to release them – he cannot let go voluntarily yet.

- He looks for fallen objects out of sight – he is now beginning to realise that they have not disappeared forever.

12 MONTHS

Gross motor development

Sitting
- The baby can sit alone indefinitely.

- She can get into sitting position from lying down.

Standing
- The baby pulls herself to stand and walks around the furniture.
- She can return to sitting without falling.
- She may stand alone for a short period.

Mobility

- The baby is now mobile by crawling, bottom-shuffling, bear walking, walking alone or with one or both hands held.
- She may crawl upstairs forwards and downstairs backwards.

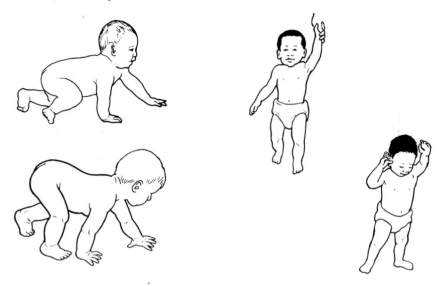

Fine motor development

- The baby looks for objects hidden and out of sight.

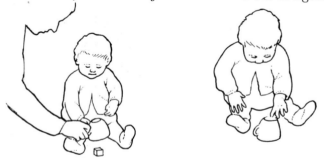

- She uses a mature pincer grasp and releases objects.

- She throws toys deliberately and watches their fall.

- She points at desired objects, and may show a preference for one hand.

- The primitive tripod grasp is used: the thumb and first two fingers.

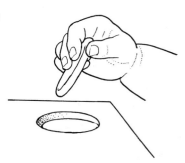

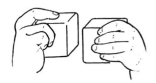

- She bangs cubes together.

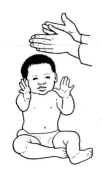

- She recognises familiar people up to 10 metres away.
- She likes to look at picture books and points at familiar objects, for example cup, ball, teddy.
- She claps hands together in delight and in play.

15 MONTHS

Gross motor development

- The baby walks alone, feet wide apart with arms raised to keep balance.

- He can sit from standing by falling backwards onto the bottom or forwards onto the arms.
- He falls easily, sometimes after just a few paces, and usually on stopping; he cannot avoid obstacles on the floor.
- He gets to standing without help from people or furniture.

- He kneels without support.

- He may climb forwards into a small chair and turn to sit.

Fine motor development

- The baby enjoys playing with small bricks.
- He builds a two-brick tower.

- He holds a crayon in a palmar grasp, scribbles backwards and forwards over the paper.
- He uses either hand but shows a preference for one.

- He enjoys brightly coloured picture books and turns several pages at once.

- He points at familiar objects in the book and pats the page.
- He uses the index finger constantly to demand drinks, food and toys out of reach.
- He often stares out of the window for long periods watching and pointing at the activities outside with interest.

- He can hold a spoon but puts it in the mouth upside down.

18 MONTHS

Gross motor development

- The baby walks confidently now, without using the arms for balance and is able to stop without falling.
- She may carry large toys.

- He runs but often falls as he is unable to co-ordinate movements to get around objects in the way.

- She likes pushing a brick trolley or similar wheeled toy.

- She walks upstairs with hand(s) held.
- She comes downstairs safely, either forwards on the bottom (one step at a time) or backwards crawling or sliding on the tummy.

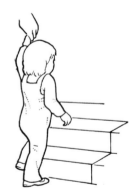

- She may walk downstairs with a hand held or holding onto the rail.

■ She squats to the floor to pick up toys.

■ She climbs into an adult-sized chair forwards and then turns round to sit down.

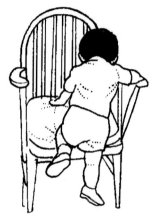

■ She tries to kick a ball, often with success.

Fine motor development

■ The baby can now use a delicate, refined pincer grasp to put small objects through small spaces.

- The tripod grasp of crayon and pencil (using the thumb and two fingers in adult fashion) is developing.
- She scribbles on paper to and fro and with random dots.

- She builds a tower of three cubes, and sometimes more.
- She tries to thread large beads and sometimes succeeds.

- She continues to enjoy picture books and points at known objects.

CHECK!

1 What is the posture of a neonate in prone and supine ?
2 What does ventral suspension mean ?
3 What is the position of the baby in ventral suspension at
   a) birth
   b) 1 month
   c) 3 months of age?
4 What is a reflex ?
5 Describe the reflex, stimulus and response of six primitive reflexes.
6 Why are these reflexes important in assessing development ?
7 What are three major elements of gross motor development at 3 months ?

8 Describe the process of head control in the first six months of life.
9 When should the baby have developed a palmar grasp?
10 What physical skills would you expect to see in a baby aged 6 months ?
11 When should the pincer grasp be present and when could it be described as mature ?
12 What aspects of gross and fine motor development are seen at 9 months of age ?
13 When should a baby be mobile ?
14 Note five elements of physical skills at 12 months of age.
15 By what age should the primitive reflexes have faded?

THINK!

1 Look at a catalogue from any major toy retailer. Examine ten different items designed for use with young babies. Consider the following points:
   a) how they stimulate development
   b) which areas of development they would encourage
   c) whether you agree with the claims made for each item in the advertising material
   d) whether babies would be able to use them effectively
   e) whether they would keep the baby's interests for long, either now or in the future.
   f) which toys you would recommend to new parents; you must be able to give reasons for your choices.
2 Think of six activities to encourage gross motor skills from 6 to 12 months of age. Remember the variations in development between these ages.
3 Think of six activities to develop fine motor skills between 12 to 18 months of age. Think carefully about why you have chosen these activities and whether they are the most suitable for this age group.

DO!

1 Write an account of physical development at 15 months.
   How would you encourage a child to progress and achieve the skills usually seen at 2 years of age?

2 Make an article to stimulate fine motor development for a child in the first year of life. Remember that all areas of development are interlinked and that children learn a great deal through sensory experience, i.e. sight, touch, taste, sound.

Remember also that this article must be attractive to a baby and should excite and encourage sensory areas. It must be strong enough to withstand vigorous activity and be safe for a young baby to play with.

Write a report including your overall aims and objectives – why you chose a particular item and how it would encourage development. Also include planning details, designs, diagrams, and so on and how you made the object.

3 Observe a baby using the article and assess (honestly and critically) how useful it is. Did you achieve your aims and objectives? Should any aspect of the item be adapted or changed to make it safer, more stimulating or more attractive ?

4 Child development study

Completing a series of observations of a specific child will:

- increase your knowledge of child development
- heighten your awareness of variations in 'normal' development
- enable you to make accurate recordings of child development
- encourage your understanding of the factors which influence development.

Find a family with a baby aged 6 months or under, who will allow you to visit them at regular intervals (preferably monthly), at a mutually convenient time. Plan to make eight visits.

Explain to the family the purpose of the study and assure them that confidentiality will be maintained.

Begin with a short history of the baby, including birth details and development since birth. Include some family details, for example brothers, sisters, position in the family, etc. Do not record names or addresses.

Make eight observations of the baby at monthly intervals. These observations should include all aspects of physical development. Ask the parents about any achievements since your last visit, as you may not see the baby demonstrate everything he is capable of at each visit.

Evaluate every observation by:

a) recording what you have seen the baby do and comparing this with what is expected at that age

b) comparing what the baby is doing at this visit with what he was capable of last time.

Include some ideas of how to help the baby extend his development.

Complete a development and weight chart to display the results of your research and compare this child's growth and development with what you have learnt about the developmental norms. Write an evaluation of your findings.

Choose one area of development to describe in detail to cover the first two years of life. Include references to your observed child. Aim to write 750–1000 words.

5 a) Look at these pictures of babies at two developmental stages. Try to assess the ages of the babies in group A and those in B.

Group A

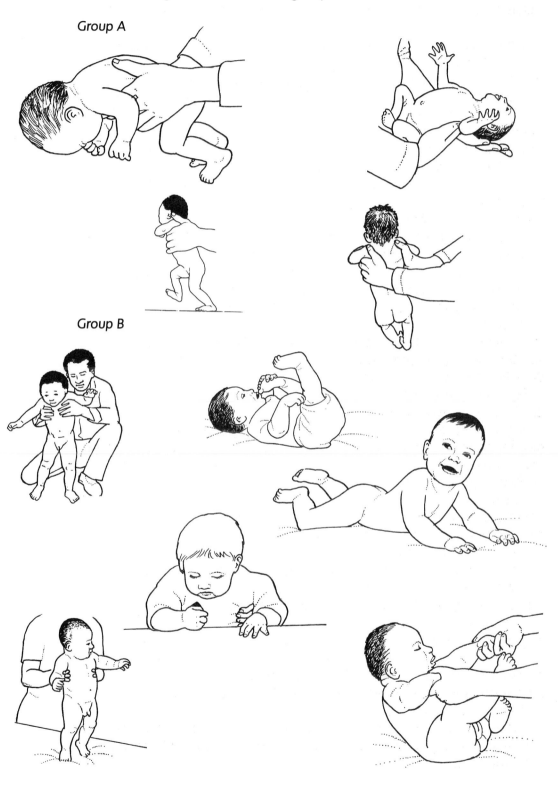

Group B

b) Do the same to assess the ages of the babies in C and D.

Group C

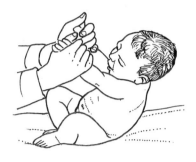
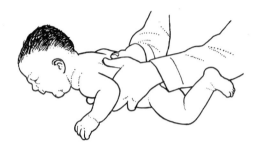

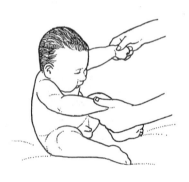
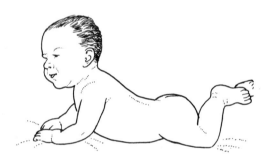

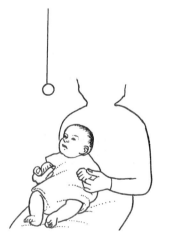

Group D

c) It is possible to see clearly the progression in development in areas of gross and fine motor skills. How would you expect a baby in C to proceed in:
   i) gross motor development?
   ii) fine motor development?
d) How would you expect a baby in D to proceed in:
   i) gross motor development?
   ii) fine motor development?

6 Look at the pictures of young children and give the approximate age by which each skill shown should have been accomplished.

a)

b)

c)

Looks for objects hidden and out of of sight

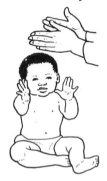

d) Claps hands in play

e) Holds crayon in palmar grasp and scribbles backwards and forwards

f) May carry large toy

g) Enjoys picture books and points at familiar objects

h) Pushes and pulls wheeled toy

i) Climbs into adult-sized chair

j) Builds tower of 3 bricks or cubes

k) Squats to pick up fallen toy

l) Walks up and down stairs with a hand held

7 a) How old is the baby in each of the following illustrations?

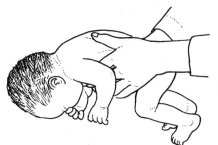

b) Prone

a) Ventral suspension

c) Supine

d) Prone

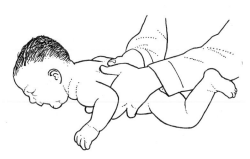

e) Ventral suspension

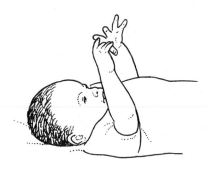

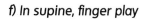

f) In supine, finger play

g) Prone, arms extended

h) In supine, lifts leg and grasps foot

b) Study the following diagrams which show the progress of gross motor skills at various stages. Label them and put them in the correct sequence.

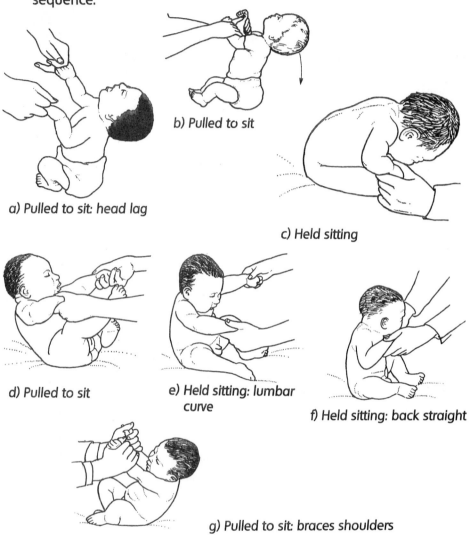

a) Pulled to sit: head lag

b) Pulled to sit

c) Held sitting

d) Pulled to sit

e) Held sitting: lumbar curve

f) Held sitting: back straight

g) Pulled to sit: braces shoulders

c) How old is the baby in the following illustrations?

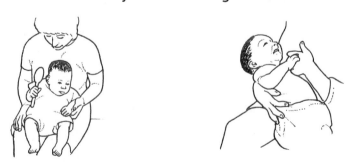

This work can all be included in a portfolio of evidence for National Vocational Qualifications.

Physical development (2) from 2 to 7 years

2 YEARS

At two years children are very mobile, and love exploring their surroundings. They enjoy pulling things apart, fitting things together, pushing in, pulling out, filling and emptying. At two years children will still often test by touch and taste.

Gross motor development

- The child runs safely.
- He stops and starts easily.

- He squats down steadily to play with or pick up a toy, and gets up again without using the hands.
- He pushes and pulls large wheeled toys; can pull along a small wheeled toy by the string and goes in the right direction.
- He can climb up onto the furniture, usually to reach something or to see out of the window.
- She is beginning to show awareness of how she relates to other objects (spatial awareness).
- She walks up and down the stairs holding on; she puts two feet on every step.

- She tries to kick a ball but usually walks into it.

- He rides a small tricycle by pushing it along with the feet; he does not use the pedals.

Fine motor development
- The child usually uses a preferred hand to hold a pencil; she draws circles, lines and dots.

- He can use a fine pincer grasp to pick up and put down tiny things.
- She can use a fine pincer grasp with both hands to do complicated tasks like peeling a satsuma.

- He carefully builds a tower of six or seven bricks.

- He likes picture books, enjoys recognising things in favourite pictures. He now turns the pages one at a time.

- She can match miniature toys on request.

3 YEARS

At three years children's motor skills are developing well. They walk and run well, managing stairs easily. Their hand/eye co-ordination is good and they can draw recognisable copies of simple shapes.

Gross motor development
- The child can stand and walk on tiptoe.
- He walks forwards, sideways and backwards.

■ She can kick a ball hard.

■ She walks upstairs with one foot on each step, down with two feet on each step.
■ She is now well aware of own size in relation to things around her.

■ She rides a tricycle using the pedals.

Fine motor development

- The child now builds a tower of nine or ten bricks.

- She can cut with scissors.

- She enjoys painting with a large brush.
- She may know colours
- She matches two or three primary colours.
- She controls a pencil in the preferred hand between the thumb and first two fingers.
- She will copy a circle.

- She can thread large wooden beads onto a large shoelace.

4 YEARS

At four years children have developed good muscle control which helps with energetic climbing, jumping, hopping and tricycle riding. They are also becoming good at tasks needing careful hand/eye control.

Gross motor development

- The child can stand, walk and run on tiptoe.

- Keeping the legs straight, he can bend at the waist to pick up things from the floor.

- He climbs trees, ladders, play equipment.

- She walks or runs both up stairs and down stairs putting one foot on each step.
- He can catch, kick, throw and bounce a ball and hit it with a bat.
- Rides a tricycle well, able to make sharp turns.

Fine motor development
- The child is able to build a tower of ten or more bricks.

- He can build three steps with six bricks, after being shown how.

- She threads smaller beads than at 3 years.

- He grasps a pencil maturely and has good control; he draws a person on request, showing head, legs and trunk.
- He can match and name four primary colours.

5 YEARS

At five years children cope with most daily personal duties and are ready for the wider world of school. They can play all kinds of ball games requiring gross motor skills and games needing appropriate placing of objects. Fine skills are well co-ordinated with control in writing and drawing.

Gross motor development
- The child moves rhythmically to music.

■ He can walk along a thin line, climb, dig and use slides and swings.

■ She plays a variety of ball games quite well.

■ He can hop and run lightly on the toes.

Fine motor development

- The child builds three to four steps with bricks from a model.

- There is good control of pencils and paint-brushes.

- She can draw a person with head, trunk, legs and eyes, nose, mouth.
- She matches 10 to 12 colours and names four or more primary colours.
- She may be able to thread a large needle and sew stitches.

6 YEARS

At six years the children have developed agility and strength. Writing is accomplished mainly by movements of the fingers and wrist.

Gross motor development
- The child can make a vertical jump of about 10 centimetres.

- He kicks a football a distance of three to six metres.
- He makes a running jump of approximately 100 centimetres.

- He rides a two-wheeled bicycle.

Fine motor development

- The child can carefully align cubes to build a virtually straight tower.

- He can catch a ball with one hand thrown from one metre.

- He grasps and adjusts the pencil as at 5 years.
- The writing hold is similar to that of an adult.
- Writing is confined to a small area of the paper.
- He draws recognisable pictures.

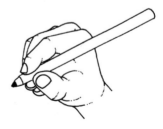

7 YEARS

At seven years children's physical progress is consistently improving; they can balance and climb the apparatus with ease. They like to read and watch television and love drawing and other tasks requiring hand and eye co-ordination.

Gross motor development

- The child can now ride a two-wheeled bicycle expertly.
- He hops easily, keeping well balanced.

- She can climb, balance and adapt physical skills to negotiate the apparatus.
- She runs around energetically playing games outside.

- She can jump off the apparatus from about four steps high.

Fine motor development

- He writes most of the letters of the alphabet.
- He draws a person with originality, for example clothed, seated.

- She can draw a diamond neatly.
- She can sew neatly with a large needle.

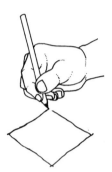

- She can build a tall straight tower with bricks.

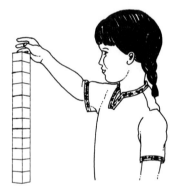

VARIATIONS IN DEVELOPMENTAL PROGRESS

The development of a child is a progression through stages. Very often an age is attached to a stage of development, such as children walking at 15 months. In reality some children will walk as early as 9 months and others as late as 18 months. This is perfectly normal. Development is not a line but an area or range. Although you will need a working knowledge of the average age at which children achieve their developmental milestones, you will always need to remember the range of achievement.

Children will progress through the stages of development at their own pace. There may be many reasons why children will do this more quickly or more slowly. Factors may include race: African and Caribbean children will often achieve the stages of gross motor more quickly than the average, sitting, standing and walking early in the range.

Children who have a condition such as cerebral palsy may achieve the stages more slowly. Progress is individual but the child will move through the stages in the same order, for example gaining head control, sitting with support, sitting unaided, pulling to stand, walking with help, walking alone. What is important is that the child is making progress through the stages.

There are other broad principles which can be applied to physical development and these are more thoroughly explained in Chapter 4 *(The principles of development)*.

THE ROLE OF THE ADULT

The adult needs to provide a safe environment for babies and children to extend their physical skills. Children need room to move around freely and the opportunity to extend their range of movement in both gross motor and fine motor skills.

There are many toys that will help with this and it is important to choose carefully with safety and the child's stage of development in mind. Many toys will be labelled as suitable for certain age groups, but bear in mind the stage the child is at and select accordingly. Providing toys and activities which stimulate development needs to be carefully undertaken. Children usually need activities which will extend their abilities but not so difficult or easy that they lose interest. However much children enjoy a challenge they will always enjoy their favourite toys. Children will work at achieving a skill, practise it and then enjoy themselves using their new found achievement.

Although bought toys can be good, there are plenty of things around the ordinary home, garden and park which can be used by adults to stimulate children's physical development: boxes to climb in and out of, saucepans and cupboards to explore, wooden spoons, buttons, cotton bobbins to sort, hideaways under the table with a long cloth. Outside in the garden or park there is room to move around, there are plants, insects, animals, mud and water to explore. All these can be observed, experienced and explored with imaginative, sensitive, adult encouragement and supervision. It is up to the adult to recognise the stage of development the child has reached and to provide the encouragement needed to help the child move forward at the pace each one needs. This pace may well vary with each child and should reflect individual needs.

Exploring the garden

At what age would you expect a child to be able to do the following:
1 Ride a tricycle using the pedals?
2 Walk upstairs and downstairs holding on and putting two feet on every step?
3 Balance on the apparatus beam?
4 Walk upstairs with one foot on each step but downstairs with two feet on each step?
5 Draw a recognisable person with head, body, arms, legs and maybe eyes, nose, mouth?
6 Build a tower of ten bricks?
7 Build a tower of six or seven bricks?
8 Hold a pencil in the preferred hand?
9 Stand, walk and run on tiptoe?
10 Match and name four primary colours?

DO!

1 Try out some simple developmental assessment for yourself. Use a set of small bricks and ask children of different ages to construct a tower. Devise a visual method to present your results and compare them with the norms.
2 Make a collection of children's drawings of people. Put them into the order of the developmental stages. Does this order correspond with the ages of the children?
3 Do 12 observations of children, one at each of the following ages: 2, 3, 4, 5, 6 and 7 years. Do six to show the progression of gross motor development and six to show the progression of fine motor development. You will be able to use these observations for your portfolio for the NNEB Diploma or as evidence for NVQ underpinning knowledge.
4 Look closely at the large apparatus and equipment which is used inside and outside at your school or nursery. Describe each item, if necessary drawing a diagram to make the explanation clearer. Evaluate each item saying how it helps to stimulate all areas of development. To do this you may need to refer to other chapters in this book. Conduct a survey amongst the children you are working with. Find out what recreational activities they take part in outside the home, school or nursery and what the children think about these activities. Write about 250 words to say:
   a) how these activities help to extend physical development
   b) why the children enjoy these activities.
5 Look at the pictures of young children on the next page and give the approximate age by which each skill shown should have been accomplished.

a) Builds 3 steps with 6 bricks after a demonstration

b) Draws a recognisable person with head, trunk, legs, arms and facial features

c) Sits and steers but cannot yet use pedals

d) Builds a tower of 9 or 10 bricks

e) Rides a 2-wheeled bicycle

f) Writes letters

1 Now you have made some observations and done some research of your own, think about developmental ages and stages.
2 From your own research can you show that variations in achieving stages are acceptable and part of normal development? Can you use your research as evidence?

Key terms
You need to know what these words and phrases mean. Go back through the chapter and find out.

Norm	Neonate
Gross motor skills	Stimulus
Fine motor skills	Posture
Prone	Symmetrical
Supine	Asymmetrical
Ventral suspension	Primitive tripod grasp
Headlag	Palmar grasp
Reflex	Pincer grasp
Primitive reflex	Spatial awareness
Voluntary action	

4 THE PRINCIPLES OF DEVELOPMENT

This chapter includes:
- **Principles of development and children's progress**
- **Five principles of development.**

Principles of development and children's progress

A principle is a basic truth or law which can be applied to a certain type of activity. It is an essential factor in the progression of the activity.

The principles of development are a set of criteria which apply to development and its continuation throughout infancy and childhood. They are relevant to all areas of development, not only physical.

Five principles of development

1 DEVELOPMENT AS A CONTINUAL PROCESS

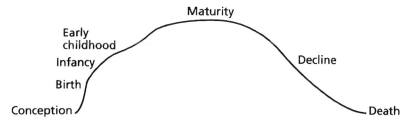

Development as a continual process, showing the steep learning curve of infancy and early childhood

From conception to maturity developmental changes are gradual, continuous and flow into each other. There are periods of very rapid change in infancy when many new skills such as walking, verbal communication and basic manipulative skills are learned, skills which form the basis of later performance. This rapid development decreases to a slower pace in the later years of childhood.

2 THE SEQUENCE OF DEVELOPMENT

The order in which new skills are acquired is always the same, but the rate at which different children acquire them will vary; for example, all children must acquire head

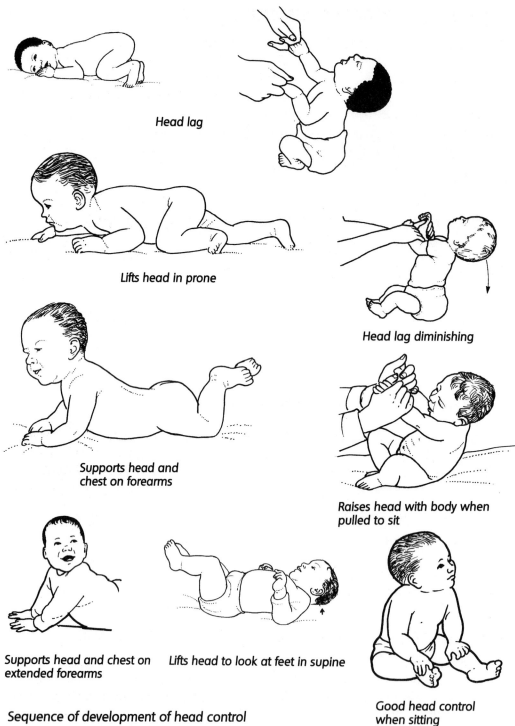

Head lag

Lifts head in prone

Head lag diminishing

Supports head and
chest on forearms

Raises head with body when
pulled to sit

Supports head and chest on
extended forearms

Lifts head to look at feet in supine

Good head control
when sitting

Sequence of development of head control

control before they can sit unsupported, so that they can balance. Some children with
a condition such as cerebral palsy may not develop head control until they are
2 or 3 years old, and only then can they learn to sit alone.

3 THE MATURITY OF THE NERVOUS SYSTEM

The central nervous system (CNS) is composed of the brain, the spinal cord and the nerves. The brain sends messages to all parts of the body down the spinal cord to the nerves which stimulate the muscles to obey the brain's command. Similarly the nerves send messages to the brain via the spinal cord; this information is constantly being transmitted and translated. The nervous system must be mature enough to be able to understand the messages it receives and to be able to send out commands.

Complete curve at birth

1 month: head and legs gaining more control

3 months: head and legs above level of the back as the nervous system matures

Ventral suspension: sequence of development

The brain is responsible for the way the body works; it stores information for future reference and helps children to make sense of the world around them. When a new skill has been learnt it is essential to give a child the opportunity and incentive to practise. Praising children in their newly gained ability will encourage them to do it again, and reinforce the information in the brain.

An example of this is toilet training. The central nervous system must be mature enough to interpret messages from the bowel or the bladder to mean that:

1 they need emptying
2 where it is acceptable to empty them
3 how to communicate this to an adult.

4 THE REPLACEMENT OF REFLEX BY VOLUNTARY ACTIONS

The primitive reflexes will mostly disappear by about three months of age; the Moro is the last to go by five months (defensive and protective reflexes remain throughout life). You may see some children with special needs who still have their primitive reflexes. This is a sign of damage to the central nervous system. These primitive reflexes must go to be replaced by voluntary control, actions which a child chooses and wants to do.

An example of this process is the fading of the palmar grasp reflex so that a baby can grasp objects with the whole hand and drop them at will, generally at about six months of age.

5 THE DIRECTIONS OF DEVELOPMENT: DOWNWARDS AND OUTWARDS

The development of gross motor (whole body) skills begins with the control of the head and works downwards, to sitting, crawling, pulling to stand, walking.

The development of fine motor (hand/eye) skills begins in the centre of the body and works outwards to the fingers, which gradually increase in ability to perform very complicated manoeuvres.

Examples of this process are the jerky, unco-ordinated movements of the arms with fists clenched developing to symmetrical arm waving with the hands open; or finger play developing to the palmar grasp, pincer grasp, then tripod grasp enabling the child to perform delicate movements such as using a spoon and fork, unwrapping sweets, threading beads, fastening buttons and so on.

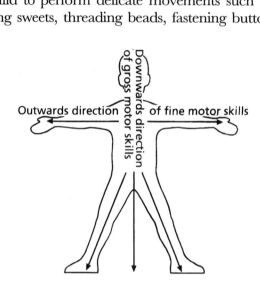

Directions of development

CHECK!

1 Describe the principles of development.
2 What is the central nervous system?
3 Why is it important in child development?

THINK!

1 Give three other examples (other than that given on page 77) of the replacement of reflexes by voluntary actions.
2 Give three other examples (other than that given on page 75) in the sequence of development.
3 Give examples of each principle of development to show that you understand the principle.

1 Observe a young child at 15–20 minute intervals for a period of at least two hours.
   Evaluate the observation in terms of all round development. Include a detailed analysis of how the principles of development relate to this particular child.
2 A friend of yours is doing a business studies course at the same college. He has recently completed an assignment on the principles of accounting and is interested to see your work on the principles of development. How could you explain this area of your studies to your friend, using examples to illustrate your meaning?

Key terms
You need to know what these words and phrases mean. Go back through the chapter to find out.

Principle	Central nervous system
Sequence	Spinal cord
Skill	Reflex action
Maturity	Voluntary action

5 MEASURING AND RECORDING DEVELOPMENT

This chapter includes:
■ **The importance of measuring and recording development**
■ **Ways of recording physical development.**

The importance of measuring and recording development

Every professional person who works with young children is responsible for their care and subsequent well-being. This framework of responsibility must include a sound knowledge of child development, so that:
- expectations of the child are realistic, reasonable and within their capabilities
- appropriate play activities are provided to stimulate the next stage of development
- children who are not making progress are quickly identified and investigated by the health visitor and/or paediatrician.

Careful observation of children is the most effective tool for assessing developmental progress, preferably over a period of time in an environment where they feel at ease, for example at home, at playgroup, in the day nursery, at nursery or primary school. The observation and recording must be structured and include all areas of development, not only what is interesting on that occasion. Sometimes 'milestones' are used to measure development, for example that children should be walking at around 15 months, but the use of these places too much emphasis on one area of development. It is vital to remember that development continues as an uninterrupted pattern of changes; the acquisition and performance of new skills must be measured against the performance of the whole child.

Many different methods have been devised to record development in a systematic manner.

Ways of measuring and recording development

There are various ways of recording a child's development:
- a narrative description of the areas of development and the skills achieved
- making tape recordings of the child's progress
- filling in charts, for example the Denver screening checklist (see opposite).

Look carefully at the samples of different charts which follow.

Denver screening checklist

Age in months	Motor	Social	Hearing and speech	Eye and hand co-ordination	Signature
1	Holds head erect for a	Quieted when picked up	Startled by sounds	Follows light with eyes	
2	Head up when prone (chin clear)	Smiles	Listens to bell or rattle	Follows ring up, down and sideways	
3	Kicks well	Follows person with eyes	Searches for sound with eyes	Glances from one object to another	
4	Lifts head and chest in prone	Returns examiner's smile	Laughs	Clasps and retains cube	
5	Holds head erect with no lag	Responds when played with	Turns head to sound	Transfers object to mouth	
6	Weight bearing and bouncing; sits with support	Turn head to person talking	Babbles or coos to voice or music	Takes cube from table	
7	Rolls from front to back	Drinks from a cup	Vocalising, makes different sounds	Looks for fallen object	
8	Tries to crawl or shuffles	Looks at mirror image	Shouts for attention	Passes toy from hand to hand	
9	Turns around on floor; stable sit	Helps to hold cup when drinking	Says *mama* or *dada*	Manipulates two objects at once	
10	Stands when held up	Smiles at mirror image	Listens to watch	Clicks two bricks together	
11	Pulls up to stand	Finger feeds	Knows 2 words with meaning	Uses pincer grip	
12	Walks or side steps around pen	Claps; waves goodbye; imitates	Knows 3 words with meaning	Retains 3 small objects	
13	Stands alone	Holds cup for drinking	Looks at picture	Shows preference for one hand	
14	May walk alone	Uses spoon	Knows own name	Holds 4 cubes	
15	Climbs upstairs	Shows shoes	Has 4–5 clear words	Places one object upon another	
16	Pushes pram, toy horse, etc.	Tries to turn door knob	Has 6–7 clear words	Scribbles freely	

continued on following page

Age in months	Motor	Social	Hearing and speech	Eye and hand co-ordination	Signature
17	Climbs on to chair	Manages cup well	Babbled conversation	Pulls (table) cloth to get toy	
18	May walk backwards; walks confidently	Takes off shoes and socks	Enjoys pictures in book	Constructive play with toys	
19	Climbs stairs up and down	Knows one part of body	Has 9 words	Builds tower of 3 bricks	
20	Jumps	May indicate bowel awareness	Has 12 words	Builds tower of 4 bricks	
21	Runs	Has bladder control by day	2-word sentences	Does circular scribble	
22	Walks upstairs	Tries to tell experiences	Listens to stories	Builds tower of 5 or more bricks	
23	Seats himself at table	Knows 2 parts of body	Has 20 words or more	Copies perpendicular stroke	
24	Walks up and down stairs; runs, walks upstairs, throws ball; cannot kick ball	Knows 4 parts of body; cup/spoon feeds; toilet by day; copies domestic tasks; tantrums	Names 4 toys; increase vocabulary; 2-word phrases; constant chatter; knows parts of body	Copies horizontal stroke; picks up crumbs; unwraps sweet; circular scribble; Stycar vision toy test; 6-cube tower	
30	Runs well straight forward and climbs easy nursery apparatus; pushes and pulls large toys skilfully but has difficulty in steering them round obstacles; jumps with two feet together; kicks large ball	Pulls down pants or knickers at toilet but seldom able to replace; very active, restless and rebellious; prolonged domestic make-believe	Continually asking questions beginning *What?*, *Where?*; uses pronouns, *I, me* and *you*	Picks up pins, threads, etc., with each eye covered separately; recognises minute details in picture books; imitates horizontal line and circle (also usually T and I); recognises self in photographs when once shown	
36	Dresses, gait stands on one foot. Note hyperactivity	Feeds self; toilet-trained; gives name; helps	Names parts of body and paints pictures. Talks to self	Stycar vision test. 9-cube tower; builds block bridge; draws circle	
48	Stands on one foot; hops, runs, climbs; rides tricycle	Alertness; friendliness; aware of surroundings; co-operation; self-willed. Eats skillfully; washes self	Gardiner-Sheridan hearing test. Note speech intelligible. Sentences. Responds to questioning	Stycar vision, near and far. Draws circle and square; grasps pencil; builds bridge; note ataxia tremor; finger and thumb opposition	

CHILD DEVELOPMENT

Name:
Address:
Date of birth:
Sex:
Clinic/Hospital (No):

A child development chart arranged by age (6 WEEKS, 6 MONTHS, 8 MONTHS, 1 YEAR, 18 MONTHS, 2–2½ YEARS, 3 YEARS, 4 YEARS, 5 YEARS) with sub-columns M V S B, across four developmental areas.

SOCIAL BEHAVIOUR AND PLAY (B)

Age	Milestones
6 WEEKS	Turns to regard speaker's face (HE); Smiles (HE)
8 MONTHS	Plays "peek a boo" (EH); Hand and foot regard (H); Puts objects into mouth (H)
1 YEAR	Waves "bye-bye" (H); Plays "pat-a-cake" (H); Indicates wants (not cry) (H); Drinks from cup (H)
18 MONTHS	Indicates toilet needs (H); Takes off shoes and socks (H); Explores environment (H); Holds spoon gets food to mouth (H)
2–2½ YEARS	Dry through day (H); Puts on clothing (H); Eats with spoon and fork (H); Plays alone (H)
3 YEARS	Dresses with supervision (H); Goes to toilet alone (H); Eats with fork and knife (H)
4 YEARS	Dresses without supervision (H); Washes and dries hands (HE); Brushes teeth (H); Shares toys (H)
5 YEARS	Dramatic group play (H); Chooses own friends (H); Comforts friends in distress (H)

HEARING AND SPEECH (S)

6 WEEKS	Startled by noise (E); Rattle 15cm at ear level (E)
6 MONTHS	Laughs, screams (H); Vocalizes (EH)
8 MONTHS	Responds to own name (H); Polysyllabic babbles (EH); Distraction hearing test (E)
1 YEAR	Understands several words (H); Uses "Mama" and "Dada" (H); Turns to name (HE); Distraction hearing test (E)
18 MONTHS	Words: 3 or more (H); Jabbers continually (EH); Obeys simple instruction "close the door" (E); Points to eyes, nose and mouth (HE)
2–2½ YEARS	Gives name (HE); Uses plurals (HE); Speech discrimination test (E); Hearing test (E)
3 YEARS	Sentences of 4 words (HE); Uses prepositions (H)
4 YEARS	Recognises colours (EH); Gives full name, sex and age (EH); Counts up to 10 (EH)
5 YEARS	Hearing test – Audiometry (E); Language test (E); Fluent and clear speech (H)

FINE MOTOR AND VISION (V)

Age	Milestones
6 WEEKS	Follows horizontally to 90° (E); Stares (EH)
6 MONTHS	Follows fallen toys (E); Fixes on small objects (E); Reaches out to grasp (palmer grasp) (HE)
8 MONTHS	Transfers and mouths (EH)
1 YEAR	Pincer grip (E); Casts (E); Points with index finger (EH); Holds 2 bricks and bangs (E)
18 MONTHS	Scribbles (HE); Delicate pincer grasp (E); Turns pages (H); Builds tower of 3 or 4 bricks (H)
2–2½ YEARS	Builds tower 8 bricks (E); Imitates vertical line (E); Picks up "Hundreds & Thousands" (E)
3 YEARS	Matches two colours (H); Threads beads (E); Copies circle (E)
4 YEARS	Draws man with 3 parts (E); Copies bridges of 3 bricks (E); Copies cross and square (E)
5 YEARS	Copies 3 steps from 6 bricks, 4 steps from 10 bricks (E); Threads beads well (E); Draws man with all features (E); Copies triangle (E)

GROSS MOTOR (M)

Age	Milestones
6 WEEKS	Prone (E); Ventral suspension (E); Moro response (E); Head control (E)
6 MONTHS	Pull to sit (E); Sits with support (HE); Downward parachute; Weight bears (E)
8 MONTHS	Crawls (EH); Forward parachute (E); Sits without support (E); Rolls over from back to prone (E)
1 YEAR	Walks alone (E); Walks holding on to furniture (EH); Pulls to stand (E); Gets to sitting (EH)
18 MONTHS	Climbs upstairs one hand held (H); Carries toys while walking (HE); Walks backwards (HE)
2–2½ YEARS	Kicks ball (EH); Jumps in place (E); Climbs and descends stairs (H)
3 YEARS	Stands on one foot 1 second (E); Pedals tricycle (E); Climbs stairs in adult manner (E); Runs fast (H)
4 YEARS	Walks heel to toe (E); Stands on one foot 5 seconds (E); Hops 2 metres forward (E); Hops on one foot (E)
5 YEARS	Walks backwards heel to toe (E); Bounces and catches ball (E); Walks downstairs 1 foot per step (H)

	M	V	S	B
USUAL AGE OF ATTAINMENT				
DATE AND AGE				
PRESENT ATTAINMENT				

* = Sheridan—Gardner Near Vision Test, Sheridan—Gardner Distant Vision Test
** = Hirschberg Corneal Light Reflection Test; Cover Test

E = Pass by examination
H = Pass by history

Hips = Check for dislocation
Testicles = Check for presence and descent

by S. LINGAM, Feb. 1984

A further example of a child development chart

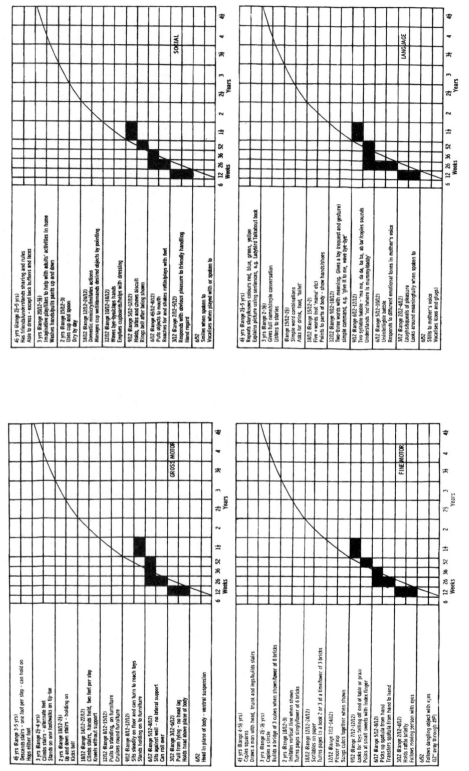

Development centile charts, showing initial good progress, followed by some areas of difficulty

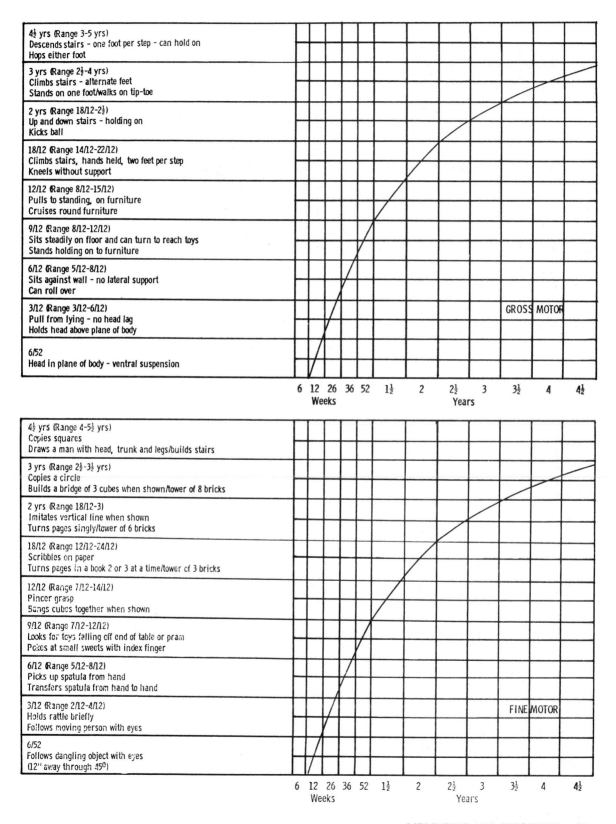

GROSS MOTOR

4½ yrs (Range 3-5 yrs) Descends stairs – one foot per step – can hold on Hops either foot												
3 yrs (Range 2½-4 yrs) Climbs stairs – alternate feet Stands on one foot/walks on tip-toe												
2 yrs (Range 18/12-2½) Up and down stairs – holding on Kicks ball												
18/12 (Range 14/12-22/12) Climbs stairs, hands held, two feet per step Kneels without support												
12/12 (Range 8/12-15/12) Pulls to standing, on furniture Cruises round furniture												
9/12 (Range 8/12-12/12) Sits steadily on floor and can turn to reach toys Stands holding on to furniture												
6/12 (Range 5/12-8/12) Sits against wall – no lateral support Can roll over												
3/12 (Range 3/12-6/12) Pull from lying – no head lag Holds head above plane of body												
6/52 Head in plane of body – ventral suspension												

6 12 26 36 52   1½   2   2½   3   3½   4   4½
Weeks   **Years**

FINE MOTOR

4½ yrs (Range 4-5½ yrs) Copies squares Draws a man with head, trunk and legs/builds stairs												
3 yrs (Range 2½-3½ yrs) Copies a circle Builds a bridge of 3 cubes when shown/tower of 8 bricks												
2 yrs (Range 18/12-3) Imitates vertical line when shown Turns pages singly/tower of 6 bricks												
18/12 (Range 12/12-24/12) Scribbles on paper Turns pages in a book 2 or 3 at a time/tower of 3 bricks												
12/12 (Range 7/12-14/12) Pincer grasp Bangs cubes together when shown												
9/12 (Range 7/12-12/12) Looks for toys falling off end of table or pram Pokes at small sweets with index finger												
6/12 (Range 5/12-8/12) Picks up spatula from hand Transfers spatula from hand to hand												
3/12 (Range 2/12-4/12) Holds rattle briefly Follows moving person with eyes												
6/52 Follows dangling object with eyes (12" away through 45°)												

6 12 26 36 52   1½   2   2½   3   3½   4   4½
Weeks   **Years**

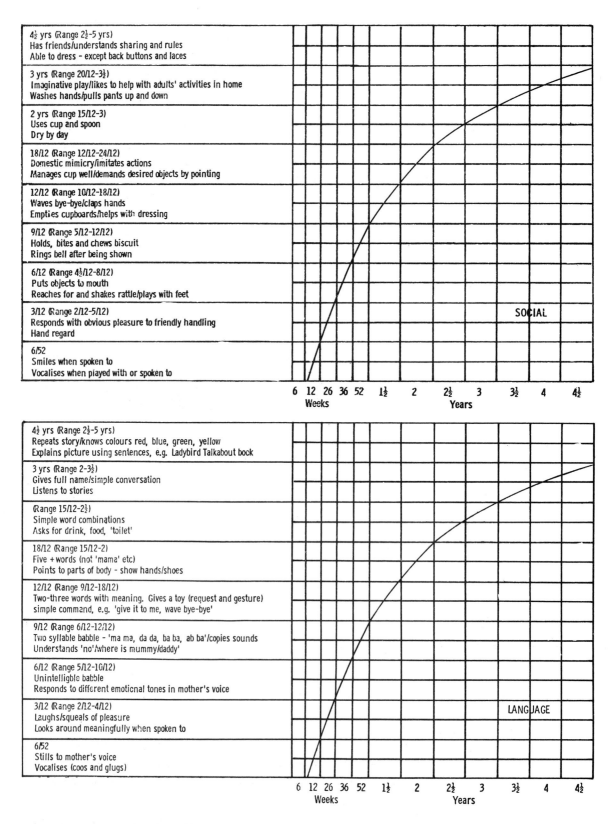

SOCIAL

4½ yrs (Range 2½-5 yrs)
Has friends/understands sharing and rules
Able to dress - except back buttons and laces

3 yrs (Range 20/12-3½)
Imaginative play/likes to help with adults' activities in home
Washes hands/pulls pants up and down

2 yrs (Range 15/12-3)
Uses cup and spoon
Dry by day

18/12 (Range 12/12-24/12)
Domestic mimicry/imitates actions
Manages cup well/demands desired objects by pointing

12/12 (Range 10/12-18/12)
Waves bye-bye/claps hands
Empties cupboards/helps with dressing

9/12 (Range 5/12-12/12)
Holds, bites and chews biscuit
Rings bell after being shown

6/12 (Range 4½/12-8/12)
Puts objects to mouth
Reaches for and shakes rattle/plays with feet

3/12 (Range 2/12-5/12)
Responds with obvious pleasure to friendly handling
Hand regard

6/52
Smiles when spoken to
Vocalises when played with or spoken to

SOCIAL

x-axis: 6 12 26 36 52 Weeks 1½ 2 2½ 3 3½ 4 4½ Years

LANGUAGE

4½ yrs (Range 2½-5 yrs)
Repeats story/knows colours red, blue, green, yellow
Explains picture using sentences, e.g. Ladybird Talkabout book

3 yrs (Range 2-3½)
Gives full name/simple conversation
Listens to stories

(Range 15/12-2½)
Simple word combinations
Asks for drink, food, 'toilet'

18/12 (Range 15/12-2)
Five + words (not 'mama' etc)
Points to parts of body - show hands/shoes

12/12 (Range 9/12-18/12)
Two-three words with meaning. Gives a toy (request and gesture)
simple command, e.g. 'give it to me, wave bye-bye'

9/12 (Range 6/12-12/12)
Two syllable babble - 'ma ma, da da, ba ba, ab ba'/copies sounds
Understands 'no'/where is mummy/daddy'

6/12 (Range 5/12-10/12)
Unintelligible babble
Responds to different emotional tones in mother's voice

3/12 (Range 2/12-4/12)
Laughs/squeals of pleasure
Looks around meaningfully when spoken to

6/52
Stills to mother's voice
Vocalises (coos and glugs)

LANGUAGE

x-axis: 6 12 26 36 52 Weeks 1½ 2 2½ 3 3½ 4 4½ Years

DEVELOPMENT CENTILE CHARTS

Development centile charts (as shown on pages 84–6) have been devised after studying and recording the progress of thousands of children. They present the information in a highly visual way and are easy to read. The figures on the bottom line (the horizontal axis) represent the age of the child, in weeks until one year of age and thereafter in years. The developmental items are listed down the side (the vertical axis) and are given an approximate age range. The blocks on the chart are filled in when a skill has been witnessed, in the space that relates to the child's age. Blocks which appear above the centile line indicate good developmental progress. Blocks which appear below the line may be indications of developmental difficulties; again the advantage of the chart is that it presents this information in a clear way which can quickly be interpreted.

Charts should always be completed regularly, so that if there are any areas of difficulty, they will be quickly detected and any necessary treatment can be given. Look at the examples of completed charts which indicate a child's initial good progress, followed by some areas of difficulty.

Values of centile charts
There are several benefits to child-care workers in using centile charts:
- the information enables the reader to compare a child with itself: it is easy to compare the previous recording and note individual progress
- a child can also be with compared with others: it is easy to note average, typical development
- the charts can record all areas of development, making it possible to see the pattern of progress: an area of advanced development can be compared with an area of less than average progress
- centile charts can identify children who are not making satisfactory progress, or are deviating from the norm; so the cause can be sought
- the information recorded in this way allows for early intervention
- the data is simple to read and to complete, and effective in measuring progress.

These charts are used by whoever is doing the assessment, wherever the assessment is done. They are used by health visitors, nursery nurses, doctors, general practitioners, paediatricians and school nurses. They are used in the home, in baby clinics, day nurseries, family centres, hospitals, GP clinics and at medical examinations and check-ups in schools.

DO!

1 Read through the following health visitor's notes recording the development of several children at varying ages.

Tahira, aged 6 months
Rolls both ways, sits for long periods with support. She adopts the crawling position but is not yet mobile. Grasps objects with a palmar grasp, transfers from hand to hand and puts to mouth. Attempts to grab objects out of reach.

Plays with her feet. She is a happy baby who shouts and vocalises, laughing and enjoying sociable company.

Jack, aged 12 months

Sits unsupported for long periods of time. He bottom-shuffles at great speed. Palmar and pincer grasp seen. Helps with dressing. Waves goodbye. Bangs cubes together and gives toy when requested. Unintelligible babble constantly, no recognisable words.

Adil, aged 18 months

Walks confidently, runs and squats to collect toys from the floor. Walks upstairs with one hand held, crawls down backwards. Kneels. Kicks a ball. Builds a six-cube tower. Uses a cup and spoon and helps with household tasks, e.g. dusting and putting rubbish in the bin. Joining words to make simple sentences, asks for required objects.

2 Look at the development charts and plot these children's development on the centile charts on pages 85–6.
3 What do the centile charts show you?
4 Are they developing within the average range?

THINK!

Make a list of ways to stimulate each of these children to help them to continue their developmental progress.

CHECK!

1 Why must professionals have a thorough knowledge of child development?
2 What is the most effective way of assessing development?
3 Where should developmental assessments take place?
4 List four ways of recording development.
5 What are the benefits of using centile charts?
6 Which professionals may use centile charts?

Key terms
You need to know what these words and phrases mean. Go back through the chapter to find out.
Milestone
Narrative
Centile chart

---

6 FACTORS WHICH MAY AFFECT PHYSICAL DEVELOPMENT

This chapter includes:
- **Antenatal factors**
- **Perinatal factors**
- **Postnatal factors.**

There are many factors which can have a positive or negative effect on a child's progress. These factors can be grouped according to the time that they occur: antenatal (occurring before birth), perinatal (occurring during birth) or postnatal (occurring after birth).

Antenatal factors

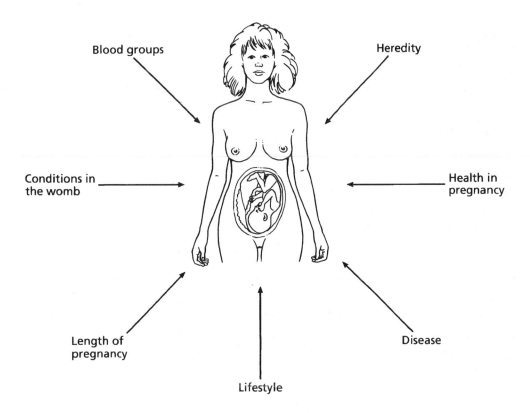

Antenatal influences on pregnancy

HEREDITY

Heredity means the transmission of characteristics from one generation to the next. Everybody is the product of their parents and bears physical resemblance to them. All children inherit their physical features and the way their bodies function. This is because the *genetic information* carried by the ovum (egg) and spermatazoon (sperm) influences a person's appearance and the way their body works.

In the centre of every cell in the body is a nucleus containing chromosomes, made up of DNA (deoxyribonucleic acid). A specific piece of genetic information is called a *gene*, and each chromosome carries many thousands of genes. Except for identical twins, no two people have the same genetic information.

The nucleus of each ovum and sperm contains 23 separate chromosomes and genes, the instructions for inheritance. When fertilisation occurs these chromosomes unite to make 23 pairs (see diagram).

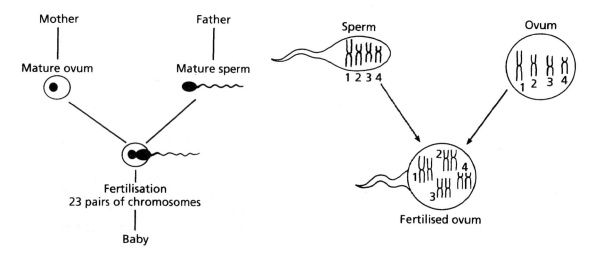

Genetic inheritance

One pair of chromosomes is called the sex chromosomes and determines whether the baby will be a boy or a girl. They are called the X and Y chromosomes. Women only pass on the female X chromosome, but men pass on either the female X or the male Y chromosome. The XX combination results in a girl, the XY combination in a boy.

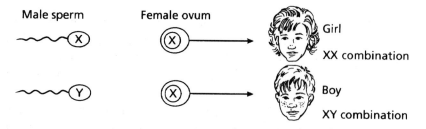

Sex determination

1 2 3   4 5

6 7 8 9 10 11 12

13 14 15   16 17 18

19 20   21 22 X Y   Boy □ ♂
                              or
                              Girl ○ ♀

Note that the male Y chromosome
is much smaller than the female
chromosome.   X X
                              23

Normal human chromosomes

So it is always the sperm which decides the sex of the baby. (Henry VIII's wives might have survived longer if he had known this!)

The chromosomes contain thousands of genes contained in DNA. These genes are the more detailed units of inheritance and carry the information for characteristics which children will inherit from their parents. Just as the chromosomes pair up, so do the genes, each matching with a gene carrying similar information. The genes will influence characteristics such as height, eye colour, hair colour, skin texture and colour, as well as the physical development of such organs as the brain and muscles, and every human characteristic.

Of course, when they pair not all genes will necessarily carry the same information. If they do, then that message will be passed to the child; for example two genes for blue eyes will inevitably produce a child with blue eyes. If the parents have different coloured eyes, and pass on genes for different colours, then the *dominant* (powerful) gene will determine the eye colour. The child will, however, still carry the information contained in the other gene and may pass this on to their own children: this is the influence of the *recessive* gene. This is the reason two brown-eyed parents can produce a child with blue eyes, or how dark-haired parents can produce a child with red hair. It also explains how some characteristics may miss generations, and children can inherit the features of their ancestors.

People who have a recessive gene are called *carriers*, but this term usually describes people who carry a gene for a particular disease but are not affected by it themselves.

It will be useful here to examine exactly what happens when genes pair, and to see how the chances of passing on either dominant or recessive characteristics are worked out.

Remember that each parent has two genes for each characteristic, but only one is present in the ovum or sperm. The pairings are entirely random (see the diagram overleaf, *The possible outcomes at fertilisation*).

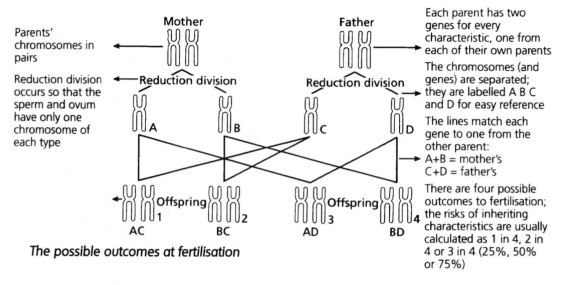

Parents' chromosomes in pairs

Mother

Father

Each parent has two genes for every characteristic, one from each of their own parents

Reduction division occurs so that the sperm and ovum have only one chromosome of each type

← Reduction division

Reduction division

The chromosomes (and genes) are separated; they are labelled A B C and D for easy reference

A   B   C   D

The lines match each gene to one from the other parent:
A+B = mother's
C+D = father's

Offspring 1 · Offspring 2 · Offspring 3 · Offspring 4

AC   BC   AD   BD

There are four possible outcomes to fertilisation; the risks of inheriting characteristics are usually calculated as 1 in 4, 2 in 4 or 3 in 4 (25%, 50% or 75%)

The possible outcomes at fertilisation

Dominant inheritance

By matching up each gene with the genes of the other parent, it is possible to calculate the chances of dominant inheritance occurring with each pregnancy. In the example illustrated below (*Dominant inheritance*) there is a 2:4 or 50% chance. Remember that this can be applied to diseases passed on by dominant inheritance.

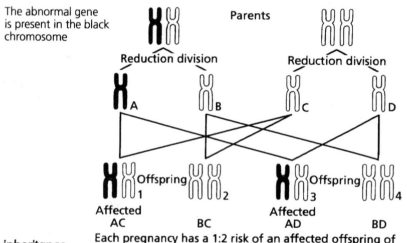

The abnormal gene is present in the black chromosome

Parents

Reduction division

Reduction division

A   B   C   D

Offspring 1 · Offspring 2 · Offspring 3 · Offspring 4

Affected AC   BC   Affected AD   BD

Dominant inheritance

Each pregnancy has a 1:2 risk of an affected offspring of either sex; thus AC and AD are affected (2:4)

Recessive inheritance

If two brown-eyed parents both carry the recessive gene for blue eyes, there is a 1:4 chance of recessive inheritance with each pregnancy. There is a 2:4 chance of recessive genes being carried by the children.

Using this combination it is possible to see how a recessively inherited characteristic or disease could appear 'out of the blue', with no recent family history. Cystic fibrosis (CF) often appears this way. 1:20 of the white British population carries the recessive gene for CF; if two people carrying the same abnormal gene reproduce, they have a 1:4 chance of having a child with cystic fibrosis.

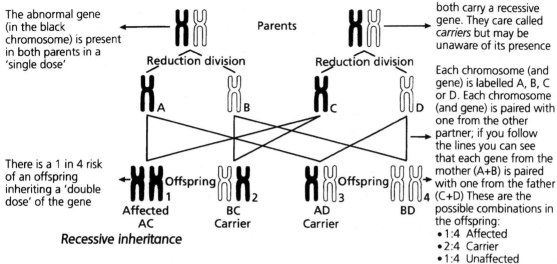

The abnormal gene (in the black chromosome) is present in both parents in a 'single dose'

Parents

The mother and father both carry a recessive gene. They care called *carriers* but may be unaware of its presence

Reduction division

Reduction division

Each chromosome (and gene) is labelled A, B, C or D. Each chromosome (and gene) is paired with one from the other partner; if you follow the lines you can see that each gene from the mother (A+B) is paired with one from the father (C+D) These are the possible combinations in the offspring:
• 1:4 Affected
• 2:4 Carrier
• 1:4 Unaffected

There is a 1 in 4 risk of an offspring inheriting a 'double dose' of the gene

Offspring 1 — Affected AC

Offspring 2 — BC Carrier

Offspring 3 — AD Carrier

Offspring 4 — BD

Recessive inheritance

Sex-linked inheritance

Some diseases are carried on the female X chromosome. These are called sex-linked disorders or X-linked disorders. Because they are carried on the X chromosome they almost always pass from mother to son.

The male Y chromosome is much smaller than the X chromosome (see the diagram *Normal human chromosomes* on page 91), and carries virtually no genetic information. This enables the X chromosome to be dominant.

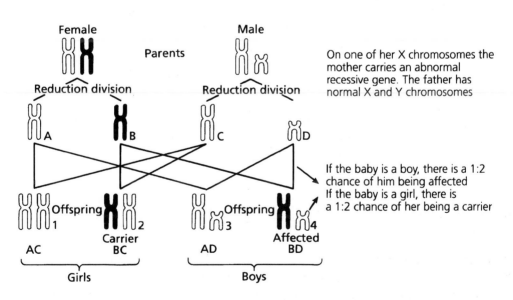

Female

Male

Parents

On one of her X chromosomes the mother carries an abnormal recessive gene. The father has normal X and Y chromosomes

Reduction division

Reduction division

If the baby is a boy, there is a 1:2 chance of him being affected
If the baby is a girl, there is a 1:2 chance of her being a carrier

Offspring 1 — AC

Offspring 2 — Carrier BC

Offspring 3 — AD

Offspring 4 — Affected BD

Girls

Boys

Sex-linked inheritance   Female parent carrier

You can see from the diagram above that with each pregnancy there is
- a 1:2 chance of each girl being a carrier or unaffected
- a 1:2 chance of each boy having the disease or being unaffected.

Haemophilia and Duchenne muscular dystrophy are passed on in this way, as is colour blindness. It is interesting to note that affected fathers cannot pass the disorder on to their sons. They can only pass the affected X on to their daughters, meaning that they will be carriers.

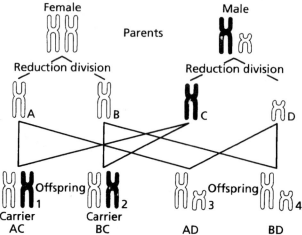

The affected male's daughters are always carriers since he must pass on his X chromosome with the abnormal gene (C) to female offspring AC and BC

Sex-linked inheritance   Male parent affected

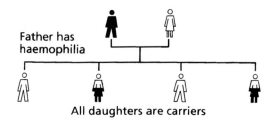

Father has haemophilia

All daughters are carriers

Haemophilia: the genetic inheritance pattern

Queen Victoria was a carrier of haemophilia and her children passed this on to many european royal families.

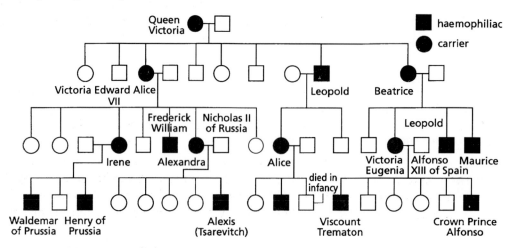

Chromosomal abnormalities

Occasionally there is an error in the chromosomes. When they unite in the fertilised ovum some may break, there may be too many or not enough. Down's syndrome is a well known chromosomal abnormality. It is also known as Trisomy 21 because there are three number 21 chromosomes instead of the usual two. Chromosomal abnormalities result in a general pattern of characteristic abnormality, affecting many of the systems of the body.

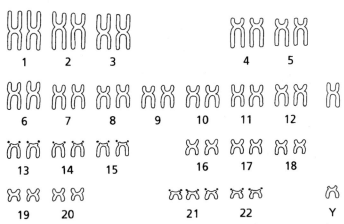

The chromosome pattern of a male infant with Down's syndrome
Note the presence of the extra number 21 chromosome, Trisomy 21.

The chromosome pattern of a male infant with Down's syndrome

HEALTH IN PREGNANCY

Infections

Some pathogenic (disease causing) organisms are so small that they can cross the placental barrier from the mother's bloodstream to the baby's, causing developmental problems and sometimes death. These organisms must be prevented if possible, to avoid often disastrous effects on the postnatal development of the child.

Rubella (German measles)

German measles has been accepted and tolerated as a fairly mild and unavoidable childhood illness. It is fairly harmless to children, but it is very dangerous to pregnant women as it can damage the developing fetus during the first three to four months of pregnancy. It may kill the fetus or result in deafness, blindness or heart disease.

All pregnant women are screened for rubella antibodies. Babies are immunised at 12–15 months with the MMR (measles, mumps and rubella) vaccine, and schoolgirls are immunised against rubella between the ages of 11 and 13 years. By preventing the illness in this way it is less likely that women will contract the disease in pregnancy.

AIDS

AIDS (Acquired Immune Deficiency Syndrome) is caused by the Human Immunopathic Virus (HIV). A mother infected with HIV may pass this virus to her child through the placenta. The child may be born with AIDS or develop it at any time. It may be weeks or years later. Because AIDS reduces the body's natural immunity the child will easily become infected with many types of germs. They may even develop a specific type of cancer. There is no known cure for AIDS at present.

Sexually transmitted diseases

Sexually transmitted diseases (such as gonorrhoea, syphilis or herpes) may affect the fetus, or the baby may become infected during the birth. All these diseases have effects on development.

Toxoplasmosis

Toxoplasmosis is caused by a parasite which infects cats who then shed infectious organisms in their faeces. Humans can catch it by changing cat litter trays and gardening without gloves on, by eating unwashed vegetables or raw, undercooked meat.

In pregnancy the virus can attack the fetus, causing blindness, and it can damage the brain resulting in epilepsy and/or delayed intellectual development. In some European countries (though not in England), pregnant women are routinely screened for the disease.

Listeriosis

Listeria is an organism which is often found in pate and soft cheeses like Brie and Camembert. It, too, can cause damage to the developing fetus.

Other infections such as virulent strains of the influenza virus may cross the placental barrier.

Diseases

Diabetes

Diabetes is a condition in which the body does not produce enough insulin to enable it to use the carbohydrate (starch and sugars) eaten in the diet. The usual treatment is to inject the correct amount of insulin to enable the body to use the carbohydrate effectively. During pregnancy this needs very careful control to monitor the mother and meet the needs of the fetus.

Babies born to diabetic mothers can be much larger than average and be immature in their development. There is also a higher risk of congenital abnormality.

Heart disease

A mother with heart disease may give birth to a baby prematurely or in poor condition. Both mother and baby need very special care in the antenatal period.

Toxaemia of pregnancy

Toxaemia only occurs in pregnancy. The word *toxaemia* means 'poisoned blood' and its diagnosis indicates the presence of *toxins* (poisons) in the blood which may affect the baby. The signs of toxaemia are:
- high blood pressure

- protein in the urine
- oedema (swelling of tissues) especially in the hands and feet
- rapid weight gain.

Mild toxaemia is common and is treated with rest and careful monitoring by the midwife and doctor. Severe toxaemia can kill the mother and baby – the only cure is to deliver the baby quickly. This may be a very early delivery and the baby will have the associated problems of prematurity and will probably be light for dates as well (see *Length of pregnancy* on page 98).

LIFESTYLE

The way the mother lives her life, the care she takes of her general health and the consideration she gives in pregnancy to the well-being of her baby will have an undoubted effect on the future development of her child.

Smoking

It is generally accepted that babies born to mothers who smoke during pregnancy will be smaller at birth than if the mother had not smoked. There is also a higher incidence of premature birth and intellectual delay.

Drugs

A drug is any substance taken into the body to produce a specific physical or psychological effect, so this will include prescribed medicines, addictions and alcohol.

Doctors must be careful when prescribing drugs to pregnant women, and should avoid any that are known to have an adverse effect on the fetus. Thalidomide is a notorious drug which caused a lot of fetal damage during the 1950s and 1960s. This was prescribed by doctors to prevent morning sickness in pregnancy. It is better not to take any tablets or medicines during pregnancy unless absolutely necessary.

Mothers addicted to drugs like heroin, cocaine, barbiturates and valium will produce babies who are also addicted. They will need to be weaned off these drugs and may be delayed in their all-round development. Some babies suffer from epilepsy as a result of their mother taking drugs during pregnancy.

Alcohol can also cross the placenta and heavy drinking can result in *fetal alcohol syndrome*, which is similar to alcoholism in adults with catastrophic results for the baby. Here too, the baby would need to be weaned off the alcohol after birth. Even moderate drinking is thought to increase the incidence of miscarriage, minor malformations and slower development in childhood.

Caffeine is a substance found mainly in coffee, but it is also present in tea. It can be addictive and excessive amounts in pregnancy are thought to affect future development of the child.

Diet

The fetus is a parasite which means that it feeds from the mother and is totally dependent on her. The baby will always take the nutrients it needs and if the diet is inadequate it is often the mother who suffers. She must eat a well balanced diet to meet the needs of the fetus and to maintain her own health.

Work

Some occupations may be hazardous during pregnancy, especially those which involve contact with dangerous chemicals, radiation or radioactive materials, lead products or other dangerous substances. There is a higher risk of abnormality in the baby if the mother operates a VDU or is a computer programmer.

Exercise

Regular exercise is good for the mother and baby. High-risk sports should be avoided at the end of the pregnancy to avoid injury either to the mother or the baby.

LENGTH OF PREGNANCY

The length of pregnancy in a human is 40 weeks. A baby born after 37–42 completed weeks of pregnancy is born at *term*. It is much better for the baby to be born at term, because then it will have completed all its fetal development and will be prepared for life outside the womb.

Sometimes babies are small or *light for dates*. This means that they do not weigh as much as expected for the length of time that they have been in the womb. A baby born at 36 weeks or before is pre-term or born early. Sometimes babies are both *pre-term* and light for dates. All these babies may have problems soon after birth which may affect their future development. Possible areas of difficulty may be:

- breathing problems
- hypothermia
- bleeding in the brain
- low levels of sugar in the blood
- jaundice
- anaemia
- infection.

There may be many other complications which affect babies born too soon. It is usually true that the longer they have had to develop in the womb, the better their chance of a future healthy life. For instance, a baby born after 34 weeks will have a better chance of survival than a baby born at 26 weeks. Neonatal intensive care is improving all the time and babies born at a very early gestational age are now surviving, but they may be affected by developmental delay.

CONDITIONS IN THE WOMB

The womb is a muscular bag which should grow to accommodate the growing fetus, the placenta, the membranes and the amniotic fluid. There should be enough space for the baby to grow.

There may, however, be more than one baby! Two, three or more babies may restrict movement and growth.

Occasionally there is a *fibroid*, a fatty growth in the womb, which may take up some of the baby's room.

Another possible complication is that a contraceptive coil (IUCD) could remain in the womb and might induce premature labour.

BLOOD GROUPS

Everyone has a blood group inherited from their parents. The four main groups are A, B, O and AB. In addition there is a substance found in the blood of some humans called the *Rhesus factor*. About 85% of the population are Rhesus positive and about 15% are Rhesus negative. The baby inherits two Rhesus genes, one from each parent. The Rhesus positive gene *D* is dominant. The Rhesus negative gene *d* is recessive.

During pregnancy fetal and maternal blood should not mix, but at delivery, or if a miscarriage has occurred, the baby's blood can enter the mother's system. The first pregnancy is usually straightforward, but second and subsequent babies may be affected if antibodies are allowed to form. If the mother is Rhesus negative and the baby Rhesus positive the mother may react to the Rhesus factor in her baby's blood and make antibodies to attack the foreign cells (the Rhesus factor in the baby's blood).

During birth some of the baby's Rh positive blood may pass into the mother's Rh negative blood. This may produce antibodies which can affect subsequent Rh positive babies

Such mothers can now be injected with Rh antibody after the birth of the baby to destroy Rh positive red cells and protect any future Rh positive babies. This injection is called Anti-D

Severely affected Rhesus babies have an exchange transfusion to replace their Rh positive blood with Rh negative

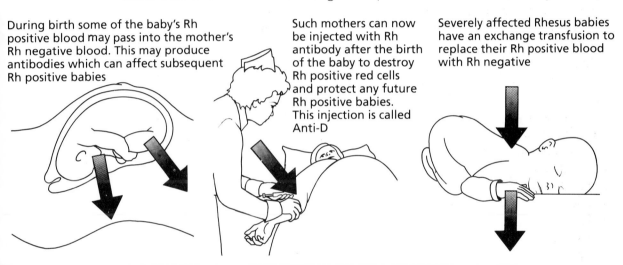

A Rhesus negative mother carrying a Rhesus positive baby

The amount of damage can vary from mild anaemia and jaundice to haemolytic disease of the newborn, which is very serious and may require an exchange blood transfusion. Fortunately this situation is now very rare because regular blood tests during pregnancy can detect antibodies in the mother's blood. An injection of Anti-D (anti-Rhesus factor) can prevent the further formation of antibodies and protect the baby.

CHECK!

1 a) How are characteristics passed from parent to child?
   b) What are the units of inheritance called?
   c) What does XX and XY mean?
   d) What is *dominant inheritance*?
   e) What is the chance of recessive genes affecting a fetus?
   f) How many pairs of chromosomes are there in a fertilised egg?
2 a) How can rubella be prevented in pregnancy?

b) Which organs might the rubella virus damage?
c) What is the name of the organism which causes AIDS?
d) How can a pregnant woman avoid getting toxoplasmosis ?
e) Which sexually transmitted diseases can affect the fetus?
f) From which sources might a person contract listeriosis?
g) What effects can diabetes have on the baby?
h) What does *toxaemia* mean? Describe the signs of this disease.
i) What commonly used substances are also drugs?
j) What effect can these drugs have on a fetus?
k) Why is the mother's lifestyle important during pregnancy?

3 a) What is the normal length of pregnancy?
b) When is a baby born *at term*?
c) Describe what is meant by *pre-term* and *light for dates*.
d) List five specific complications may affect a pre-term or light-for-dates baby.
e) What does *viable* mean?

4 What conditions in the womb could affect fetal growth and development?

5 a) What is the Rhesus factor?
b) What problems might the Rhesus factor cause in pregnancy?
c) What special care are Rhesus negative mothers given during pregnancy?

THINK!

1 Think of all the characteristics you have inherited from your parents.
2 Investigate a family in detail: your family or the family of a friend. Try to explain how the pattern of genetic inheritance has affected all the family members.
3 Think of routine tests and observations which may be carried out at antenatal clinics to detect the early signs of toxaemia in pregnancy.
4 Think of jobs which may be unsuitable for a woman to undertake before or during pregnancy.

DO!

1 Make a family tree to show how the members of your household have inherited their hair and eye colour.
2 Find out about chromosomal abnormalities. Choose one and write about all the effects this may have on a child's development.
3 Using your knowledge of dominant and recessive inheritance, work out the following patterns of transmission of the Rhesus factor. Remember that the Rhesus negative gene is recessive.

1	Mother	dd	Father	DD
2	Mother	dd	Father	Dd
3	Mother	dd	Father	dd

Perinatal factors

The birth process is much safer now than it was 100 or even 50 years ago. Improvements in antenatal care by trained midwives and doctors can prevent, detect and treat any abnormalities very effectively. The *infant mortality rate* (the number of babies who die in the first year of life) and the *maternal mortality rate* (the number of mothers who die within a year of childbirth as a direct result of the pregnancy, labour or delivery) have declined, due partly to improved social conditions, but they remain higher than average in areas of deprivation.

It is, however, impossible to remove all the hazards at delivery: the unexpected can always happen and the delivery of a baby can only be called 'safe' when it is all over! Adverse events at delivery can be fetal distress, effects on the baby of anaesthetics or analgesics or an abnormal presentation.

FETAL DISTRESS

The baby may become distressed due to *anoxia*, lack of oxygen. If this persists it can cause damage to the brain. (Some cases of cerebral palsy are thought to be caused by anoxia.) This situation may require a quick delivery, using one of the following methods:

- forceps: spoon shaped cups put around the baby's head to lift it out
- ventouse extraction: a suction cap to pull the baby out
- Caesarian section: an incision into the uterus to remove the baby.

ANAESTHETICS AND ANALGESICS

A general anaesthetic, or painkillers used too close to the birth, may result in a baby who is slow to breathe and may require resuscitation.

ABNORMAL PRESENTATION

The most straightforward way for a baby to be born is head first, but sometimes babies present as bottom, legs and feet, face, shoulder or other part of the body coming first. This will prolong labour and may result in a tired mother and a shocked baby. Anoxia may occur during the birth.

The passage down the birth canal continues to be the shortest yet most hazardous journey humans ever make.

CHECK!

1 Why are pregnancy and birth safer now than they were 100 years ago?
2 What does the *infant mortality* rate mean ?
3 What complications might arise at delivery?
4 What does *anoxia* mean ?
5 How may anoxia affect development?

Postnatal factors

Postnatal factors are those which affect a child from birth onwards. Everything that happens to a child throughout childhood can affect the progress they make.

ENVIRONMENT

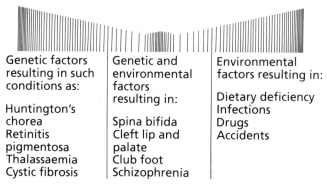

Genetic factors resulting in such conditions as:	Genetic and environmental factors resulting in:	Environmental factors resulting in:
Huntington's chorea Retinitis pigmentosa Thalassaemia Cystic fibrosis	Spina bifida Cleft lip and palate Club foot Schizophrenia	Dietary deficiency Infections Drugs Accidents

Inadequate nutrition and infections are still common world wide

Causes of disease

A person's environment means their total surroundings: the family, the community and the country they live in, and must include their culture, religion and education.

The amount of potential given to a child is decided by heredity (see page 90); the environment determines the extent to which that potential develops. If a child has the genetic information to grow to 150 cm, the outcome will not be affected by however much food, care and stimulation is provided; but these contributory factors will determine whether or not a child achieves their maximum – the best they can. By offering children the opportunity to fulfil their potential in all areas of growth and development they are given a good basis for life (see Chapter 10, *Emotional and Social Development*).

PERSONAL AND COMMUNITY HYGIENE

Hygiene means taking all measures necessary to promote health. The World Health Organisation defines health as 'a complete state of mental, physical and social well-being'. This is a very difficult goal to reach, but children must be given the chance to have total health. Meeting a child's health needs means providing the opportunity for:

- a well balanced diet
- rest and sleep
- exercise
- fresh air
- exposure to a certain amount of sunlight
- a safe environment to prevent injury
- protection from infection
- personal and communal cleanliness
- positive mental health and self-esteem
- constructive use of leisure.

HORMONES

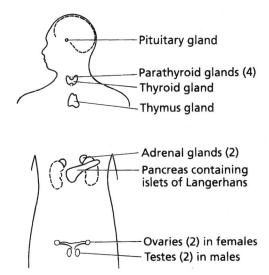

Hormonal influences on development

A hormone is a chemical substance which is made in one part of the body and carried in the bloodstream to act on tissues or organs in another part. It is a chemical messenger. Hormones are usually produced in *endocrine* (ductless) glands; these glands pass their secretions directly into the bloodstream, for distribution around the body, to their 'target' organ.

Pituitary gland

The pituitary gland is the size of a pea and is situated at the base of the brain. It is called the 'master of the orchestra' of endocrine glands because it regulates, or controls, their hormone production. The hormones it produces affect:

- the rate of growth (it can cause giantism or dwarfism if it produces too much or too little)
- the development of the reproductive organs and secondary sexual characteristics
- blood pressure
- urine production.

Thyroid gland

The thyroid gland produces the hormone thyroxine. The function of thyroxine is to regulate:

- general growth rate
- bone development
- the nervous system
- muscle development
- circulation of the blood
- the function of the reproductive organs.

Insufficient thyroxine before birth causes *cretinism* with the following effects:

- poor growth
- slow movements and clumsiness
- intellectual delay
- a large and protruding tongue.

If the condition is recognised and treated early the child should progress to develop normally.

Parathyroid glands

The parathyroid glands produce the *parathyroid* hormone. Its function is to control the use of calcium and phosphorous. These are vital for healthy bones and teeth, for efficient muscle action and blood clotting. Too much parathyroid hormone causes softening of the bones and weak muscles. Too little parathyroid hormone causes painful muscle cramps.

The pancreas

The pancreas produces the hormone *insulin*. Its function is to control the amount of sugar in the bloodstream. Too little insulin causes *diabetes* (see page 96).

Adrenal glands

The adrenal glands produce the hormones: adrenalin and cortisone. Their function is to control certain body minerals affecting growth and assist sexual maturation.

Adrenalin is the 'fight or flight' hormone which is active at times of stress, It provides the strength to fight or the energy to run away!

The testes and ovaries

The testes in the male produce the hormone *testosterone* and the ovaries in the female produce *oestrogen* and *progesterone*. The function of these hormones is to control the development and functioning of the reproductive organs.

INFECTIONS AND IMMUNITY

Several childhood illnesses can affect growth and development. Some of them are controlled by an immunisation programme:

- diphtheria
- tetanus
- whooping cough (*pertussis*)
- polio
- measles
- mumps.

Before birth a baby is protected by the mother's immunity: her antibodies to infections pass through the placenta into the baby's bloodstream. After birth babies need to develop their own immunity which depends upon their own immune system:

- the thymus gland produces thymic hormone which helps children to make antibodies. This gland is large in childhood but shrinks away during adult life

- tonsils and adenoids are areas of lymphatic tissue which protect the child from infection. They are the first line in defence in the respiratory tract, as they are situated in the throat and at the back of the nose. They can become enlarged and cause discomfort for some children, but doctors prefer now not to remove them because they have such an important function in fighting infection. They too shrink in size in adulthood
- *leucocytes* (white blood cells) fight infection throughout life.

CHECK!

1 What decides the amount of potential given to a child?
2 What does *hygiene* mean?
3 List six health needs.
4 What is a hormone?
5 What type of gland produces hormones?
6 Why is the pituitary gland important ?
7 Which gland produces thyroxine?
8 What are the functions of thyroxine?
9 Which hormone is produced in the pancreas?
10 What is the function of adrenalin?
11 Which hormones do the testes and ovaries produce?
12 Which diseases are controlled by immunisation programmes?
13 How can children develop their own immunity ?

THINK!

1 Think of as many ways as you can of meeting the health needs of children.
2 What might be the results of the failure to provide for a child's health needs?

DO!

1 Choose one factor from each of the groups (antenatal, perinatal and postnatal) which affect development . Describe the possible positive or negative influence these factors can have on a child's developmental progress.
2 Using the information gained from this chapter, write a letter to a friend who is planning to have a baby, informing her of how she can achieve the best of health before becoming pregnant and how she can maintain this good health during pregnancy.
   Include explanations of how she can avoid health problems before the baby is born and prevent illness in the baby after birth.

Key terms

You need to know what these words and phrases mean. Go back through the chapter to find out.

Congenital	Insulin
Heredity	Toxaemia
Inherit	Toxoplasmosis
Deoxyribonucleic acid (DNA)	Premature
Chromosome	Light-for-dates
Gene	Hypothermia
Ovum	Anaemia
Spermatozoa	Rhesus factor
Conception	Jaundice
Sex chromosomes	Viable
Recessive gene	Infant mortality rate
Dominant gene	Maternal mortality rate
Sex-linked inheritance	Fetal distress
Placental barrier	Anoxia
Rubella	Hygiene
AIDS	Hormones
Listeriosis	Endocrine gland
Diabetes	Immunity

SECTION 2
Language and cognitive development

7 AN INTRODUCTION TO LANGUAGE AND COGNITIVE DEVELOPMENT

> **This chapter includes:**
> - **Introduction**
> - **Who's who in psychology**
> - **Nature versus nurture.**

Introduction

The following three chapters will look in detail at the way in which children acquire skills of communication *(language development)* and the growth and process of their thinking and understanding skills *(cognitive development)*. Examining the work of psychologists who have used scientific methods to study these aspects of children's development helps us to understand the sequence and pattern of growth in these areas. Such studies are very influential: the way that we organise and provide for the care and development of young children is directly linked to the research and findings of psychology.

It is very difficult to examine and understand children's cognitive development without looking at the way that language develops alongside it. The link between the development of language and the child's ability to think and understand in an ever more complex way is very clear. As children grow up and become aware of the variety of experiences that surround them they need to organise their thoughts, to make connections and to pose questions about what they experience. Language is the tool that human beings use to unravel these mysteries: as their powers of language increase so do their abilities to make some sense and order of the world. Language is necessary for us to move away from the limitations of thinking and understanding in simple concrete images; it offers us the possibilities of complex abstract and symbolic thought.

THINK!

1 What does the word 'movement' mean to you when you hear it (or read or write it)?
2 Ask others in your group to share their thoughts.
3 Did you all have the same response?
4 Did some of you respond with a concrete image; for example a wheel turning, a child running?
5 Were some responses more abstract, for example a dizzy feeling after a roundabout ride, The Green Movement?

None of these responses is right or wrong. The range of answers shows how language enables us to link common threads in apparently unconnected examples to form an idea of movement.

Language enables us to conceptualise, that is, to organise our knowledge and experience into the concept of, for example, 'movement'. Without the ability to use language to order and define our experience, our understanding and thinking would be very limited indeed.

The development of children's language and thinking go hand in hand and must be considered alongside each other.

CHECK!

1 What do you understand by the term *cognitive development*?
2 Why are cognitive and language development linked?
3 Explain why language is necessary to enable us to think in complex ways.
4 What do you understand by the term *concept*? Give an example of a concept.

Who's who in psychology

The following pages give a brief outline of some of the major figures whose work has been very influential in the field of child care. Further reference to some of these figures is made in the subsequent chapters of this section.

THE PSYCHOLOGISTS

Sigmund Freud

Sigmund Freud lived and worked in Vienna. He began his work at the end of the nineteenth century and continued until his death in 1939. He was a physician who was interested in examining the minds of his patients whilst trying to identify the cause of their physical symptoms. He used techniques of hypnosis, dream analysis and free association. This same approach is used in *psychoanalysis* today and Freud is often referred to as the father of psychoanalysis. Freud's methods and findings were very controversial at the time. He is most famous for recognising the influence of the unconscious or *subconscious* mind on human behaviour. One of the ways he used to prove the existence of the unconscious was to examine 'slips of the tongue', arguing that the unconscious mind was responsible for making these remarks, often against the wishes and interests of the conscious mind. Nowadays we might refer to these remarks as 'Freudian slips'.

Freud is also influential because of the links he made between the development of the personality in later life with early childhood experiences, and in particular the child's relationships with its parents or carers. Much of Freud's work has been criticised or even ridiculed, but the stress by child-care workers on the importance to the child of the impressions and experiences of their early years is directly linked to Freud's findings.

John Bowlby

John Bowlby studied the process of attachment between mothers and their babies. His theory of *maternal deprivation* was very influential in the 1950s and 60s, both in an assessment of the kind of provisions made for the institutional care of children and in shaping attitudes to how children should be cared for and who should be doing the caring. (Bowlby's theories and responses to them are examined fully in Section 3, *Social and emotional development*.)

Jean Piaget

Jean Piaget lived between 1896 and 1980, was Swiss and a biologist by training. He observed his own children at play and then a wider sample of other children. He used these observations as the basis for his theory of cognitive development, which identifies particular stages of development and the kind of learning that is within the child's understanding at each stage. He also stressed the child's interaction with the environment as a crucial factor in learning.

Piaget's work has been criticised and many of his findings challenged. In spite of this, most early years' provision is very closely allied to Piaget's findings on intellectual development, which will be examined in more detail below.

Lev Semyonovich Vygotsky

A Russian psychologist whose studies of children's learning were carried out in the 1920s and 30s, Vygotsky's work looked at the importance of the social world in children's learning and stressed that learning progresses through social interaction and communication. (See also *zone of proximal development* on page 143).

Jerome Bruner

Jerome Bruner has suggested from his studies that adults can support or 'scaffold' children's learning and that through this support the children achieve tasks of which they might be incapable alone. Having achieved with support, the child may then attempt and achieve the task without the adult's support.

THE BEHAVIOURISTS

The theories of the psychologists discussed briefly above have at least one thing in common, that children's learning is linked to clearly defined stages of development and that children will proceed through these at varying speeds. There are other perspectives on how and why children learn. One of these approaches is that of the *behaviourists*, who believe that learning takes place through a process called *conditioning*. Ivan Pavlov and BF Skinner belong to this school.

Ivan Pavlov

Pavlov's work is based on his experiments with dogs. The dogs became so familiar with the bell that was rung before their food was set down that they would salivate at the bell before the food appeared, in anticipation of this food. The dogs were *conditioned* to associate the bell with food so that their reflex response to the food (salivation) was triggered by its ringing. This type of response is called *classical conditioning*. Only behaviour which is mainly automatic, like reflexes, can be conditioned in this way.

BF Skinner

The basis of Skinner's theories is his work with rats who had to learn to press levers to obtain food. He found that the rats learned how to press the levers and that this behaviour was *reinforced* by receiving the reward of the food pellets. The rats soon learned that to obtain another reward (food) they would have to perform the task again. These kinds of experiments led to the theory of *operant conditioning* where the subject needs to perform a desired behaviour which is then reinforced with a reward. Just about any kind of behaviour can be conditioned in this way and the technique has an obvious application in behaviour modification programmes. *Positive reinforcement*, where behaviour that is desired is rewarded, has been shown to be more effective than *negative reinforcement* which punishes undesirable behaviour. This is because punishment may limit an undesirable response but it will not reinforce a positive behaviour with which to replace it.

CHANGING ATTITUDES

Taken on their own, none of the psychological studies glanced at here can explain all of the complexities surrounding how and why children learn. By considering some of these findings we can see the influence of these thinkers on the way that we approach children's learning. Our knowledge about the way in which children learn does not stand still: studies are continually examined and re-evaluated so that those who work with children can make informed decisions about what they do and why they do it.

Nature versus nurture

Are children born with predetermined intellectual capacity or does the environment that surrounds them encourage the development of these abilities? This is basically the subject of the nature *versus* nurture debate and it can be relied upon to provoke much discussion amongst those who are involved with children's learning.

Those who uphold the *nature* side of the argument say that intelligence is innate and that the child's genetic inheritance determines intellectual achievement and, to some extent, personality.

The supporters of *nurture* hold that it is the quality of the child's environment in the crucial early years that has much to do with the growth of intelligence.

The exercises which follow may make the debate appear more simple than it really is; it is likely that both nature and nurture play a significant part. Scientists are continually discovering more about the factors that make us who and what we are and they are sure to find out more about the scope of our genetic inheritance. As child-care workers you have no influence on the child's 'nature', but it is your role and responsibility to provide a rich and stimulating environment that will 'nurture' all children and enable them to fulfil their potential.

1 In your own words, write down what the nature versus nurture debate is about.

THINK!

A 6-year-old child of musical parents is already showing a real interest in music and is able to play a number of simple tunes on the piano. If you believed that *nature* was the strongest factor in this case you might say that the child has inherited this musical talent from her musically able parents, that her ability was genetically determined. But someone on the *nurture* side of the fence might say that this child had grown up in a household where music was valued, where she was encouraged from an early age to join in with family music activities and that it was her environment which was responsible for her musical aptitude.

Which factor do you believe is more important?

DO!

1 Talk this last case over with another student.
2 Think of three more examples and write down factors that you might put for both the nature and the nurture sides of the argument.
3 Which side can you make the strongest case for?

Key terms

You need to know what these words and phrases mean. Go back through the chapter and find out.

Cognitive development	Positive reinforcement
Conceptualise	Negative reinforcement
Behaviourist	Nature
Classical conditioning	Nurture
Operant conditioning	

---

8 LANGUAGE DEVELOPMENT

> **This chapter includes:**
> - **What is language?**
> - **Bilingualism**
> - **Psychology and language development**
> - **Sequence of language development**
> - **Talking with children**
> - **Planning for children's language development**
> - **Factors affecting language development.**

What is language?

Language is the main way in which human beings communicate. We are the only species which has the ability to use language. Other species do communicate but in ways specific to their needs, for example, by making their fur standing on end to communicate danger, spraying their territory to mark it out or growling to deter attackers.

Humans live in a very complex world and need a complex system of communication. Language is this complex system. Language is also needed to satisfy the human need to communicate feelings, complex needs, thoughts and ideas.

Spoken language is a structured set of sounds; written language is a structured set of symbols. These symbols are shared and understood by everyone who speaks the same language. Consider the word *pain*. In English this means suffering or distress. In French (pronounced *pan)* it means bread. Therefore what *pain* means to an individual, and how it is pronounced, depends upon which language the individual was brought up to speak.

Language is learned, and the ability to operate well within society is affected by the ability to use language effectively.

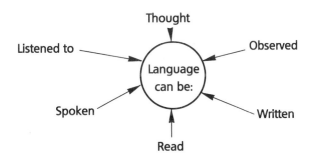

The forms of language in the diagram are used at different times for different situations. The ability to use all these expressions of language requires a high level of skill. Young children need the opportunity to acquire these skills.

THINK!

1 Which of these skills would you expect a nursery-aged child to have?
2 Which of these skills would you expect an infant-aged child to be developing?
3 Why do you think that there is a difference in these answers?

SPOKEN LANGUAGE

The raw materials of spoken language are sounds. These sounds come together to form words. Combinations of words are brought together in special and complex ways to form sentences. The meaning in a sentence is communicated by the way in which words are combined. Look at the following:

> The dog bites the man.
> The man bites the dog.

The same words are used each time but because the order of the words is altered, so is the meaning of the second sentence.

So that there is shared understanding of what is being said there are some rules that everyone needs to learn and use. These include pronunciation and grammar.

Pronunciation

Pronunciation is the way that words are said and may vary depending on which part of the country you come from. These accents add interest and diversity to language and the variations are not usually so different that people cannot be understood.

THINK!

1 How many accents can you recall?
2 Can you identify which part of the country they come from?
3 Are some accents thought to be 'better' than others?
4 How might people be stereotyped because of their accent?
5 What do you think about this stereotyping?

Grammar

To be able to communicate exactly what is meant the speaker must normally use the correct grammar. Try the following exercise.

THINK!

1 *The table is in the classroom.* How would you say that there is more than one table?

2 *I am playing my guitar.* How would you say this if you did this yesterday? Can you think of two ways of saying this?

3 *I run across the road.* How would you say this if it happened an hour ago?

4 Think carefully about how you changed the sentences. What did you change?

5 How did you know what to change?

Once you have learned these rules you rarely get them wrong when you are speaking even if you cannot identify the grammatical rules.

NON-VERBAL COMMUNICATION

When people are speaking and listening there are many clues besides the actual spoken words which are picked up to help us interpret the interaction:

- tone of voice
- body posture (how and where we stand)
- gesture, body movements (such as a shrug)
- facial expression
- eye contact.

This non-verbal communication may have several functions:

- to replace speech, for example, a finger on the lips
- to signal an attitude, for example, yawning when someone is talking to you
- to aid verbal communication, for example, pointing when saying 'that one'
- to express emotion (emotion is often evident in facial expression).

As with other aspects of language there is a general shared understanding of non-verbal signals. Moreover, they are often sent out, received and understood without us being consciously aware of them.

It is important to realise that there are some cultural differences in non-verbal communication which could result in misinterpretation: in some cultures, for example, children are expected to avoid eye contact when being addressed by an adult, whereas other cultures might interpret such behaviour as insolence on the part of the child.

LISTENING

Although most people are born with the ability to listen and take it for granted, it is in fact quite a complex skill. Listening involves sifting out and selecting relevant information from all the sounds around us.

Like all other skills children need to practise listening carefully. This demands good powers of concentration. This skill is often called *active* listening.

DO!

1 List four activities which involve active listening.

2 What is your role in these activities?

3 What other ways can you think of which would help a child to listen carefully?

THINKING

Language is the main tool that human beings use for thinking. Thinking can be done without language but at a very simple level: we can recall pictures, images and tactile sensations. However, these ways of thinking and recalling information are not complex enough for all that is demanded of human beings. A more flexible and efficient way of using and manipulating information in many different ways is needed: language is this flexible and efficient way of thinking.

Language and cognitive development are therefore very closely linked.

THINK!

Many concepts are stored in the memory and recalled as a word. A whole range of meanings and possibilities are recalled by one word.
1 What do these words mean to you?
   - Movement
   - Shape
   - Sound
2 Did you recall a range of meanings for each word?
   These words mean many things and would therefore be impossible to store as one picture or image.

DO!

1 Ask other people what meanings the words *movement*, *shape* and *sound* mean to them.
2 Represent this information on a chart or graph.
3 Suggest reasons why we need to store information as words. Give examples from your findings.

WRITTEN LANGUAGE

Letters, words and sentences are symbols used to represent the spoken word. The understanding of these symbols has to be shared with people who speak and write in the same language. For example, in English this combination of symbols

APPLE

is used to represent this object.

In Punjabi this combination of symbols ਆਦਮੀ is used to represent this object.

So that there is a shared understanding of how to write, there are rules which everyone needs to learn. In   standard English there are the following rules:
- you write on each line from left to right
- you start at the top left-hand corner
- the spacing between the letters in words and the words in sentences is standardised
- words are spelled in the same way
- appropriate punctuation and grammar are necessary.

Some of these rules will be different in other languages.

Learning all these rules as well as developing the fine motor skills needed for writing is a difficult task. Children need plenty of practice.

Reading
Once language is written down it can be read by making sense of the symbols.

DO!

Use the symbols below to decode the sentence which follows.

A = 1	G = 7	M = 13	S = 19	Y = 25
B = 2	H = 8	N = 14	T = 20	Z = 26
C = 3	I = 9	O = 15	U = 21	
D = 4	J = 10	P = 16	V = 22	
E = 5	K = 11	Q = 17	W = 23	
F = 6	L = 12	R = 18	X = 24	

4,5,3,15,4,9,14,7   9,19 1,14   9,13,16,15,18,20,1,14,20   5,1,18,12,25
18,5,1,4,9,14,7   19,11,9,12,12.

Although decoding is an important skill, reading is not just a matter of decoding symbols. There are many *cognitive* skills needed so that the symbols can be understood. Again the link between language and cognitive development is important. As with writing, there are rules that need to be learned and applied when reading so that the reader can understand the text. These rules are learned over a period of time and children need plenty of practice at them. In English, for example, in reading, as for writing:
- the reader progresses from left to right
- the top left-hand corner is the starting point
- there are patterns in words that reflect sound (phonics) or shape (look and say)
- punctuation ensures that the text makes sense.

Language in our world
Language is not just learned in school or when someone is trying to teach it to us. We live in a literate world so language is all around us in all aspects of our daily life. We are constantly bombarded with language in all its forms, spoken, written, to read and to listen to.

1 What are the standardised rules in reading?
2 What are the standardised rules in writing?
3 Why are these rules necessary?

DO!

1 Investigate how these rules are different in other languages.
2 How may this affect a child's acquisition of written English?
3 Go for a walk in your local area.
4 Make a note of all the different ways that you can see or hear language being used (do not forget thinking!).

Bilingualism

Many children in Britain today will come from homes where English is not the first or the only language of the family. The child may grow up in a setting where English is never spoken, where English is sometimes spoken or where English is used between some members of a family while others converse in another language. The child will need to become confident and fluent in the language that is spoken in the child-care settting (usually English) so that she can participate fully in the experience. This can only be done if there is awareness and understanding of the child's linguistic background on the part of the child-care workers. With this, appropriate provision can be made for the development of language skills in English and in the child's first or home language.

GLOSSARY OF TERMS

Monolingual	Bilingual	Multilingual	British Sign Language
Speaking one language, for example a child who speaks only English	Speaking two languages, for example a person who speaks Welsh to his family and Welsh-speaking friends but converses in English with colleagues at work.	Speaking many languages, for example a nursery nurse who speaks English with her colleagues, converses with her family in Punjabi and communicates with a deaf child in sign language (see below).	A distinct visual, gestural, language. It has an independent grammar different from spoken English. It has precise rules governing location, shape, direction, orientation and speed of movement of the hand. It uses head and body movements, facial expression and direction of eye-gaze to convey meaning. Like any language it has regional variations. BSL is the first or preferred language of the deaf community, which in the UK comprises 50 000 people. British Sign Language is used in Britain; deaf communities elsewhere in the world will have developed their own sign language.

NB British Sign Language does not have a written form although you may find line drawings of individual signs in some children's reading books.

Do not confuse *fluency* in spoken language with *literacy* in that language. Many people may not be able to read and write in a language that they can nevertheless speak fluently.

CHECK!

1 Read through the previous section again.
2 Write down definitions of the terms *monolingual, bilingual, multilingual.* Try to give examples from your own experience of people who fit these linguistc groups.
3 What do you understand by the term *linguistic background*?

NEEDS OF BILINGUAL CHILDREN

It is not helpful or accurate to categorise all bilingual children as having the same needs or experiences. What they do have in common is the experience of using and needing to use more than one language, but there will be other factors that might be quite different. Some examples are given below.

- A child from a Pakistani background whose grandparents settled in Britain in the 1950s has grown up in an extended family where her parents speak to her in English, and where she converses with her grandparents in Punjabi. At school she talks in English with teachers and sometimes in Punjabi to her classmates. After school she also learns to read and write in Arabic, the language of the Koran.
- The 4-year-old son of a German student on a 2-year study programme attends a suburban playgroup where the playgroup workers are encouraging him to use his few words of English. His mother usually speaks to him in German but is also introducing more English at home.
- A 6-year-old from Manchester has moved to rural mid-Wales where her parents have opened a restaurant. All of the children in her class speak Welsh as their first language and, although there are some English lessons, Welsh is the main language of the school and of the playground.
- A 3-year-old whose family are refugees from South East Asia are housed in temporary bed-and-breakfast accommodation. The child attends a local authority day nursery and is very withdrawn. His parents communicate with the staff through an interpreter, but this service is not often available.
- A 4-year-old hearing child whose parents are profoundly deaf uses British Sign Language with her parents at home and with their friends at the Deaf Club. In school and with her brother she communicates in spoken English.
- A 5-year-old Bengali child has recently moved to a small village school from a large city school where many languages were spoken and valued. His last teacher felt that he was progressing well. In his new school he is the only child for whom English is a second language. There is no ESL (English as a Second Language) support for him and he is slipping behind in his school work.

1 Read the case studies again.
2 What similarities are there in these experiences?
3 What differences are there?
4 Consider each individual child. What are the needs of each one?

MEETING THE NEEDS OF BILINGUAL CHILDREN

It is important that the needs of children whose first language is not English are understood and met in the child-care setting. All children will experience some feelings of anxiety on the first days in an unfamiliar setting, such as school or playgroup. These anxieties are bound to be increased if the child is surrounded by an unfamiliar linguistic environment as well. If such children are to benefit from their experiences in nursery, school or day care, staff need to make sure that they understand, build on and value the children's first language (or mother tongue) capabilities.

You need to remember the following points:

- many children who do not speak English fluently will be very capable in their first language
- do not label children who speak little or no English as having language problems or language delay. Their lack of competence is in English, not language
- a child may be able to use language to conceptualise in their mother tongue but not in their second language
- the non-verbal language in English (the intonation, rhythm, use of gesture and eye contact) may be quite different from that of the child's first language
- a bilingual or multilingual child will thrive in an atmosphere where language diversity is valued
- speaking more than one language is a positive attribute and should be regarded as such.

Any child unable to communicate in the language of the child-care setting (English, in most of the case studies above) will be disadvantaged. Specialist help needs to be available to ensure that the child learns and practises English. Given the right kind of support and an attitude of understanding from the staff, the child will soon acquire the necessary skills in English that are needed to take full advantage of all that is going on.

In our enthusiasm to get children competent in their second language, we should make sure that the development of the first language is fostered too. Studies show that children who are given an opportunity to develop their first language to an advanced level can transfer reading and writing skills to their second language quite readily. However, children who are introduced to the complex skills of reading and writing in a language that they do not understand might have difficulty in making similar progress.

SUPPORT FOR BILINGUAL CHILDREN

The kinds of support available for bilingual children varies a great deal from area to area. Funding is available from the Home Office via the Local Authority to support the needs of children from the New Commonwealth, in effect those whose families come from the Indian sub-continent or from the Caribbean. This means that there are many bilingual children who are excluded from this source of support: those from EU countries for example, who rely on local initiatives to provide services to support their acquisition of English.

Here are some examples of the kinds of support that might be available:

- English as a Second Language (ESL) staff: these are teachers and classsroom assistants (often nursery nurses) who work alongside members of staff in schools and nurseries where there are children who would benefit from a one-to-one relationship and small group work on developing English skills. Where there are substantial numbers of children whose first language is not English a member of an ESL team may be assigned to a particular establishment. In other cases, where there are fewer such children, a number of sessions per week might be allocated.
- mother tongue (or heritage or home language) teachers, assistants or language instructors: some local authorities employ staff whose job is to support and encourage the acquisition of the child's first (or home) language. This builds on the process that has already begun at home and allows for the growth of confidence and skills in language and in thinking.
- bilingual assistant (often a nursery nurse): these assistants are usually employed in an establishment where many of the children have a common first language. The assistant works alongside the other staff, translating instructions and information for the children and also sharing stories, nursery rhymes or games, allowing the child access to the whole curriculum. The bilingual assistant can provide reassurance for the child and can be helpful in supporting a flow of information to and from parents, particularly when settling children into new situations.
- Saturday or community schools: these are usually run by members of a local community, including parents, who are anxious that the cultural identity of the community is maintained by keeping the language alive. This is in particular for children who are the second generation of their family to have been born in Britain. These schools sometimes have a religious function as well, for example learning extracts from the Koran.

DO!

1 Investigate the linguistic background of the children in your placement or workplace.
2 How many languages are spoken by children and by staff?
3 Are there children who are bilingual or multilingual? Under what circumstances do they use their 'other' languages?
4 Listen to the children. Do you hear a variety of accents and dialect words?
5 Find out what kind of support is available locally for children for whom English is their second language.

LANGUAGE DIVERSITY

We are part of a world where there are many different languages, accents, dialects and other ways of communication, both written and spoken. It would be limiting for children only to be aware of their own language and ignorant of the existence of others. By promoting a positive atmosphere that celebrates language diversity we can enrich the language experience of all children while at the same time valuing the experience of the bilingual child. This is an enriching experience for all children and is of as much benefit to the child in the monolingual environment as it is to the child who is already surrounded by many languages.

The following ideas are suggested for promoting language diversity in a child-care setting. It is important to value language diversity everywhere, not just in establishments where a variety of languages are spoken.

- Present welcome signs and greetings in a variety of languages.
- Choose dual-language books for your book corner (include sign language too). Draw children's attention to the differences in text and script.
- Teach songs and nursery rhymes in a number of languages. Get help from parents and friends if you need it.
- Make books in the children's own language.
- Listen to tapes of songs and poems and stories in many languages.
- Make a display of printed materials containing as many different languages and scripts as you can find. Get children to help by bringing in things from home.
- Choose stories from all around the world. Find someone who can tell the story in another language; tell the English version alongside this.
- Encourage children to learn simple greetings in languages other than their own.

Try to think of some more ideas to add to this list.

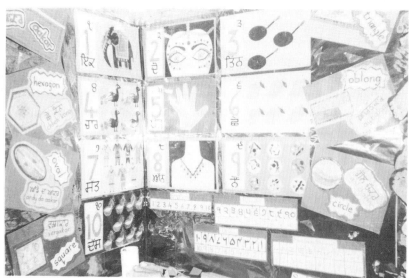

Language use in a child-care setting

DO!

1 Think of a setting that you are familiar with: a nursery, playgroup or infant school classroom and suggest some ways to provide an environment that would promote language diversity.

2 Draw a diagram and include on it any ideas that you may have which might widen the range of the children's language environment. Identify children and adults on the diagram and suggest what they might be doing.

Psychology and language development

Many psychologists have studied and researched how human beings acquire language. Some have concluded that language is predominantly a genetically inherited skill. Others believe that language is learned after a child is born. This is part of the nature *v* nurture debate (see page 111).

Nature		Nurture
Our ability for language is genetically determined.	Language is learned *after* we are born through a process of reinforcement.	Social interaction is important in the acquisition of language skills
Noam Chomsky Chomsky believes that we are born with all the appropriate physical and intellectual capabilities for the acquisition of language: ■ speech-producing mechanisms: tongue, lips, palette, breath control ■ the intellectual ability to understand complex grammar. ■ parts of the brain that enable understanding of language. He calls this a Language Acquisition Device or LAD.	BF Skinner When children utter sounds and words which are part of the language that they will eventually speak, they are greeted with a positive response. This positive response is the reinforcement. It encourages the child to repeat the sound or word. Sounds and words that are not part of the language that the child will eventually speak are not reinforced and are therefore extinguished. This is called *operant conditioning.*	L.S. Vygotsky Vygotsky stressed the importance of the relationship between speech and writing. He saw children's early attempts at writing as significant. Children progress from drawing things to drawing speech. This will not initially be recognisable as writing but conceptually children have understood what writing is: the setting down or drawing of speech. This development occurs through interaction and communication with other people.

The nature–nurture debate on language is inconclusive. It seems likely that learning language has elements of both nature and nurture: there is some genetic sensitivity to language but that children's experiences after birth are very important in their development of language.

Children progress from drawing things to drawing speech

1 What is the *nature* argument for language acquisition?
2 What is Chomsky's LAD?
3 What is the *nurture* argument for language acquisition?
4 How does operant conditioning relate to language acquisition?
5 Why is children's drawing important in the development of language skills?

DO!

1 Read back through the nature–nurture debate on language acquisition.
2 What are the problems associated with each argument?
3 Decide for yourself what you think is the combination of nature and nurture in children's language acquisition. Give reasons for your answer.
4 Compare your conclusions with those of others. How similar are they?

Sequence of language development

Children's language develops through a series of identifiable stages. These stages are sequential, as outlined below. The level of children's development depends partly on their chronological age, but their experience of language from an early age is, however, just as important a factor. If children are exposed to a rich language environment this will be reflected in their language development. Children who have not had this opportunity will not have had the same chances for development. It is important to take this into account when assessing a child's stage of language development.

Children who are bilingual may develop their languages at a slightly slower rate than children who are monolingual. This is to be expected as they have much more to learn. Given an environment that promotes language development, bilingual children will become proficient in both languages.

Approximate age	Developmental level
Birth	Involuntary cry
2–3 weeks	Signs of intentional communication: eye contact
4 weeks onwards	Cries are becoming voluntary, indicating for example, unhappiness, tiredness, loneliness Children may respond by moving their eyes or head towards the speaker, kicking or stopping crying
6 weeks onwards	Children may smile when spoken to Cooing and gurgling begin in response to parent or carer's presence and voice, also to show contentment
1–2 months	Children may move their eyes or head towards the direction of the sound
3 months	Children will raise their head when sounds attract their attention

Approximate age	Developmental level
4–months	Playful sounds appear: cooing, gurgling, laughing, chuckling, squealing; these are in response to the human voice and to show contentment Children respond to familiar sounds by turning their head, kicking or stopping crying Shout to attract attention
6 months	The beginning of babbling: regular, repeated sounds, e.g. *gegegegeg, mamamam, dadada.*; children play around with these sounds. This is important for practising sound-producing mechanisms necessary for later speech Cooing, laughing and gurgling become stronger Children begin to understand emotion in the parent or carer's voice Children begin to enjoy music and rhymes, particularly if accompanied by actions
9 months	Babbling continues and the repertoire increases Children begin to recognise their own name May understand simple, single words, e.g. *No, Bye-bye* Children continue to enjoy music and rhymes and will now attempt to join in with the actions, e.g. playing pat-a-cake
9–12 months	Babbling begins to reflect the intonation of speech Children may imitate simple words. This is usually an extension of babbling, e.g. *dada* Pointing begins. This is often accompanied by a sound or the beginnings of a word. This demonstrates an increasing awareness that words are associated with people and objects
12 months	Children's vocabulary starts to develop. First word(s) appear, usually names of people and objects that the child is familiar with. They are built around the child's babbling sound repertoire Children understand far more than they can say. This is called a *passive* vocabulary. Spoken words are referred to as an *active* vocabulary They begin be able to respond to simple instructions, e.g. 'Give me the ball', 'Come here', 'Clap your hands'
15 months	Active vocabulary development remains quite limited as children concentrate on achieving mobility Passive vocabulary increases rapidly Pointing accompanied by a single word is the basis of communication
18 months	Children's active vocabulary increases; this tends to be names of familiar things and people Children use their language to name belongings and point out named objects Generalisation of words is difficult, e.g. *cat* can only be their cat, not the one next door One word and intonation is used to indicate meaning, e.g. *cup* may mean, 'I want a drink', 'I have lost my cup', 'Where is my cup?'. The intonation (and possibly the situation) would indicate the meaning to people who are familiar with the child Children will repeat words and sentences

Approximate age	Developmental level
21 months	Both passive and active vocabularies rapidly increase; the passive vocabulary, however, remains larger than the active Children begin to name objects and people that are not there: this shows an awareness of what language is for Sentences begin. Initially as two word phrases, e.g. 'Mummy gone', 'Coat on' Gesture is still a fundamental part of communication Children begin asking questions, usually 'What?', 'Who?' and 'Where?'
2 years	Both active and passive vocabularies continue to increase Children can generalise words but this sometimes means that they over-generalise, e.g. all men are *daddy*, all furry animals with four legs are *dog* Personal pronouns (words used instead of actual names) are used, e.g. I, she, he, you, they. They are not always used correctly Sentences become longer although they tend to be in *telegraphic* speech, i.e. only the main sense-conveying words are used, e.g. 'Mummy gone work', 'Me go bike' Questions are asked frequently, 'What?' and 'Why?'
2 years 6 months	Vocabulary increases rapidly; there is less imbalance between passive and active vocabularies Word use is more specific so there are fewer over- and under-generalisations Sentences get longer and more precise, although they are still usually abbreviated versions of adult sentences Word order in sentences is sometimes incorrect Children can use language to protect their own rights and interests and to maintain their own comfort and pleasure, e.g. 'It's mine', 'Get off', 'I'm playing with that' Children can listen to stories and are interested in them
3 years	Vocabulary develops rapidly; new words are picked up quickly Sentences continue to become longer and more like adult speech Children talk to themselves during play: this is to plan and order their play, which is evidence of children using language to think Language can now be used to report on what is happening, to direct their own and others' actions, to express ideas and to initiate and maintain friendships Pronouns are usually used correctly Questions such as 'Why?', 'Who?' and 'What for?' are used frequently Rhymes and melody are attractive
3 years 6 months	Children have a wide vocabulary and word usage is usually correct; this continues to increase They are now able to use complete sentences although word order is sometimes incorrect Language can now be used to report on past experiences Incorrect word endings are sometimes used, e.g. *swimmed, runned, seed*
4 years	Children's vocabulary is now extensive; new words are added regularly

Approximate age	Developmental level
4 years *continued*	Longer and more complex sentences are used; sentences may be joined with *because*, which demonstrates an awareness of causes and relationships Children are able to narrate long stories including the sequence of events Play involves running commentaries The boundaries between fact and fiction are blurred and this is reflected in children's speech Speech is fully intelligible with few, minor incorrect uses Questioning is at its peak. 'When?' is used alongside other questions. By this stage children can usually use language to share, take turns, collaborate, argue, predict what may happen, compare possible alternatives, anticipate, give explanations, justify behaviour, create situations in imaginative play, reflect upon their own feelings and begin to describe how other people feel
5 years	Children have a wide vocabulary and can use it appropriately Vocabulary can include colours, shapes, numbers and common opposites, e.g. big/small, hard/soft Sentences are usually correctly structured although incorrect grammar may still be used Pronunciation may still be childish Language continues to be used and developed as described in the section on 4-year-olds; this may now include phrases heard on the television and associated with children's toys. Questions and discussions are for enquiry and information; questions become more precise as children's cognitive skills develop Children will offer opinions in discussion

Talking with children

The most important factor in children's language development is interaction with other people. It is important that people who work with young children adopt practices that contribute positively to children's language development. There is a recognised link between the quality of adult input and the quality of children's language. Listed below are some important points to remember when talking with children. However, these are only practical points. A sensitivity towards children's needs and knowledge of them as individuals are the basis of positive interaction.

The tone of your voice	Does it convey warmth and interest in the child?
How quickly you speak	Do you speak at a pace that is appropriate for the child or children you are talking with?
Listening	How do you show the child that you are listening? Eye contact and getting down to the child's level show that you are listening. Becoming involved in the conversation also indicates that you are listening and interested.

Waiting	Do you leave enough time for the child to respond? Young children may need time to formulate their response. It is important to remember that pauses and silences are part of conversation.
Questions	Do you ask too many questions? This may make the conversation feel like a question-and-answer session, especially if your response is 'That's right'. What type of questions do you ask? *Closed* questions require a one-word answer and do not give the child the opportunity to practise and develop their language skills. *Open* questions have a range of possible answers and do give the child the opportunity to practise and develop their language skills.
Your personal contribution	Do you contribute your own experience and/or opinions to the conversation? Conversation is a two-way process. It involves both people sharing information. This should be the same with children. It is important that the choice of what to talk about is shared.
What do you talk about?	How much of what you say is management talk? How much is conversation and chatting? How much is explaining? How much is playful talk? Children need to be involved in a wide range of language experiences to enable them to practise and develop their own language.
Developing thought	Do you ask for and give reasons and explanations when talking with children? Do you encourage the child to make predictions in real and imaginary situations? Do you encourage the children to give accounts of what they are doing or have done? Children's language and cognitive skills can be developed in this way.
Who do you talk to?	You must talk to all children within the group. All children need the opportunity to practise their language. There will be a range of developmental levels within every group of children and it is important that each child's needs are met.

DO!

1 Read the following three conversations between an adult and a child. The dots indicate a pause.

Conversation 1
(Three children are playing at a clay activity.)

Adult   What are you playing with?
Child   Clay.
Adult   What are you making?
Child   Dinner.
Adult   What does the clay feel like?
Child   ...Cold...wet.

Adult   Is it smooth?
Child   Yes. . .

Conversation 2
(A child arrives at nursery.)
Adult   Hello, James. . .What have you brought with you?
Child   . . .my Fluffy. . .
(The adult sits down on a chair near to the child.)
Adult   Have you brought it to show to us?
Child   Yes.
Adult   Let me have a look . . . He's lovely . . . I've got a teddy that looks just
         like Fluffy . . . Little brown eyes *(The adult points to them.)* . . . A big
         nose . . . I take mine to bed with me . . . What do you do with Fluffy?
Child   . . . Go to bed with him . . . Bring him to nursery . . . Take him to
         Nan's . . . My Nan makes toys . . .
Adult   Does she . . . What does she make?

Conversation 3
(A child comes in from playing outside.)
Child   I don't like it outside.
Adult   Why not? *(She is tidying the room.)*
Child   It's cold.
Adult   No it's not . . . Fasten your coat up . . . *(She continues to tidy up.)* . . .
         What have you been playing with?
Child   . . . The bike and on the grass . . . with Simon . . .
Adult   What did you do with Simon?
Child   . . . Played . . . *(The child wanders off.)*

2 Make a list of the positive and negative aspects of communication for each
   conversation.
3 Which of the conversations demonstrates the best adult communication
   skills? Give reasons for your choice.

DO!

1 Tape yourself talking with a child who is under 7 years of age.
2 Listen to the tape and assess your communication skills: refer to the section
   on talking with children on page 127.
3 What is the child's stage of language development? Give reasons for your
   answer backed up with examples from the tape.
4 Suggest ways in which you can improve your communication skills.
5 Suggest ways for enhancing the child's communication skills.

Planning for children's language development

Children learn and develop their language skills through interaction with other people.
Adults therefore have a vital role to play in children's language development through

talking and listening to them. Careful consideration also needs to be given to the activities and experiences provided for children. Appropriately planned activities or experiences provide the opportunity for children to use their existing skills and develop others.

Before planning it is necessary to assess each child's level of development. This can be done through careful observation of the child. Once the level is established, relevant experiences and activities can be planned to meet the child's needs. During the experience or activity the adult needs to adopt a variety of strategies to promote each child's language development.

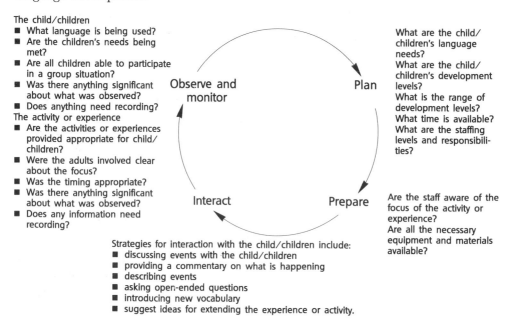

The child/children
■ What language is being used?
■ Are the children's needs being met?
■ Are all children able to participate in a group situation?
■ Was there anything significant about what was observed?
■ Does anything need recording?
The activity or experience
■ Are the activities or experiences provided appropriate for child/children?
■ Were the adults involved clear about the focus?
■ Was the timing appropriate?
■ Was there anything significant about what was observed?
■ Does any information need recording?

Observe and monitor

Plan

What are the child/children's language needs?
What are the child/children's development levels?
What is the range of development levels?
What time is available?
What are the staffing levels and responsibilities?

Interact

Prepare

Are the staff aware of the focus of the activity or experience?
Are all the necessary equipment and materials available?

Strategies for interaction with the child/children include:
■ discussing events with the child/children
■ providing a commentary on what is happening
■ describing events
■ asking open-ended questions
■ introducing new vocabulary
■ suggest ideas for extending the experience or activity.

The monitoring, planning, preparation and interaction with children is a continual process. As children develop their language skills the adult needs to respond to their changing needs.

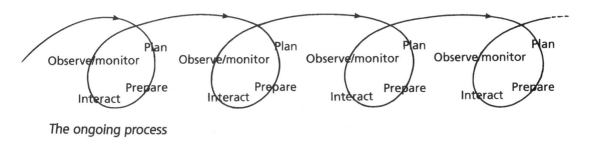

Observe/monitor   Plan   Prepare   Interact
Observe/monitor   Plan   Prepare   Interact
Observe/monitor   Plan   Prepare   Interact
Observe/monitor   Plan   Prepare   Interact

The ongoing process

CHECK!

1 What is involved in observing children's language?
2 What is involved in planning experiences or activities to promote language development?

3 List the ways in which an adult can interact with a child to promote their language development.

THINK!

1 Why is it important for an adult to be aware of each child's level of language development?
2 What are the different observational techniques that could be used to establish this?
3 Why is it important that all the adults involved with the child are aware of the focus of the language work?

DO!

1 Choose an appropriate experience that promotes language development of a child or children within a specified age group.
2 Refer to the section on interaction on page 127. List specific examples of how you would interact with the child to promote their language development.

Factors affecting language development.

To develop language successfully children need a rich stimulating environment that provides the opportunity for experiences appropriate to their level of development. There are a number of factors that influence the quality of the language environment:
- the presence of positive role models
- the opportunity for the children to practise their language skills
- positive feedback to enable the children to pick up language and to adjust and refine their language skills.

DO!

Below are four outlines of care situations for young children:
   a) a 2½-year-old child who is at a day nursery for the whole day
   b) a 3-year-old child who attends a nursery unit attached to a school for half the day; she spends the other half of the day at home
   c) a 2-year-old child who is cared for by a bilingual childminder; the childminder also cares for three other children: two more 2-year-olds and a 4-year-old. All the children are being brought up bilingually
   d) a 3-year-old only child who is at home all day with her mother.
Answer the following questions for each particular child. Your answer should make reference to the factors that affect development and the language development sequence.
1 Who provides the child with positive role models?
2 How are the positive role models provided?

3 What opportunities may the child may have to practise their language?
4 How could the child's language development be encouraged through feedback?

All children come to a care setting with different experiences. This includes their experience of language. Because the experiences that a child has had are so influential in their development, the pace that children develop language is not uniform. Within any group of children there will be a wide range of proficiency in language. This could include children who have delayed language development in relation to the expected range of norms; it could also include children who are way beyond the expected range of norms. It is important that each child is treated as an individual and their needs assessed and met.

When a child's language development is delayed there are a number of agencies who may be involved in meeting the child's needs. The extent of provision for children with language delay will vary from area to area. Some of the agencies who may be involved are listed below:
- health visitor
- speech therapist
- Portage worker/scheme
- language unit
- nursery
- individual classroom support
- support from charitable organisations, for example Barnardos, The National Children's Home
- local initiatives.

DO!

1 Investigate one of the agencies outlined above.
2 What help and support are they able to provide?
3 How can this help be accessed for a child who needs the support?

Key terms
You need to know what these words and phrases mean. Go back through the chapter and find out.

Monolingual | Mother tongue teachers/assistants
Bilingual | Bilingual assistant
Multilingual | Language Acquisition Device
British Sign Language

---

9 COGNITIVE DEVELOPMENT

What is cognitive development?

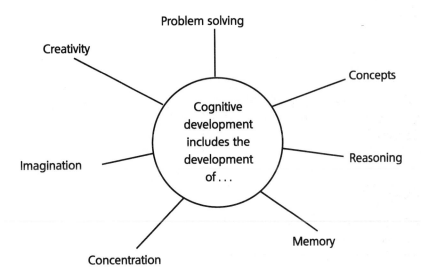

IMAGINATION

Imagination is the ability to form mental images, or concepts of objects not present, or that do not exist. It is fairly easy to conjure up images of, for example a beach, outer space, grandparents, school, chocolate.

The imagination is the basis for many of the activities we regard as enjoyable:
- books
- films and television
- dance
- art
- music
- design.

These are part of the culture of a society. They are often the basis for activities which people choose to be involved in, in their own time. They provide relaxation and add to the quality of life.

Imagination is also part of the following activities:
- problem solving
- innovative and original thought.

Change comes about through new and innovative ideas and by finding solutions to problems. Imagination is an important aspect of ideas. The idea might be an invention, for example the telephone, television, the car, the aeroplane. All these started as ideas in someone's imagination. The idea might also be a solution to an existing problem which might be an everyday or individual problem, scientific or medical problem, society or world problem. The process is the same: solving problems in new or unusual ways requires imagination.

Imaginative play in young children also contributes to the development of other important skills. Through using their imagination to play children develop the ability to use one object to represent another, for example using a doll to represent a baby, using a pan to represent a hat, using sand and toy cars to represent a race track. This is called *symbolic* play: one object is being used as a symbol for another.

This skill is transferable. If a child can use symbols in a play situation they can transfer this skill to learning to read and to write, as reading and writing involve use of the same skill of using symbols, in this case letters and words to represent the spoken word (see Chapter 8, *Language development*).

CHECK!

1 What is imagination?
2 Name some things that imagination is needed for.
3 Explain why imagination is important.
4 What is symbolic play?
5 Why is symbolic play important?
6 How does the ability to symbolise help children learn to read and write?

Children and imagination

Children do not need to be taught to be imaginative. Their play is full of examples where they are using their imagination. Here are some examples; there are many more:
- during creative activities such as painting or collage
- being someone, or something, else in role play
- creating an object or design
- thinking up a story or poem
- creating objects from large empty boxes
- moving to music or dancing
- making music
- listening to stories.

It is important that these imaginative skills are nurtured, which means giving children the opportunity to express and develop their ideas. Your role is to provide the time, space, materials and encouragement to enable the children to do this.

Role play

Role play involves the child becoming somebody, or something else. Imagination is an important part of this play. The child may be imitating someone, or something, that she has seen, for example a shop assistant, a doctor, a waiter, a television character. Children also create new, sometimes unique, characters or situations in their play. The child creates these new characters and situations in her imagination.

Role play enables children to discover, enquire, organise and make sense of their environment. They can practise and develop their communication skills; feelings can be explored. All this can be done in a safe environment because they can opt out of the play at any time. This is an important part of their all-round development.

CREATIVITY

Being creative is a way of expressing imaginative ideas in a personal and unique way. When people write books, make films, play or write music, act, dance, paint, create beautiful buildings or gardens or find innovative solutions to problems we say that they have been creative.

There is a lot of debate about what creativity is and whether it is taught or innate. It is hard therefore to say precisely what is and what is not creative, but for something to be described as creative it should have a number of the following features:

- use of the imagination
- begin with an open-ended outcome
- be a personal expression of ideas
- be unique in its process and product
- have the process equally important as the product.

THINK!

1 What do you do now that could be described as creative?
2 Why do you get involved in this activity?
3 What are the benefits of this activity to you?
4 Are there any creative activities that you used to be involved in when you were younger?
5 If so, why are you not still involved in them?

DO!

1 Collect information about creative activities people in your group are involved in now, and creative activities they were involved in when they were children.
2 Represent this information on a graph.
3 Write up your findings and suggest reasons for them.

Children and creativity

Creative activities for children provide the opportunity for them to think beyond what is obvious and to develop their own ideas. This is an important skill for later learning. Children do not need to be taught to be creative. They need the time, space, materials and encouragement to develop their own ideas. This is important: being creative is the expression of personal ideas, not copying or imitating someone else's ideas.

Sometimes it is enough to provide children with the opportunity to be creative and allow them to play without any intervention, for example putting out a range of different sizes and shapes of boxes and letting the children develop their own play themes and ideas.

At other times adults may have more influence in the activity by providing a framework for it. It is important that the framework still allows the child the opportunity to develop their own ideas. Frameworks can be provided in many different ways:

- by the type of materials provided
- by the introduction of a theme for the activity
- by suggestion while the child is engaged in an activity
- by the siting of the activity
- through group work: the child works within the framework agreed by the group.

CHECK!

1 What is creativity?
2 List some activities that require a person to be creative.
3 What features should a creative activity have?
4 Do children need to be taught to be creative?
5 How can you provide a framework for a creative activity?
6 Why is copying not creative?

PROBLEM SOLVING

The ability to solve problems is another aspect of cognitive development. Problem solving does not just mean complex problems; it also includes everyday problems that all people come across, for example which route to take on a journey or how to put objects into a bag so that they all fit. Experience of the world and of how things work means that most problems are quickly solved.

When older children and adults are faced with a problem they draw together all that they know about a situation to enable them to solve it. Logic is used to assess possible solutions: for example, to fit things into a bag you need to know about, sizes, shapes, capacity, tessellation (how items fit together) and rotation. You will very quickly be able to assess the problem and come up with a range of ideas to solve it. Young children need to develop these skills. Their knowledge and experience of the world is more limited than older children and adults, so they have less information to draw on to enable then to solve a problem that they face.

There is a developmental sequence in children's ability to solve problems.

Trial and error learning is the earliest stage in development. The child is trying out solutions to a problem in a random way and will try and fail, try and fail until they arrive at a solution. This will probably involve returning to the problem many times. At this stage the child is not able to identify the problem clearly that they are attempting to solve. Trial and error learning can be very frustrating for a child and in this case careful adult intervention is needed to suggest ways forward for the child.

The next stage in development is a growing ability to identify the problem facing them and work out a possible solution before they try anything out. Children begin to be able to predict what might happen. This *hypothesis* is based on their increasing knowledge and experience of the world. The greater their knowledge and experience the more accurate the hypothesis becomes.

CHECK!

1 What is problem solving?
2 What is trial and error learning?
3 What is a hypothesis?
4 What is the developmental sequence in problem-solving skills?
5 Suggest reasons for the difference in how young and older children solve problems.

1 Observe a child under 2 years old attempting to do a jigsaw puzzle.
2 Observe an older child doing a jigsaw puzzle.
3 What are the differences in their approach to the problems of fitting each piece?
4 Make a list of the things that the child must know to be able to solve the problems of fitting each piece.

CONCEPTS

If we are going to look at the way in which children acquire an ability to think in ever more complex ways we need to examine how they form *concepts*. Concepts are the way in which all information is organised. As children develop a wider range of concepts they build up their knowledge about the world. They form basic concrete concepts through their interaction with the environment and these increase in complexity as their experiences widen.

For example, a young child may first meet and name the concept of 'wet' through bathtime and understand wetness as the feel of water on the skin and hair. The concept develops further when the child is out in a shower of rain and feels the wetness of his anorak and his socks. In the sand tray water is added to the dry sand and the child extends his understanding of 'wet' to the wetness of the sand. More and more experiences of wetness will give the child a comprehensive understanding of the concept of 'wet'.

A whole range of meanings and possibilities are recalled by the concept of 'wet'.

All concepts will be built up in a similar way and it is the role of adults to ensure that opportunities for experiences to assist in this development are provided for children. More abstract concepts such as 'time' or 'speed' will take much longer to understand reliably. Those that are even further away from concrete experiences, such as 'freedom' and 'justice', are impossible for the young child to grasp.

Piaget's theories of cognitive development

Piaget's work on the development of children's thinking is the basis for the way that we provide care and education for young children. His theory looked at the way that children use their everyday experiences to build up an understanding of their world.

He said that the child passed through particular stages on the way to an ever more complete and complex understanding of their surroundings. Using what he found out from observing children, he identified the kind of learning of which the child was capable at each of these stages. Some of the details of these findings have been challenged by more recent psychological studies. Nevertheless there is still much in Piaget's work that enables us to understand the development of children's thinking and the part that we can play in this process.

Hard soft red slow stretchy under transport furniture

1 Choose two of the above concepts and think of activities that would enable 4-year-olds to develop and extend an understanding of them.
2 Write down your suggestions and use them when you have the opportunity.

KEY TERMS USED BY PIAGET

Piaget used a number of key terms in his theories:

- *Cognition*: the process through which logical thinking develops
- *Schema*: all the ideas, memories and information that a child might have about a particular object. These schemas are formed through the child's interaction with the outside world
- *Assimilation*: the way in which a child takes in the important elements of their experiences
- *Accommodation*: the process that involves fitting what the child has learned from new experiences into existing schemas
- *Adaptation*: the result of the interaction of assimilation and accommodation. The child now knows more about the world and can act upon it.

An example follows of these terms in context: a child is used to playing with bricks. Her present *schema* for bricks tells her that bricks can be different sizes and different colours but that they are all the same shape. One day some L-shaped and arch-shaped bricks are introduced to the brick box. She investigates these new additions, playing with them alongside the familiar items she knows as bricks *(assimilation)*. She soon discovers that she can use these new toys in much the same way as the bricks she has already *(accommodation)* but that the different shapes present her with new possibilities and problems in her building *(adaptation)*. Through this experience the child's original schema for bricks has changed considerably.

Two further terms used by Piaget are:

- *Equilibrium:* the need for balance between assimilation and accommodation. A child needs to have plenty of opportunity for assimilation, to experiment, explore and become familiar with one experience before another one comes along. The child can become confused if they have not yet accommodated or organised current experiences into their thinking
- *Operations:* Piaget's term for a framework or structure that he believed must exist so that schemas can be combined in an orderly and logical way. This is essential to the development of more complex thought, for example the ability to speculate.

1 Read through Piaget's key terms again. Check that you understand the meanings.

1 Devise another example that explains assimilation, accommodation and adaptation. Discuss this with a fellow student.

PIAGET'S STAGES

Piaget identified four distinct stages of cognitive development, each with its own characteristics. It is important to remember that the ages given are approximate and intended only as a guide.

Sensory-motor (birth–2 years)

At the sensory-motor stage the child:

- learns principally through the senses and through movement
- is *egocentric:* he can only see the world from his own viewpoint
- becomes aware of *object permanence*, that objects continue to exist when not in view; this awareness occurs at around 8–12 months
- uses abilities intelligently and begins to learn through trial and error methods.

Pre-operations (2–7 years)

Now the child:

- uses words for communication, thinking, imagining
- uses symbols in play, for example a doll for a baby, a lump of playdough for a cake
- still sees everything from her own point of view (this inability to *decentre* has been challenged by later research)
- believes that everything that exists has a consciousness, even objects (*animism*); at this stage the child may blame the table that she's bumped her head on
- understands right and wrong in terms of what will happen after an event; expects that everyone will share this view *(moral realism)*.

Concrete operations (7–11 years)

By this stage the child:

- can see things from another's point of view, i.e. can *decentre*
- is capable or more complex reasoning but needs concrete objects to assist this process, e.g. uses apparatus to solve mathematical problems
- knows that things are not always as they look; understands *conservation*
- knows the difference between real and pretend
- can understand and participate in play with rules.

Formal operations (12–adult)

Characteristics of this stage include:

- the ability to think logically
- abstract thought with no need for props.

NB Research shows that many adults never reach this level of thinking.

PIAGET AND PLAY

Recognition of Piaget's stages can help us plan and provide for the kinds of play experiences that are most appropriate for each stage of development. At the *sensory-motor* stage, play involves:

- using the senses
- being self-absorbed
- movement
- lots of practice, often of the same skill. Piaget used the term *mastery* to describe the child's need to persevere and achieve.

Play for children at the *pre-operational* stage involves:

- using symbols, e.g. a cardboard box for a house
- using language to communicate, with oneself, with others, with objects
- make-believe and fantasy
- games with simple rules
- being alone sometimes, more often with others.

By the *concrete operations* stage, play involves:

- more complicated rules
- taking responsibility and roles
- an awareness of the difference between fantasy and reality
- an ability to think of other people
- working with others, sharing decisions.

THINK!

For each of the kinds of play listed above:
1 Describe three activities that take into account the stage of development.
2 Write down why you chose each activity and where it might take place.

EXPERIMENTS IN THINKING

Piaget developed his principles of cognitive development from his observations of children who were asked to solve particular problems. If we pose similar problems to children their responses will enable us to identify the stage of their cognitive development. The most famous of these are the conservation test and the test for decentring, the mountain test.

Conservation

Piaget argued that a child at the pre-operational stage does not understand that a quantity of a substance can be presented in a variety of different ways and provided that nothing is added or taken away, the amount remains the same. Children at this stage are likely to be tricked by the visual appearance of the substance and say that the amount has changed. They are unable to *conserve*. There are a number of ways of testing for conservation. Here are some examples.

Conservation of mass

Playdough is used to make two balls of the same size. The child is asked if there is the same amount of playdough in each ball. If the child agrees that the amounts are the same, the adult rolls one of the balls of dough into a sausage shape, making sure that the child can can see what is happening. The child is then asked again whether one of the dough shapes has more in it than the other, or if they are both the same. The child who has not yet learned to conserve will be misled by the appearance of the dough and say that there is more in one than the other.

Conservation of capacity

Conservation of capacity can be demonstrated in much the same way, by using the same amounts of liquid in a tall thin beaker and a short squat one

Conservation of number

Two equal rows of counters (or buttons or sweets) are set out in front of the child. She agrees that each row contains the same number of counters. When the adult, again in full view, moves the counters so that one line is longer than the other, the child who is unable to conserve number is likely to say that the longer line contains more counters.

Decentring

Piaget's test to show whether a child was able to take another's point of view – the ability to decentre – was his famous mountain experiment. A model comprising three mountains with different features was placed before the child .The child was asked to describe the model from her point of view saying which mountain was furthest away, closest, and so on. A doll was then placed alongside the model, with a different perspective from that of the child. The child was then asked to describe the mountain scene from the point of view of the doll (see the illustration below). Piaget believed that the inability of the child to describe the mountain scene from the doll's perspective showed that she could not yet *decentre*.

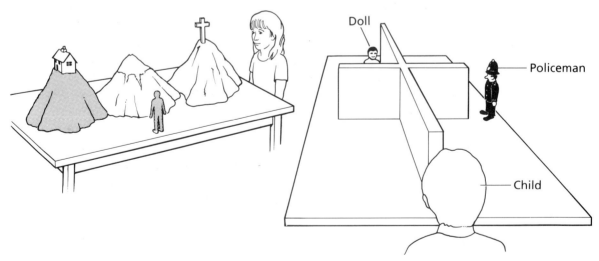

Decentring – the mountain test, and the later doll test

More recent experiments to test the child's ability to decentre have given different results. Martin Hughes' model contained two dolls, a policeman (in a fixed position) and a boy (who could be moved). The child was asked to move the boy doll to a position where the policeman could not see it, thus looking at the model from the policeman's point of view. Children who were unable to see Piaget's mountain from the doll's point of view had much more success in hiding the boy doll from the policeman. It is thought that Piaget's task seemed irrelevant to the children and that they did not understand what they were being asked to do. Hiding the doll from the policeman seemed much more straightforward and showed that if there was enough reason to do so, the child could decentre and see the world from another's perspective.

RECENT DEVELOPMENTS

Piaget's theories of cognitive development, although influential, have been constantly re-examined and modified. Piaget stressed the importance of the environment in children's learning, seeing children as instinctively and actively curious about their surroundings. His theory that children learn most effectively through first-hand experiences has provided the rationale for the discovery-learning, or 'learning by doing', child-centred approach to education. The child is seen as an individual who, through interaction with an environment that provides the right kind of learning experiences, progresses according to his stage of development.

Vygotsky's studies on the ways that children learn emphasised not just the individual child but the social context of learning. His findings showed that children had a great deal to learn from each other through interaction and communication. Unlike Piaget, Vygotsky felt that the child's level of ability should not be judged merely on what they could do alone but on what they were capable of with help. He used the term *zone of proximal development* to explain those tasks that might be beyond the child's capability alone but that were possible with assistance. The child might then be provided with a more challenging and stimulating environment than if left to discover and learn alone.

The work of Jerome Bruner pays particular attention to the role of the adult in children's learning. He sees the adult's role not just as a provider of a rich environment for children to discover, but as having an active part to play alongside them by *scaffolding*, that is providing a structure that supports this learning. There are links here with Vygotsky's work, but the emphasis in Bruner's work is on the skilled adult, tuned in to the child's capabilities who can offer the support to enable the child to break out of a repetitive activity, consolidate what has been learned and move on to the next step.

Recent studies have found that there are aspects of children's learning that Piaget did not take into account in his initial work on cognitive development. The effects of social interaction with other children and the involvement of skilled and sensitive adults have been shown to have a significant bearing on the way that children learn.

CHECK!

1 Re-read the summaries of Piaget's stages.
2 Make a chart showing how Piaget saw that children's thinking developed.

3 Write down definitions of the following terms:
object permanence, decentre, animism, conservation.

THINK!

Have you seen a baby call for a toy that is just out of sight but that she knows is there? This demonstrates that she has grasped the concept of *object permanence.*

1 Find some other examples from your own experience with children that you can link to Piaget's theories of cognitive development.

DO!

1 Try out Piaget's conservation experiment for yourself a with a young child. Use two pieces of playdough and make sure that the child watches as you roll one of the pieces into a different shape.
2 What happened?
3 Do your findings agree with Piaget's?
4 See if you can devise a test for conservation of capacity using different shaped beakers.

The role of the adult in promoting language and cognitive development

The nature/nurture debate shows that children's learning is influenced by their environment. It is important, therefore, as with language development, that adults who work with children are aware of how to plan, prepare and monitor children's activities and also how to interact with children during the activities. Careful consideration of the environment provided for children can contribute to them reaching their potential. The principles outlined in the following diagram are similar to those outlined in Chapter 8. *Planning* is based on observation and monitoring of the children's needs and development. It is also based on observation of practical considerations of the use of space, time, equipment and staff.

Preparation is based on careful planning so that the environment provided meets the needs of the children across the developmental range. Again practical considerations are important when preparing an area.

Interaction with the children takes account of their individual developmental needs. Some of this information is gathered through observation and must be incorporated into the planning. Practical considerations of staff time are an important issue here.

Observation and *monitoring* provide valuable information on the children. This forms the basis of planning and preparing the area and also interacting with the children.

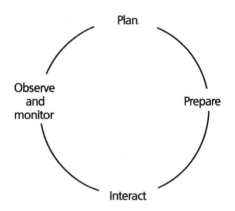

What are the children's needs?
What are the children's developmental levels?
What is the range of developmental levels within the group?
What space is available?
How much time is available?
What are the staffing levels and responsibilities?
Is there a current theme/topic?

Plan

What learning is taking place?
Is the activity at the appropriate level for the children?
Were the children's needs met?
Were all the children able to participate in an activity?
Was an appropriate space used for each activity?
Did the children have enough time?
Was staff time used appropriately?
What is significant about what was observed?
Does anything that was observed need to be recorded?

Observe and monitor

Are all the necessary equipment and materials accessible?
Is the activity attractively presented and inviting for the children?
Is the available space used appropriately?

Prepare

Interact

Ways of interacting with children include:
■ talking with the children
■ asking questions
■ offering encouragement
■ playing alongside the children
■ offering suggestions and guidance to extend the children's learning. This may include suggesting the use of other equipment where appropriate.

This is an ongoing process; the areas are interdependent, as illustrated by the diagram on page 130.

DO!

1 Plan three activities for children to encourage the development of either cognitive or language skills. Include details of the activity as outlined above in the adult's role.

> **Key terms**
> You need to know what these words and phrases mean. Go back through the chapter and find out.
>
> | | |
> |---|---|
> | Imagination | Operations |
> | Role play | Sensory-motor |
> | Creativity | Concrete operations |
> | Problem solving | Formal operations |
> | Trial and error learning | Conservation |
> | Hypothesis | Decentering |
> | Schema | Object permanence |
> | Assimilation | Zone of proximal development |
> | Adaptation | Scaffolding |
> | Equilibrium | |

SECTION 3
Social and emotional development

10 AN INTRODUCTION TO EMOTIONAL AND SOCIAL DEVELOPMENT

This chapter includes:
- **What is emotional and social development?**
- **The connection between ages and stages of development**
- **'Normal' development**
- **Theories of development**
- **Emotional and social needs.**

Introduction

Children begin to develop emotionally and socially from birth. These two areas of development are closely linked to each other and development in one area is strongly affected by development in the other. Both areas involve the growth of children's feelings and their relationships with others.

We will also look at a number of different theories about:
- why and how development happens
- children's emotional and social needs in their early years
- ways in which carers can meet these needs
- the benefits of this to children.

What is emotional and social development?

EMOTIONAL DEVELOPMENT

Emotional development includes:
- the growth of children's feelings about and awareness of themselves
- the development of feelings towards other people
- the development of self-image and identity.

SOCIAL DEVELOPMENT

Social development includes:
- the growth of the child's relationships with others.
- *socialisation*, the process by which children learn the culture or way of life of the society into which they are born
- the development of social skills.

Children's development in both areas follows a path towards emotional maturity and independence. Maturity means being fully developed and capable of control. Achieving independence involves the development of skills that lead to less need of other people for help or support.

DEVELOPMENTAL LINKS

In this book the different areas of development are studied separately, but it must be emphasised that all areas of development are linked. They affect and are affected by each other. Some examples of the close links that exist between different areas of development are:

- walking: a stage of physical development that gives greater independence and increases possible social contacts
- talking: a stage of language development that enables children to move from non-verbal communication with close carers to being able to communicate with other people in more complex ways
- coping with separation from main carer(s): a stage of emotional development that enables children to have a wider range of experiences and relationships. This also increases their opportunities for play and learning.

There are close links between the different areas of development

THINK!

What is included in the culture or way of life of a society? For suggestions to help with this answer, see Chapter 11, *Socialisation.*

CHECK!

1 What in your own words is social and emotional development?

The connection between ages and stages of development

There is wide variation in the chronological age (the age in years and months) at which children reach developmental stages. Some of the most important things to remember when studying these are:

- there are recognisable stages of emotional and social development that children reach and through which they pass
- children pass through them at different ages: one child will be able to do things at an earlier age than another. The fact that one child is younger than another when they reach an observable stage need be of no significance at all; it does not necessarily mean that they have any developmental problems
- the development of any skill depends on the maturation of the nervous system (see Chapter 4, *The principles of development*).

DO!

Carry out some research of your own by doing the following:
1 Make a list of some recognised developmental stages that you are aware of (for example smiling at carer, sitting unsupported, starting to talk, playing happily without a main carer present). Try to include some social and emotional milestones.
2 Ask the carers of a small number of children at what age their children reached these stages.
3 Make a chart to show the variation in their ages of development.
4 Using your results, write a conclusion about ages and stages of development.

'Normal' development

It is clear that children vary in the age at which they reach different stages of development, and in their rates of development. As stated earlier in this book, in Chapter 3, it is nevertheless useful to describe an average age at which children might be expected to reach specific developmental stages. The word average means a medium, a standard or a 'norm'. The word 'normal' is linked to that of a norm or average, but it is not very helpful to use the word 'normal' to describe development, since we might then describe anything which does not fit this pattern as 'abnormal'. This is clearly not an appropriate way to describe developmental delay. It is more appropriate to describe children as not having reached the stage of development expected at their age.

NORMATIVE MEASUREMENTS

In order to establish average ages for development, the observations of many people in different professional fields have been put together. These have been used to describe an average or norm against which any individual child's development can be measured. These measurements are called *normative measurements*. An example of this is the observations of children's first social smile that have led to an understanding that the average age for this to happen is around six weeks. There are advantages and disadvantages of using normative measurements, as outlined below.

Advantages
Using averages or norms of development is useful because:
- it satisfies the curiosity of carers about what a child should be doing at a given age, and it helps them to know what to expect
- it gives background information and a framework within which to assess developmental delay
- it helps people to assess a child's progress after an injury or illness, and can be used to decide whether the child needs additional help and stimulation.

Disadvantages
The disadvantages of using norms of development are:
- carers may be tempted to think that children are 'good' when they are level with the norm and 'bad' if they fall behind it
- carers and other people may wrongly think that children have disabilities, when in fact they are simply slow to develop in certain areas.

THINK!

1 Why is it not helpful to talk about 'normal 'development?

CHECK!

1 What is a normative measure of development?
2 What are the advantages and disadvantages of using average measurements of development?

Theories of development
WHY DOES EMOTIONAL AND SOCIAL DEVELOPMENT OCCUR?

It is very useful for anyone involved in the care of children to stand back and ask why emotional and social development occurs, because:
- it increases our understanding of both how and why development occurs
- it illustrates the importance of the role of the adult carer in encouraging healthy development.

There are many theories about development (ideas that people have about how and why development occurs). The two basic theories are:
- development happens because human beings are genetically programmed to develop in a certain way. These are called biological theories (the *nature* argument)
- people learn their responses and skills. These are called learning theories (the *nurture* argument).

People tend to use a combination of these theories to guide their practice with children. Below is an outline of some of the theories of social and emotional development.

BIOLOGICAL THEORIES

A biological or genetic explanation of how social behaviour and personality develop includes the following points:

- we are born with a definite personality and this determines how we respond and behave
- our temperament, sociability, emotional responses and intelligence are determined by what we inherit from our biological parents
- the way we behave and the pattern our development takes is programmed in our genes, and is sometimes affected by chemical changes in our bodies
- the way we mature and change follows a pre-set programmed pattern.

Support for this theory can be illustrated by the observation of parents who have more than one child. They comment that their children develop very different personalities and social skills even though they have grown up in the same environment.

It is interesting, however, to look at what happens to children who have little or no contact with other people as they grow up. There are two main ways that this separation occurs:

- a child may be abandoned or lost in a deserted place and cared for by animals
- a child may be locked away and given enough nourishment to stay alive, but little or no human contact.

Such children have occasionally been discovered, and case histories have been written about them.

It may be surprising to learn that when found, these children are hardly recognisable as human. They do not walk or run, physical skills that we would expect to develop naturally. They also have no recognisable language. They do not eat with their hands or use a toilet. To begin with they do not respond or relate to the people caring for them. These children demonstrate that very few skills, even physical ones, develop automatically. They show clearly that in the absence of other people, children do not develop social skills or recognisable human emotional responses.

Although there is a common belief that some aspects of children's personalities are inherited, most evidence points to the fact that children learn most of their social skills and emotional responses. Physical development on the other hand is more strongly influenced by genetic inheritance.

THINK!

1 How does the development of children who have grown up without frequent human contact seem to be affected? Is there anything surprising about this?

DO!

1 Go and find any references you can to children such as those described

above, sometimes referred to as *feral* children. Examples you might use are Kaspar Hauser, Amala and Kamala or Jeannie (the subject of a recent TV programme).

LEARNING THEORIES

The learning group of theories hold that children develop as they do because they have contact with other people and learn from them. With regard to emotional and social development learning theories hold that:
- children develop by learning from their experiences
- the only things babies are born with are some primitive reflexes; they do not have any social behaviour that is instinctive, or occurs automatically
- the environment, rather than inherited characteristics, is of the greatest importance in determining how children develop emotionally.

How children learn social behaviour is covered in detail in Chapter 11, *Socialisation*. This includes how children learn:
- by being rewarded or punished
- by copying or pretending they are other people
- by experiencing pressure from their peer group.

There is much evidence which points to nurture, or learning, being a very important factor in determining how children develop socially and emotionally.

PSYCHOANALYTICAL THEORIES

Sigmund Freud (see Chapter 7), working at the beginning of the twentieth century, was the founder of modern psychoanalytical theory. Many others have since built on his ideas.

Psychoanalytical theories are in some respects a mixture of biological and learning theories. They hold that:
- children are born with a set of needs, for example the need for love, affection and security (dependency needs)
- these needs appear at different ages and stages through childhood
- children develop healthily only if these needs are met
- a child's future development can be badly affected if at any stage the appropriate needs are not met.

A good example of a need is that of the infant to be near a familiar carer. Children need this for many reasons. Through it they develop a sense of security and trust. If this need is not met, and infants have a large number of carers when very young, they may find it difficult to learn to trust people. This in turn may have a profound effect on the way they relate to people later both as children, and adults. This aspect of development is covered in detail in Chapter 13, *Bonding and attachment*.

It is useful to look at children in terms of their basic needs. Understanding these needs enables adults to know how to care for them appropriately and increases carers' awareness of how they can encourage healthy development. An outline of emotional and social needs is given in the next part of this chapter.

1 Imagine yourself working in a family home or in a nursery. Think of some of the emotional needs of the children you are caring for. Describe how you might meet these needs during the day.

1 What are the names of the three main theories which explain how and why children develop emotionally and socially?
2 Briefly explain the main points of each of these theories.

CONCLUSIONS

There are several conclusions to be drawn about theories of development:
- there are a range of different theories about how and why a child learns to behave
- it is not necessary to believe one theory entirely and reject the others: they can all be useful in different circumstances to help to explain behaviour and development
- learning and the environment (nurture) play a relatively greater part in emotional and social development than heredity and biological factors (see chart)
- an awareness of these theories can help carers to find the most appropriate way to respond to and care for children.

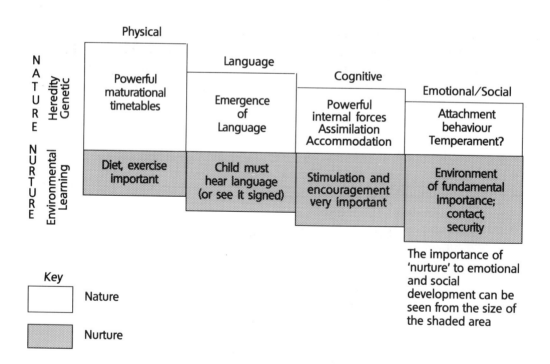

The relative influence of nature and nurture on the different developmental areas

Emotional and social needs

From the beginning of life, through to maturity, children have several emotional and social needs which may be met, to some extent, by all the people they have contact with. However, their primary carers, that is those with whom they have a close bond of attachment, are the most significant and influential. This is especially true in the early and formative years. These emotional and social needs are discussed below.

LOVE AND AFFECTION

Children need unconditional love, affection and acceptance. They need to know that, no matter what they do, they will always be loved. This need is met by children experiencing, from birth onwards, a stable, continuous, dependable and loving relationship with a small group of carers.

In the early years, close physical contact is protective as well as affectionate. When babies are in their carer's arms, a loud noise will startle them far less, and a mild digestive upset will be endured more easily. Love and affection are essential to all aspects of children's development, not just social and emotional.

Early relationships which are consistent, unconditional, affectionate and loving encourage children to:

- value themselves and therefore develop a positive self-image and self-concept (see also Chapter 12, *Self-image and self-concept*)
- develop trust, and as a result become emotionally involved with other people
- receive and give affection
- care for others, including in time their own children
- adjust their behaviour to please a loved person
- develop a moral conscience (an understanding of right and wrong) as they feel shame and guilt when they do something they know their carer would disapprove of
- respond increasingly to adult expectations and become a socially acceptable member of society.

Love and affection provide protection and security

1 In what circumstances may it be difficult for a carer to meet a child's need for love and affection?
2 What are the possible effects on children's development when their need for love and affection is not met?
3 How may a lack of love and affection influence children's intellectual development?

SECURITY

A child needs to feel secure in order to cope with all that is new and changing in their world. This need can be met in the early years by:

■ the experience of a stable family life and family relationships; this gives a child a sense of having a past, a present and a future (personal continuity). It encourages children to develop a coherent self-image and self-concept, a view of themselves that fits together and makes a complete whole

■ the security of a familiar place and familiar routines; these provide a predictable and dependable framework from which they can venture out. Notice the contrast between a young child's usual behaviour at home, and their behaviour in an unfamiliar place

■ having access to familiar objects, which can be a teddy bear, comfort blanket or other favourite toy; these objects can give reassurance and a sense of security. Children show a strong desire to retain them or return to them during a stressful experience.

Familiar objects give reassurance and a sense of security

CHECK!

1 How can a child's sense of security be encouraged?
2 Why is this sense of security important?
3 Why is it important for children to have a coherent self-image?

1 In what circumstances may it be difficult for children to develop a positive and coherent self-image?

CONSISTENT CARE AND REASONABLE GUIDELINES

Children need to be able to rely on consistent care by their primary caregivers. They need to be given reasonable guidelines for appropriate behaviour in a variety of situations. This need is met by carers when they:

- demonstrate consistent attitudes and behaviour. Children do not learn underlying values if similar behaviour causes different reactions in their carers at different times. For example, if children are consistently forbidden to touch the TV controls, they learn that they are not toys. If, however, they are allowed to play with them sometimes but not at others, they are getting inconsistent messages. In this case they are both more likely to constantly test the adult's response and less likely to learn the underlying principle, that some things are not toys and must not be touched
- give consistent discipline that is appropriate to what the child has done, and also allow the child to make up for what they have done
- seek to develop their children's self-control and self-discipline; these are more likely to develop if carers reason with children and discuss their expectations of them. Children are less likely to develop self-discipline if they have to obey an adult unquestioningly out of the fear of punishment, the carer withholding affection or emotional threats. This is because the children are never being taught the reasons for what is right and wrong
- have reasonable expectations of their children based on knowledge of their age and stage of development
- give reasonable guidelines for acceptable behaviour and explain these freely.

Imagine being in a room where the walls move outwards when you push them. Although this may bring an initial sense of power, even an adult would ultimately feel insecure. If each time a child pushes for what they want, the adult gives in, the child will have less and less idea of what is reliable and firm. They may feel an initial sense of extreme power, but eventually they will feel insecure and uncertain.

1 Why is it important for children to develop self-control?
2 Why do controls, reasonable guidelines and expectations help children to feel secure?

PRAISE, ENCOURAGEMENT AND RECOGNITION

To grow from a helpless infant into a self-reliant, self-accepting adult requires an immense amount of emotional, social and intellectual learning. Children need the motivation of praise and encouragement to achieve this. They need to feel valued and recognised for themselves as well as for their accomplishments and achievements. This need is met if carers respond to their children by:

- praising them for effort more than for achievement
- showing pleasure at their successes
- seeking to develop a good relationship with them, which will result in their children wanting to behave in a way that will please them
- actively encouraging them in all aspects of their development
- demonstrating that they recognise their individuality, for example by not comparing them to other children
- having reasonable levels of expectations of them, based on their age and stage of development; too little expectation can lead children to adopt too low a standard of effort and achievement. Too high a level of expectation can make them feel they cannot live up to what is expected. This can lead to children feeling discouraged and making less effort
- allowing them to make mistakes and fail without expressing disapproval
- demonstrating a positive, optimistic attitude towards them.

THINK!

1 How can carers actively encourage their children?
2 Can you remember situations in your childhood when you were praised? Do you remember how you felt?
3 Why is it important for children, especially those with learning difficulties, to be recognised and accepted for what they are? Why do they need to be given praise for effort rather than achievement?

DO!

1 List some reasons why carers may be unable or unwilling to meet their children's need for praise and recognition.
2 Choose one day when you are working with children and make a brief record of the number of times you praise children for their efforts, and the situations in which this occurred. Assess whether you have been more positive than usual! Think back over the day and list any situations in which you could have been more positive and praised a child more.
3 List some of the non-verbal ways in which you have reassured and encouraged children during the day.

APPROPRIATE RESPONSIBILITY

For children to learn how to act in a responsible way, they need to be given appropriate responsibility. This need is met by carers encouraging and enabling children to:

- gain personal independence; children can do this initially through learning to feed, dress, wash and toilet themselves
- become increasingly independent by doing more and more for themselves
- have their own possessions over which they are allowed to have absolute ownership

- exercise choice appropriate to their age and stage of development, for example in food, play, clothes, choice of friends, study and hobbies
- understand the results of their own decisions and choices
- meet and interact with peers.

Children who are given appropriate responsibility and encouraged to be independent are more likely to become confident and accept responsibility as they mature.

THINK!

1 Why do carers of disabled children often experience difficulty in providing them with appropriate responsibility?
2 What may be the result for disabled children of this difficulty?
3 Why does helping children to understand the results of their own actions develop a sense of responsibility? Why is this important?
4 Why is it important for children's growing independence and responsibility that they mix with peers?

Key terms

You need to know what these words and phrases mean. Go back through the chapter and find out.

Social development	Self-image and self-concept
Emotional development	Unconditional
Maturity	Personal continuity
Independence	Socially acceptable
Chronological	Coherent self-image
Normative measurement	Significant adults
Theories	Self-reliance, self-acceptance
Biological theories	Optimistic
Learning theories	Peers
Psychoanalytical theories	Moral conscience
Bonding and attachment	

11 SOCIALISATION

What is socialisation?

Socialisation is the process through which children learn the way of life, the language and the behaviour that is acceptable and appropriate to the society in which they live. It starts at birth and continues throughout life, and is fundamental to the social development of any child. Throughout the process children learn how to behave appropriately in a large number of social roles.

The process of socialisation

The process of socialisation involves children learning from the experiences and relationships they have during childhood. A process is a continuous series of events that leads to an outcome; the socialisation process enables children to learn how to behave in ways that are expected and appropriate to their society. Through it they learn to become adult members of society.

How behaviour is learned during the process of socialisation

There are several different ways in which children learn the behaviour that is expected of them. These are outlined under the four headings which follow.

REWARDS AND PUNISHMENT

Adults encourage acceptable behaviour in children by rewarding it. A reward can be a very simple thing like a smile, saying thank you, or giving praise or a hug; it also includes giving children things like toys, food, or a treat; children can also feel rewarded by the feeling they get when they please an adult. Children want rewards to be repeated, and this encourages them to repeat the behaviour that brought the reward.

Adults discourage behaviour by punishing or ignoring it. Punishments, like rewards, can take a variety of forms: they include telling children they are wrong, physically or emotionally hurting them, ignoring or isolating them or depriving them of something they want.

There are many different views about the relative effectiveness of rewards and punishments in changing behaviour.

COPYING AND IMITATION OF ADULTS

Children learn how to behave by copying people in different roles. They use them as role models. For example, children copy what their mothers or fathers do and learn a lot about the roles of men and women. The idea that children develop partly by copying behaviour has implications for child-care workers who may themselves be used as role models.

ROLE PLAY

Children enjoy pretending to be someone else; they act as if they are another person, which is called *role play*. They often copy the adults who are close to them or the ones they see on the television. When they do this they may not be able to tell whether or not the adult's behaviour is socially acceptable. This may happen, for example, when children copy violent parents in their play or general behaviour.

PEER GROUP PRESSURE

There can be very strong pressure on children from their peers to behave in a certain way. Children change their behaviour when they are with their peer group, and may behave in a way that they have already learned is unacceptable to adults. A peer group can punish a child who does not conform by excluding the child from the group or by making the child feel different. To some children fear of this can be stronger than fear of adult punishment. This peer group pressure can be a form of bullying. There is an increasing awareness of the different forms that bullying can take, and a greater commitment by many schools to introduce policies to try to prevent it.

DO!

1 Read this example of reinforcement.
   A child in a nursery asks to read her book to you. You know that the child can read very few words. The policy of the school is to encourage reading in this way because it helps development of reading skills. The child reads a few words correctly and you help her with a few. Which response would encourage her to want to look at books again?

a) 'That wasn't very good, you didn't know many words.'
b) 'I think you are very clever, well done. Would you like to show me another book?'

Have you chosen response (b)? If you have, you are agreeing with the theory that children are more likely to repeat desired behaviour if they are rewarded.

2 Think of some rewards that can be used at home, or in a nursery or a school to encourage desired behaviour. Write down the rewards, say when they could be used, and why you think they could be effective.

THINK!

1 Think of some of the things that you do, and ways that you behave when you are with children. Make a list of the ones that make you a good role model.
2 Are there any things that you do that are inappropriate for a child to copy? Think whether there is something you should do about it!
3 What can an adult do to try to prevent bullying?

CHECK!

1 What are the main things that children learn during the socialisation process?
2 Write in your own words some of the processes through which children's behaviour is influenced.

Primary and secondary socialisation

It is useful to look at two periods in the process of socialisation:
- *primary* socialisation which occurs in the early years of life
- *secondary* socialisation which takes place as children grow older.

These two periods overlap in a child's life. A child does not leave one and go into the other; the first merges into the second. Anyone working with children may be involved in either or both of these periods.

Primary socialisation and the care of children

Primary socialisation is the name given to the first part of the socialisation process which takes place in the early years of a child's life. It is a very important period, involving the child learning basic patterns of behaviour, skills and responses which are appropriate and acceptable both within the family and wider society. This will lay the foundation for the future social development of the child.

Primary socialisation takes place in the early years of life within the child's close family

The role of the adult

The main influences during this early period are the people closest to the child. These people are usually the child's close family, together with any substitute carers, for example a child minder, a nanny or a day-nursery officer. The following diagram shows those people who may be involved in the primary socialisation process.

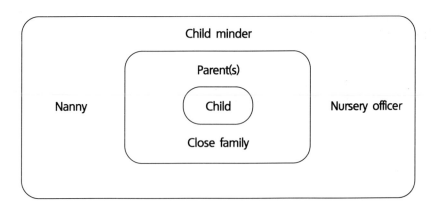

Research has shown that it is better for children to have close contact with a small number of main carers during this early period. This enables them to experience continuity and consistency in the way they are handled. It also helps them to build up a pattern of acceptable behaviour: they learn what is right and wrong from the adults around them. If children receive conflicting messages about appropriate behaviour during this early period they cannot establish a consistent pattern of behaviour. Research has shown that having a limited number of carers also helps emotional development (see Chapter 13, *Bonding and attachment*).

This knowledge has been reflected in recent legislation. The Children Act (1989) has clear guidelines about the ratios of staff to children required in day-care settings; the younger the children the higher the ratio of staff required. The act also gives guidelines about a suitable environment and accommodation for children.

SECONDARY SOCIALISATION AND CHILD CARE

Secondary socialisation begins when children are exposed to influences outside the family and close environment. They develop friendships, mix with their peers, go to school, watch the television, read, join clubs and begin to learn the rules for behaviour in wider society. These activities lay the foundation for children becoming adult members of that society. The following diagram shows the main influences during the secondary socialisation process.

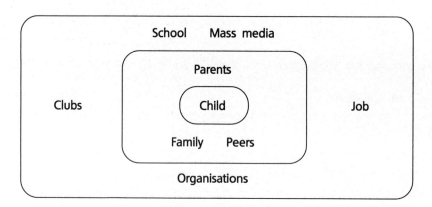

The role of the adult

Growing children need to be encouraged and enabled to develop a range of relationships and interests. This can be done by extending the child's experiences beyond the immediate family and close social group. Through this children develop the ability to adapt to a variety of situations. They therefore become increasingly independent and socially mature.

DO!

1 Imagine that you are caring for an infant during a typical day in a nursery. Make a list of any basic social skills that you will be helping the child to develop.
2 Think of ways that the staff in a nursery and/or an infant school could help children to develop wider social awareness. Record your ideas, which should include the following:
   - places the children could visit
   - visitors the staff could invite to the school
   - topics the children could investigate
   - ways in which displays could be used.
3 Suggest other ways that children can be stimulated to take an interest in their social environment.

Socialisation and culture

An important aspect of the socialisation process involves children learning the culture of their society.

WHAT IS CULTURE?

Culture is the learned, shared behaviour of people in a society. It includes a shared language, values, norms and customs.

Values are beliefs that certain things are important and to be valued, for example a person's right to their own belongings.

Norms are the rules and guidelines which turn values into action. They tell a person how they should behave or do something. Children forming a queue to go into dinner because it is safer way to proceed is an example of a norm in a school. The value that this is based on is society's belief that children are precious and should be protected from harm. This use of the word norm differs from that described in Chapter 10.

A *custom* is another word used to describe particular norms. Customs are special guidelines for behaviour which are followed by groups of people. The origins of custom often go back a long way into the past. An example of a custom is the celebration, by most people, of birthdays.

The role of the adult

In the early stages of the socialisation process, children learn acceptable behaviour from the people who are very close to them. This is usually their close family, but also includes the substitute carers (see diagram on page 163). Part of the carer's role is to teach children appropriate behaviour. Such teaching has to be repeated until children behave automatically in certain situations, for example remaining on the pavement and not running into the road, or greeting familiar people. Sometimes it is sufficient to reinforce rules and customs by rewarding children. It may also help to explain to them the reasons that certain behaviour is expected. In this way carers are also helping children to understand the values underlying the teaching.

Schools, play groups and nurseries also have norms and customs. It is important in any group that rules are kept by everyone, that is that the norms are shared. Social contact would be very unpredictable without this, as we would have no way of knowing how people were likely to behave.

DO!

1 List some other norms (or rules for behaviour) that you may be involved in teaching young children. Try to write beside them some of the values or beliefs that they are based on.

Socialisation and child care in a multicultural society

A multicultural society is one whose members have a variety of cultural backgrounds. If equal opportunities for all are to be promoted, it is essential that anyone caring for children examines the particular rules and customs of their establishment. There is a need to distinguish between rules that are essential (for example rules concerning safety and mutual respect) and those that are not (for example those connected to dress, food and religious customs). Rules can be inessential and culturally biased. Many establishments have now adopted a multicultural approach to caring. They encourage understanding and respect for the customs of all children and their families. This approach ensures that all children are given equal opportunities and that no one experiences discrimination.

Many establishments now encourage understanding and respect for the customs of all children and their families

POSITIVE SELF-IMAGES: THE ROLE OF THE ADULT

Through the process of socialisation children build up pictures of themselves and images of how others see them. All children need to develop a positive identity (see Chapter 12, *The development of self-image and self-concept*). One of the ways they do this is by seeing positive images of themselves in everyday life and in special roles. An image in this context is the way a person is shown in media such as print or film. For example everyone values a good doctor. Portraying a black doctor in a positive role in a book or on television will help a black child's positive self-identity. Such portrayal of black people also enables white children and adults to build up positive images of black people in society.

When children are not of the dominant ethnic group in a society, they may find it more difficult to see positive visual images of themselves. Their teachers, people on the television, children and adults in books are more likely to be of the majority ethnic group, or, in the case of Britain, white. The need for a positive identity has been recognised in The Children Act (1989). This legislation recognises for the first time every child's right to be part of a community that is free from racial discrimination and a society that values different backgrounds and encourages a sense of identity. The importance of this principle, and its relevance to every aspect of children's care, is emphasised throughout the guidance to the act. When people provide day care for children they are required to:

- take account of their religious persuasion, racial origin and cultural background
- have a commitment to treat all children as individuals and with equal concern
- enable children to develop positive attitudes to differences of race, culture and language.

DO!

1 Draw up an action plan to show how any school or nursery can enable both staff and children to learn about the rules and customs of people who come from a variety of social and cultural backgrounds. Remember to include activities, resources, visits, visitors and displays.

Socialisation and social roles

During the process of socialisation children learn an increasing number of social roles. This means that they learn the appropriate behaviour associated with different social positions. This learning may include the behaviour appropriate to being a daughter or a son, a sibling, a grandchild, a school pupil, a friend or a member of a club.

The learning of social roles helps children to:

- know how to behave in a wide range of social situations
- know how to expect other people to behave
- understand that people will respond differently to them according to the person's role; for example they will understand that a teacher will behave differently to them from a grandparent, and they will be able to cope with this difference
- perceive their social world as structured and predictable, and therefore have a feeling of security
- be aware that they have a place and belong in a social system.

The following table shows the potential stress associated with the learning of roles.

Cause of stress	Meaning	Example	Adult role
Role transition	Children move from one role to another	Change from pre-school to school child	Provide preparation and support
Role loss	Lose one role completely	From an only child to having a sibling	Give special attention, understanding, make allowances
Role conflict	Meeting the demands of one role clashes with another	Peer group encourages behaviour not approved by carer	Show understanding, provide firm boundaries

The role of the adult

Adult carers can help children to learn about social roles by:

■ giving them opportunities for imaginative play where they can explore their social world in a safe manner
■ providing a good role model themselves
■ making clear to the child what behaviour is appropriate and expected
■ supporting them at times of potential stress associated with the learning of roles.

THINK!

1 Try to think of some further examples to those shown in the table of children experiencing role transition, role loss and role conflict.
2 How might you tell from the behaviour of a young child that they were experiencing difficulty accepting the birth of a sibling?

Socialisation and the learning of gender roles

Sex-role stereotypes are still present in society. Stereotyping occurs when people think that all the members of a group have the same characteristics, for example boys are tough and active, girls are soft and passive. Stereotypes develop in children's minds when they learn what behaviour is expected of a boy or a girl. Although the process is weaker than in the past, by the time children are five or six they appear to have a clear awareness of gender differences and the behaviour that goes with them. These ideas are firmly held by the time they are seven or eight.

Children learn rules about how boys and girls behave from a variety of people and other influences. They learn from their adult carers, other children, and from television and the mass media in general.

Children are disadvantaged by sex-role stereotyping when it limits the opportunities available to them. This happens if children believe they cannot do something because of their gender, or when those around them believe this. Developing an awareness of stereotyping is vital for those who care for children.

AVOIDING SEX-ROLE STEREOTYPING

No one can argue with the fact that there are physical differences between girls and boys. If, however, you are aiming to provide an environment for children that avoids gender bias, it is preferable to ignore the differences and to concentrate on the many similarities between girls and boys. It is also preferable to avoid dividing children into groups according to their gender.

Dividing children into gender groups increases the likelihood of differences being emphasised. When this happens children are seen in terms of their gender first and as individuals second. One of the problems created by stereotyping is that children (and adults) begin to believe the picture others have of them and start to behave in the way that is expected. If a girl repeatedly hears a teacher asking for 'a nice strong boy' to carry something and 'a nice tidy girl' to clear up she may begin to believe she is not strong and that her role is to clear up after others. Children sometimes see differences

It is preferable to concentrate on the many similarities between girls and boys

between gender emphasised in books. Girls have traditionally been portrayed as passive and domesticated, boys as active and dominant. Teachers and other adults are increasingly aware of this bias and avoid using such books.

If you avoid making any divisions between children on the basis of their gender, you will be more likely to provide an environment in which all children reach their full potential.

DO!

1 a) Read the following list of characteristics and group them into two columns according to those which you think have traditionally been given to girls and to boys:

aggressive	ambitious	competent
caring	warm,	noisy
tactful	dominant	illogical
gentle	expressive	quiet
robust	skilful	active
sensitive	assertive	sentimental.

  b) Think of some job or tasks or activities which have traditionally been given to girls and to boys and add these to the columns.

  c) Add any adult jobs that are commonly seen as belonging to men or women.

  d) Write your own comments about the stereotypical roles that you have recorded.

2 Record any ways in which boys and girls have traditionally been or still are divided unnecessarily. (It used to be common in schools for girls and boys to have separate entrances, line up separately and be grouped on the register according to gender.)

3 Many authors are now very aware of the need to avoid bias. Look at a range of children's books and decide whether they present people in stereotypical ways according to gender.

4 Write down the ways in which a school or nursery can present positive images of both genders. Think of the staff, activities, books, displays, visitors, and any other means that can be used.

Socialisation and social status

RELEVANCE OF FAMILY STATUS

To what extent does a family's social status affect a child's early socialisation? How far does this influence the child's potential to be successful in their society? Social status is the value that a society puts on a particular role. In most societies people who have power also have higher social status. What constitutes or makes up high social status varies between societies: in some societies religious leaders have the most power and highest status, in others it is military leaders, or business people, or politicians, or people with inherited wealth and status.

In all societies there are some people who are more successful than others. Success is usually measured in terms of the power that a person has. Power includes:

■ having easy access to things that are valued (for example wealth, education, health)
■ the potential to influence directly what happens to other people (for example religious, military, political power).

The possibility of any child achieving success (that is high social status) within any society depends firstly on the openness of that society. An open society is one where the structures of the society (for example the education system, job opportunities) enable a person to change their social status within their lifetime, such as the child of a grocer or a circus performer being able to become prime minister in Britain. A closed society is one in which it is impossible for a child to move beyond the social status of their birth family, for example the Hindu caste system in India, when rigorously applied to people's lives.

There are clear indications in the case of Britain that it is, at least in part, an open society. The state provides education for all children (though some families choose to pay for it). Through education people can achieve higher social and economic status. With the introduction of comprehensive education, educational success for all children has been made progressively more possible.

Despite this, a large body of research shows that success in education and in society are not directly linked to children's ability. Children from families of lower social status are less likely to achieve success in the education system. Whatever the intentions, children do not appear to experience equality of opportunity.

INFLUENCE OF THE FAMILY

The question may be asked why a child from a family who has low social status is less likely to do well at school. This is a very difficult question to answer because it leads to the possibility of generalising and stereotyping a whole group of people. It is important, however, to ask the question if our aim is to promote equality of opportunity for all. Only by finding out the causes of inequality can we begin to compensate some children for elements that are missing in their lives.

Children who are successful at school are more likely to be:

- brought up in a secure and loving environment
- have parents or carers who see the value of educational achievement
- experiencing a language-rich environment with opportunities for play.

A secure and loving environment

Children brought up in a secure and loving environment are more likely to be responsive, confident, and to behave in a socially acceptable way, have high self-esteem, and be more willing to learn (see Chapter 13, *Bonding and attachment*). Families from all social backgrounds can provide security and love for their children.

The experience of life of some families, however, disturbs their ability to put the needs of their children first and to provide security during the crucial period of primary socialisation. This may be because of difficult relationships within the family; these can exist in any social group. Relationship difficulties may also be linked to the stress caused by living in long-term poverty, poor housing or a run-down environment. Many people, however, continue to achieve a happy secure home for their children in these circumstances.

Supportive parents or carers

Parents or carers who see the value of educational achievement are more likely to encourage their children's intellectual and social development. They recognise the value of encouraging socially acceptable behaviour, realising that this is more likely to lead to success at school. They visit the school and show interest in their children's progress. It is possible for any family, regardless of social status, to do this.

Carers who have themselves achieved through the education system inevitably have a greater understanding and knowledge of how to succeed. They are more likely to feel at ease with teachers because they are similar to them. There is less to prevent them, both practically and psychologically (in the mind), from going into school to see how their child is progressing or from helping in the classroom.

Children who experience a language-rich environment with opportunities for play establish early speech and thought patterns which are essential to the development of literacy skills (reading and writing) when they go to school. They have a good experience of play which is essential to their future intellectual development.

An environment rich in language

Carers who have a close and loving relationship with their children are more likely to spend time with them, establish language-rich communication patterns and encourage play. Children from any social background can be deprived of this if their parents' attention is directed elsewhere. Parents may be distracted from close contact with their children by the demands of their jobs and careers, by their own physical or mental health or by their personal, social or economic circumstances.

Parents of a higher social status are more likely to be able to pay for care for their children to compensate for the inadequate amount of time they themselves can give their children. This care may be by a nanny or a nursery. The disadvantages experienced by some children from families with low social status, whose carers cannot pay for care, is recognised by some local education authorities. Given limited financial resources, they aim to develop nursery education primarily in areas of high social deprivation. The aim is to enable children to have play experiences and language stimulation which will help them to benefit later from statutory education.

Children have very different experiences during socialisation, some of which directly affect their potential to be socially successful. Some of these differences are common to all social groups; others, notably those that are affected by economic status, are more likely to occur within a specific social or economic group.

The following points can be made in conclusion to this discussion of socialisation:
■ infants and young children become truly human through contact with other people. This is one of the reasons that working with and caring for young children is important and responsible work
■ children need close contact with carers during primary socialisation
■ the learning process is continuous
■ caring adults help children to develop social skills, relationships, rules for behaviour, maturity and independence
■ it is essential that a carer integrates into their practice a knowledge of the social and cultural backgrounds of children in their care.

DO!

1 Write two lists of roles in the society in which you live, one listing roles of high social status, the other low.
2 Look at the lists and try to suggest the reason why one group has high status and the other low.
3 Find out more about the Hindu caste system.

THINK!

1 Examine some of the experiences of children during the socialisation process. Why do you think that some children are more likely to achieve success within the education system and later in society?
2 What practical and psychological reasons might parents or carers have to prevent them establishing close contact with their child's school? How many of these are linked to their social or economic position?

> **Key terms**
> You need to know what these words and phrases mean. Go back through the chapter and find out.
> Socialisation   Reinforcement
> Social status   Role models

Key terms *continued*

Role play
Primary socialisation
Secondary socialisation
Culture
Values
Norms

Multicultural society
Equal opportunities
Positive self-image
Social role
Sex-role stereotyping
Social status

12 THE DEVELOPMENT OF SELF-IMAGE AND SELF-CONCEPT

This chapter includes:
- **Introduction**
- **Children's self-image and self-concept**
- **Stages in the development of self-image and self-concept (1) Birth–1 year (2) 1–5 years and over**
- **Encouraging the development of a positive self-image and self-concept.**

Introduction

WHAT IS SELF-IMAGE AND SELF-CONCEPT?

Another important strand in social and emotional development involves the development of self-image or self-concept. This is the picture we have of ourselves, the way we think other people see us and the characteristics that make us separate and different from others. It could also be referred to as our personality. If child-care workers understand the importance of having a positive self-image and the need to value themselves (self-esteem), they are more likely to develop self-esteem in children.

DO!

1 Write down six positive things about yourself. If you found that difficult it could mean that you have low self-esteem.
2 Ask someone you know to write down six positive things about you and do the same for them. (This may be the first step towards improving your self-image.)

Children's self-image and self-concept

Children's self-image or self-concept is their understanding of themselves: their view of who they are and what they are like. It includes both their thoughts and their feelings about themselves. Eventually it also includes how they think others see them

Stages in the development of self-image and self-concept (1) Birth–1 year

Children's self-concept is established gradually over the first few years of their life. By recognising and understanding the stages in this development child-care workers can encourage the process and also enable children to feel worthwhile and valued. This is vital to their emotional well-being. Children's self-image and self-concept will also influence their relationships, through to adulthood.

BIRTH TO 1 MONTH

New babies are not aware of themselves as separate beings. They do not realise that people and things exist apart and separate from them. It is thought that carers are perceived only as 'relievers of their distress', whether this is hunger, pain or loneliness. Gradually children learn to recognise themselves as separate individuals, through interaction with their carers (for detailed explanation of this interaction see Chapter 13, *Bonding and attachment*).

Children also learn to differentiate between themselves and other people or things by exploration, using their five senses. Through these early relationships and exploratory experiences children gradually come to a realisation of who they are – their personal identity – and what they think and feel about themselves – their self-image and self-concept.

THINK!

1 Describe the type of interaction between a 1-month-old baby and carer that will encourage a baby to see themselves as worthwhile and valuable. You may need to refer ahead to Chapter 13 for help with your answer.

1–3 MONTHS

During this stage children start to recognise their carer's face, hands and voice. They may stop crying if they sense (that is hear, see or feel) their carer. This implies that they are beginning to be aware of their separateness, of the carer existing independently of themselves.

Early recognition of a child's sensory impairment will enable carers to adapt their approach to meet the child's needs, for example by using sign language with deaf

The baby makes a response

children. Carers who themselves have a sensory impairment are often skilled in adapting to accommodate the different needs of such children (see Chapter 13, *Bonding and attachment*).

This period will probably see the first 'social smile', the baby's response to a person separate from themselves.

During this stage babies learn that touching a toy feels completely different from touching their own hand. In feeling the difference, they learn that the moving thing they see is their own hand, a part of them.

Is this part of me?

When they are held during feeding, changing and cuddling, babies learn that there are two kinds of feeling: one that comes from outside themselves, and the other, for example when they touch their own hand or chew on their own toes, that does not. These exploratory experiences start the process of differentiation between themselves and other people or things.

THINK!

1 What experiences could be provided for a baby aged 1–3 months that would:
   a) encourage them to discover where they begin and end
   b) develop their awareness of other people, separate from themselves?

3–6 MONTHS

Once children have distinguished themselves as separate, they will start to build a picture or image of themselves. Gradually they discover what kind of person they are and what they can do. This picture of themselves can be either:
- a positive self-image: the child feels they are valuable and worthwhile
- a negative self-image: the child feels worthless and useless.

Children measure their own worth by the responses of adults and children who are significant to them. They need to experience the approval and acceptance of these people to develop feelings of self-approval and self-acceptance.

At this stage infants still react to the world as if they alone make things exist or disappear. If they are looking at something, it exists; if they don't see it, it doesn't exist. If something or someone disappears from their view, babies will keep looking at the place where they were before they disappeared, as if waiting for them to come back. If they do not return, the baby will probably forget about them. If it is a person who is important to them they will probably cry.

The end of this period may see the beginning of stranger anxiety and separation distress (see Chapter 13, *Bonding and attachment*). This implies that babies recognise their separateness, and feel vulnerable without the support of the attachment relationship. If carers meet babies' needs at this stage, they will help to reinforce the babies' view of themselves as separate, but worthwhile.

THINK!

1 How can adults enable children aged 3–6 months to feel accepted and approved of at this stage in their development?
2 What are babies' needs at 3–6 months?
3 How can these needs be met in a way that confirms infants' views of themselves as separate but worthwhile?

6–12 MONTHS

Children of 6–12 months are more able to join in play activities because of their developing physical skills. Infants will develop a positive self-image as they are encouraged and enabled to learn by experience. Play, at this stage, can be enhanced by the involvement of an interested adult. Their responses to the child, both positive and negative, will influence the child's self-image. Infants are aware of the feelings and emotions of other people. They experience all these emotions as reactions to themselves. They do not have the knowledge that would help them to see that anger and disappointment are not always caused by them. Infants start to feel towards themselves what they sense in others around them.

During this stage children are learning that people and things have a permanent existence. Even if they cannot see them, people and things still exist. This awareness is reinforced through games such as peek-a-boo: the infants are discovering that people and things that disappear are still there, but have to be looked for.

By the end of this stage babies are aware of themselves as persons in relation to other people. They start to realise that they are separate beings and that people and things exist apart from them. They show this development in many ways, for example:

■ enjoy looking at themselves and things around them in a mirror.
■ usually know their name and respond to it
■ appreciate an audience and will repeat something that produced a laugh before
■ begin to imitate actions they have seen others do
■ respond affectionately to certain people
■ recognise other people's emotions and moods and express their own
■ learn to show love to others, if they have been shown love themselves.

These behaviours indicate that infants have become aware of themselves as separate from others, and have formed a definite image of other people who are significant to them.

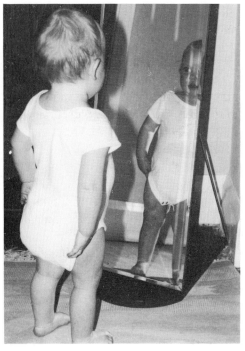

Is that me?

DO!

1 Observe a baby of 6–12 months from time to time over a few weeks. Note down the behaviours that demonstrate their growing understanding of their separateness and that of others.
Evaluate your observation and make some suggestions about how to develop the child's understanding in these areas over the next few months.

1–2 YEARS

Children are aware of themselves as persons in their own right and begin to exert their will, sometimes in defiant and negative ways.

Children's memory skills for objects and people are improving. By the end of their second year, they can remember whole situations and ideas as well as concrete things. They could, for example, demonstrate their memory of a trip to the park with grandma. They could demonstrate that they remember the things in the park (the slide, swings, etc.), the fact that they went with grandma and that they enjoyed coming down the slide.

This growing intellectual ability enables them to know people by what they do, for example the person who dresses them, the one who smokes a pipe and so on, and it also enables them to define people outside themselves and remember them.

The importance of language

Children's developing language skills enable them to express their needs more specifically and to express their will. Their growing understanding of language can have a positive or negative effect on their emerging self-image and self-concept. What is expressed to a child and how it is expressed are both significant.

Infants learn to feel toward themselves what they sense in the responses of others. This applies both to them and their activities and efforts. Children begin to feel unworthy, incompetent, afraid and useless if:

- others are impatient with their attempts to do things for themselves
- they are not allowed to explore and make new discoveries for themselves
- they always sense fear when they attempt new physical skills.

Infants' self-image is fragile at this stage. Even if others are generally encouraging and approving, their feelings about themselves can swing dramatically. One moment a child may feel very powerful and successful, having learnt a new skill. The next moment they may feel small and weak when they find they cannot do what they have tried or seen another person do.

Appropriate encouragement and praise for the effort children make at this stage is vital. Encouragement and praise for effort is more likely to develop a positive self-image than praise for achievement. This is especially true for children with learning difficulties, who may not be able to achieve in certain areas.

The importance of encouragement

Children need to be encouraged to feel proud of any new accomplishments or independence skills, in effect to feel proud of themselves. Their feelings about themselves will have a significant effect on their relationships with other people.

Between 18 months and 2 years children begin to call themselves by their name and talk about things as 'mine'. They recognise that some things belong to them and they can distinguish between 'mine' and 'yours'. They think of themselves as separate individuals and are learning to understand themselves in relation to others.

Towards the end of this period a child may be involved in playing alongside other children. They may form strong attachments to other children of the same age or older, although peers have not yet become very significant to their developing self-image. By the age of 2 some children have become sensitive to the feelings of others and display social emotions such as sympathy if a person is hurt. This implies that children understand how such experiences make them feel, and is an indication of their growing self-awareness.

THINK!

1 Why does praising a 1–2-year-old for effort encourage a positive self-image more than praising for achievement?
2 Why is this particularly important to children with learning difficulties?
3 How do our feelings about ourselves effect our relationships with other people?

4 How can the development of social emotions be encouraged in 1–2-year-old children?

DO!

1 Read the following sentences which might be spoken to a child of 1–2 years:

'You've done it wrong again.'

'Silly boy!'

'I don't think you can do that.'

'It's OK, but you spoilt it at the end.'

'You should have thought about that before.'

'How could you be so stupid?'

'That won't work!'

'It's too hard for you; I'll do it.'

a) Why would these phrases have a negative effect on a child's self-esteem?

b) Write a list of phrases that would have a positive effect on a child's self-esteem.

Stages in the development of self-image and self-concept (2) 2–5 years and over

2–3 YEARS

Between 2 and 3 years children continue to develop their understanding of who they are and what they are like. They do this largely by observing and imitating the behaviour of people around them, particularly those that are significant to them.

This is shown through role playing and imitating actions and behaviours they have observed in others, such as feeding a doll or talking on the telephone.

Is anyone there?

This need for role play has implications for disabled children who also need to be able to model themselves on adults who are like them, rather than always see themselves as different from the significant adults in their world. Pretending they are someone else (role playing) helps children to take the point of view of others, to observe others and to generalise about the important aspects of other people's behaviour.

Such behaviour implies that children have developed a self-image and a view of other people separate from themselves. It may demonstrate something of what children think and feel about themselves in relation to other people.

DO!

1 Observe some 2–3-year-old children at this stage of development during role play. Record the roles they take on and what they convey about their understanding of other people's thoughts and feelings. Note any indications of their perception of themselves, which they may act out.

I can do this myself

The development of independence

Another feature of this stage is that children are becoming significantly more independent, and are really beginning to think of themselves as having their own identity, separate from others in their world. Children will respond well to having certain things set apart as theirs, for example their own coat hook with their name and picture on it. These things confirm children's separateness, individuality and value.

With improved motor development, children learn self-help skills such as feeding themselves competently. They learn to use the implements of their cultural group: this may involve using chapatis and their hands, chop sticks or spoons and forks.

They learn to take care of their own toiletting, wash their own hands and begin to undress themselves. These are important steps toward self-reliance, socialisation and consequently towards competence and self-worth.

THINK!

1 In what practical ways could you help to encourage children of 2–3 years to see themselves as separate individuals with value and worth:
a) in the home situation

b) in a day-care setting?
2 How could you encourage children to be independent and self-reliant when they are developing self-help skills such as dressing, washing, feeding?

Growing self-awareness depends on the development of children's memory the experiences they encounter and also on the development of language.

Children who are encouraged to use language will develop more confidence in their own ability. This is because language enables children to:

■ explain how they feel, and to express more complex emotions than they could by non-verbal communication
■ receive reassurance and explanations
■ handle problem situations.

For example if a child in hospital does not have access to language they will be limited in their ability to explain in detail how they feel or what worries them. Similarly carers will be limited in their ability to reassure the child or prepare them for what may happen.

DO!

1 Think of an activity that can be done with 2–3-year-old children at this stage in their development that will encourage them to express their thoughts and feelings using language.

Dealing with negative behaviour

There are some suggestions that children's behaviour in the middle of this stage is rigid and inflexible. They do not like change, cannot wait and will not give in, often doing the opposite of what they are told. In fact there may be good reason for these behaviours. Children are just beginning to understand themselves and the world they live in. They are discovering that they have a will of their own and may practise exerting it!

The responses and reactions of adults at this time are vital to the child's emerging self-concept. Children need to be given clear guidelines for acceptable behaviour, but should not be 'put down' in a way that has a negative effect on their self-image. Being exposed to too many things they cannot do can also have a negative effect. Tasks that present children with a manageable challenge will give the opportunity for success and consequent enhancement of self-esteem. Too much frustration and consequent failure may produce a negative self-image and low self-esteem. This is one reason why disabled children, or those with learning difficulties, are more likely to have low self-esteem and a negative self-image.

DO!

1 What other factors may contribute toward developing a negative self-image in a disabled child?
2 How can carers counteract this effect?

3–4 YEARS

At 3–4 years children are more conscious of and concerned about others. This is because of their growing awareness of their own identity in relation to other people. They are beginning to understand that other people have feelings, just as they do. At this stage children usually enjoy being with other children. They begin to make strong attachments to individual children. They learn to sympathise with other children, and can be encouraged to think about their own and other people's feelings. Those who work with children are likely to find that a child with a positive self-image is easier to manage in a group situation.

Children continue to test out their self-image and that of others through role play. They also use role play to express their understanding of themselves and others' roles, behaviour and attitudes. Children can be involved in simple drama and take on characters and feelings. Role play can be used to help children understand other people's thoughts and feelings.

THINK!

1 How can children be encouraged to think about other people's feelings?

DO!

1 Make a list of the reasons why children with a positive self-image are easier to manage in group situations.

Peer group influences

During this period children test themselves out in different roles, for example as leader or follower. Through this process they learn more about who they are and what they are like. At this stage the reactions and responses of peers are very important to children and their self-concept will be affected by them. Comments like 'Here comes that dummy' and 'Oh no, it's that stupid boy again' will have a negative effect on a child's self-esteem and confidence. An insight into children's views of themselves may be gained from observing if, and how, they join in group activities.

DO!

1 Undertake an observation of children of 3–4 years testing themselves out in different roles, for example as leader, follower, comic.
2 Observe one child in the 3–4 age group known to have low self-esteem (this may be a disabled child) and note the reactions and responses of other children to them.
3 Draw up a plan of action to help develop this child's self-esteem.

Giving permission to fail

Children's feelings of confidence and self-worth will be strengthened by encouraging them to develop independence skills and also by letting them try to do things by and for themselves. Children need support to learn to accept their mistakes and not let them affect their feelings of self-worth. They need to be given permission to fail with the message that it is perfectly acceptable to make mistakes.

Between the ages of 3 and 4, the foundation of children's self-concept is established. By 3 years children have a fairly steady self-concept; they call themselves 'I' and have a set of feelings about themselves. The self-concept they have at this stage will influence how they respond to relationships and experiences both now and in the future. Their self-concept continues to be affected by the attitudes and behaviour of those around them. They still see themselves as they think others see them. It is therefore important that they are made to feel cared for, worthy and acceptable to their carers. This is especially important when they are being controlled or corrected. They need to feel that while some actions are unacceptable, their participation in such activities does not make them bad people.

Valuing cultural background

In this period children are beginning to learn the way of life of the culture into which they have been born. An important part of learning self-worth and self-confidence involves learning to value and be proud of their own cultural background. Children should never be made to feel that what they learn in their own cultural setting is less valuable than what they learn in other cultural settings.

THINK!

1 How can children be encouraged to value their own cultural background?
2 Why is this encouragement so important?
3 What may be the effects on a child's self-esteem of a day-care setting that does not value the child's home culture?

DO!

1 Write an action plan for a school listing the things that could be done to encourage all children to value one another's cultural identity.

Dealing with negative behaviour

By this stage fear of punishment should be less important to children than their own internal set of standards. These are the standards by which they judge themselves, and that guide their behaviour. Rules should be explained, so that children can understand and apply the appropriate rule to themselves. Praise for trying to do what they feel is right will be more effective than punishment for doing wrong. If children misbehave they should be given a chance to explain why they did so. This shows respect for the development of their inner conscience.

THINK!

1 How do children acquire their own set of internal rules for behaviour?

2 How can this process be encouraged?

3 Why is praise for effort toward positive behaviour more effective than punishment for negative behaviour?

Avoiding gender stereotypes

From 3 years most children know their own gender and start to learn society's ideas about attitudes and activities that are appropriate for each gender. To construct their self-concept children need to identify with an adult role model of the same gender, but models of either gender should present children with choices of behaviours, activities and goals, not with stereotyped roles, such as men going out to work and women taking care of the home. Seeing men and women doing non-stereotypical things allows children of either gender to see that they can do and be anything they want. They do not have to be limited by their gender.

Disabled children need to identify with disabled role models to construct their self-image. It is not unknown for disabled children to think that they would grow out of their disability!

THINK!

1 Why are gender role models important to the development of children's self-concept?

2 Why do children need male and female role models in child-care settings? Why is this difficult to provide?

3 In what ways can child-care settings present children with choices of behaviours and attitudes rather than stereotyped roles?

4–5 YEARS PLUS

By 4–5 years most children have developed a stable self-concept. This is likely to be based on their own inner understanding and knowledge about who they are. If it is based only on other people's views, it will not be stable, but will change according to other people's ideas of them. So if children at this stage see themselves as likeable, they will not change this view of themselves when, from time to time, other children say that they do not like them.

Internalising social rules

At this stage social rules, for example not taking other people's things without their agreement, have been *internalised* (taken in and understood) by children. They do not have to be told what is right and wrong all the time. This does not mean, however, that they will always obey these internalised rules.

Children start to rely on their own judgement of their behaviour. They are beginning to understand the words 'good' and 'bad' in terms of consequences. They learn best if things are explained in terms of themselves as well as others, for example 'If you share your toys with Zaida, she will share hers with you'. Although children may not be able fully to put themselves into someone else's situation they can understand if the explanation is given in terms of themselves.

Summary of the development of self-image
Between the ages of 4 and 5 children are likely to have developed:
- a stable self-concept
- internalised social rules
- awareness of others, particularly other children
- the desire to see a task through to completion for their own self-satisfaction
- willingness to do things to increase their own feelings of competence and self-worth
- willingness to model themselves on someone similar to themselves who is competent in some area that appeals to the child
- an inner conscience by which they judge their own behaviour (although this is still fragile at this stage)
- an ability to do things for themselves without support
- sensitivity to the needs of others
- responsibility for other people and things
- a desire for acceptance by other children.

Encouraging the development of a positive self-image and self-concept

It is obvious that in this area of development children are fundamentally affected by the thoughts and actions of others. The following guidelines summarise in a practical way some of the principles involved in encouraging the development of a positive self-image and self-concept.

TWENTY GOLDEN RULES

1 From the earliest age, demonstrate love and give children affection, as well as meeting their all-round developmental needs.
2 Provide babies with opportunities to explore using their five senses.
3 Encourage children to be self-dependent and responsible.
4 Explain why rules exist and why children should do what you are asking. Use 'do' rather than 'don't' and emphasise what you want the child to do rather than what is not acceptable. When children misbehave explain to them why it is wrong.
5 Encourage children to value their own cultural background.
6 Encourage children to do as much for themselves as they can, to be responsible and to follow through activities to completion.
7 Do not use put-downs or sarcasm.
8 Give children activities that are a manageable challenge. If a child is doing nothing, ask questions to find out why. Remember that they may need time alone to work things out.
9 Give appropriate praise for effort, more than achievement.
10 Demonstrate that you value children's work.
11 Provide opportunities for children to develop their memory skills.

12 Encourage children to use language to express their own feelings and thoughts and how they think others feel.
13 Provide children with their own things, labelled with their name.
14 Provide opportunities for role play.
15 Give children the opportunity to experiment with different roles, for example leader, follower.
16 Provide good flexible role models with regard to gender ethnicity, and disability.
17 Stay on the child's side! Assume they mean to do right rather than wrong. Do not presume on your authority with instructions such as 'You must do this because I'm the teacher and I tell you to', unless the child is in danger.
18 Be interested in what children say; be an active listener. Give complete attention when you can and do not laugh at a child's response, unless it is really intended to be funny.
19 Avoid having favourites and victims.
20 Stimulate children with interesting questions, that make them think.

Key terms
You need to know what these words and phrases mean. Go back through the chapter and find out.

Self-image	Bonding and attachment
Self-concept	Differentiate
Self-identity	Exploratory experiences
Self-esteem	Role models
Self-approval	Role play
Self-acceptance	Significant others
Self-awareness	Culture
Self-reliance	Conscience
Positive/negative self-image	Gender
Stable self-concept	Stereotyped roles
Personal identity	Internalise
Sensory impairment	Social rules

13 BONDING AND ATTACHMENT

<table>
<tr><td>

This chapter includes:
- Introduction
- What is a bond of attachment?
- What causes bonds of attachment?
- Present understanding of causes bonds of attachment
- Conditions necessary for the formation of bonds of attachment?
- How the bond of attachment develops
- Disability and the formation of bonds of attachment
- How we know if attachment has occurred
- The importance of bonds of attachment
- A poor or weak bond of attachment.

</td></tr>
</table>

Introduction

Children's social and emotional development is significantly influenced by their early relationships. In this chapter we will look, in detail, at the nature of these early relationships and how they affect children's social and emotional development. We will consider the special bond that develops between infants and the person or people who care for them.

What is a bond of attachment?

The term *bond of attachment* is used to describe an affectionate two-way relationship that develops between an infant and an adult. When the bond is established an infant will try to stay close to that adult, and will appear to want to be cared for by them. By the end of their first year, infants will show a marked preference for that person and may show *stranger anxiety* (fear of other adults). Infants may well become distressed and show *separation anxiety* if they are separated from those adults to whom they are attached.

Experiencing a bond of attachment is crucial to children's healthy social and emotional development. Therefore we need to understand why and how these bonds develop and why they are so important.

What causes bonds of attachment?

BIOLOGICAL OR INSTINCTIVE EXPLANATIONS

Biological or instinctive explanations suggest that the bond of attachment occurs naturally as a result of innate or inborn urges or instincts on the part of the baby and their carer.

Instincts

Instincts are patterns of behaviour that are not learned. They exist in all members of a particular species. Different instincts and reflexes exist in different species; some birds have a homing instinct that enables them to find their way back from distant places to their home or base. Humans and animals are born with certain instincts and reflexes that automatically make them behave in certain ways; for example if you tripped and fell, your hand would automatically reach out to cushion your fall. See Chapter 3, *Physical development* for information about the reflexes of newborn babies.

Why do babies form a bond of attachment?

Our understanding of why babies form bonds of attachment has developed in part from the work of John Bowlby, an influential British child-psychiatrist (see the section *Who's who in psychology* in Chapter 7). Although some of Bowlby's ideas have been modified over the years, they remain fundamental to an understanding of bonding and attachment.

John Bowlby conducted a major investigation of attachment bonds during the 1940s and 1950s. He studied why and how babies make attachments and concluded that babies have a biological need, or instinct, to form an attachment to the person who feeds and cares for them. Bowlby maintained that this was a survival instinct. Without it the helpless infant would be exposed to danger and might die.

Imprinting

Is there a critical or sensitive period in the life of babies, during which the bond of attachment will occur? Konrad Lorenz was an *ethologist*, who studied the biological reasons for animal behaviour. His work appeared to confirm Bowlby's idea that we are born with an instinct to attach to our mothers. It also suggested that there is a critical or sensitive period during which an instinctive bond will be formed. During the 1930s he observed that newly hatched greylag geese followed the first thing they saw after hatching. It appeared to be an instinctive reaction.

Lorenz also noticed a group of newly hatched goslings following him. Lorenz called this specific behaviour *imprinting*. Imprinting is a rapid form of attachment. This imprinting is said to occur only during a 'sensitive period' in the animal's life, for example immediately after hatching. This would suggest that, in the case of human infants, there is a critical or sensitive period, during which the bond of attachment will occur.

What causes mothers to form bonds of attachment with their offspring?

The notion that all women have 'maternal instincts' used to be widely accepted. These instincts are said to be innate and to motivate a mother to love and care for her child. They are thought to be connected to a woman having the physical attributes needed to carry and deliver a child.

OTHER INSIGHTS INTO THE CAUSES OF BONDS OF ATTACHMENT

A number of experiments on rhesus monkeys were conducted during the 1960s and

Do humans have a similar need to imprint?

1970s by Margaret and Harry Harlow. In one experiment they isolated eight monkeys in two cages that each contained two substitute or surrogate mothers, one made of wire mesh, the other of wood and covered in towelling. Four monkeys were put into a cage where the wire mesh model had the feeding bottle attached, the other four into a cage where the feeding bottle was attached to the towelling-covered surrogate. All eight monkeys clung onto the towelling model for around 15 hours a day, whether or not it had the bottle attached. No animal spent more than an hour or two in any 24 on the wire model.

The infants seemed to need the comfort they received from contact with the towelling-covered surrogate

The Harlows concluded that contact comfort was more important than feeding. This was especially true when the animals were afraid. If frightening objects, such as a mechanical teddy bear or a wooden spider, were put in their cages, the monkeys would cling onto their substitute mother. When put into a test room containing various toys, monkeys would explore and play so long as the cloth mother was present. If it was not there, or if the wire model was there, the monkeys would rush across the test room and throw themselves face downwards, clutching their heads and bodies. They clearly received no comfort from the wire surrogate.

Bowlby concluded that 'contact comfort' or affection is very important to the formation of a bond of attachment. The adult's demonstration of physical affection is crucial. From the experiment with the monkeys it would seem to be more important to the emotional development of the baby than nourishment.

THINK!

1 Is the idea of 'love at first sight' true with regard to babies?
2 Do all women have maternal instincts?
3 What are the implications of the widely accepted view that all women have maternal instincts for the following groups:
   a) prospective mothers?
   b) mothers who do not feel affection for their baby?
   c) women who do not choose motherhood?

DO!

Look through various child-care magazines and books. See if any mention is made of mothers who may not feel warmth and affection for their baby.
1 What advice is offered to them?
2 What image of motherhood is portrayed?
3 What do the pictures illustrate about parenting?

CHECK!

1 Describe the two substitute mothers in the Harlows' experiment.
2 How much time did the infant monkeys spend clinging to the towelling model?
3 How much time was spent on the wire model?
4 What conclusions can be drawn about the infant monkeys?
5 What does this experiment imply about the importance of physical affection to human infants?

Present understanding of causes of bonds of attachment

SENSITIVE RESPONSIVENESS THEORY

The idea that there is a simple instinctive urge that binds mothers and carers and their babies is not now widely accepted. We may be born with an instinctive predisposition or preference for forming relationships with our care givers, but these urges are far more flexible than simple imprinting.

Humans rely much less on instincts than animals do. Babies are more able to learn and change their behaviour in response to what they have learned.

Many psychologists now believe that human infants are born with some skills that allow them to attract and keep someone's attention. They appear to be programmed to become aware of, and to respond to, people around them. They seem to prefer things that are human, like voices and faces. From an early age babies give out strong signals that draw adults to them, and make them respond, for example crying, smiling, gazing, grasping.

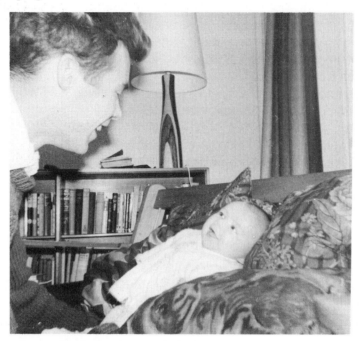

Infants seem to prefer things that are human

The carer's role in forming attachments
An adult must want both to become emotionally involved and to spend time with a child. A bond of attachment is not formed in five minutes. Carers who are sensitive to the signals given by the infant encourage the bond to occur and develop.

Making multiple attachments
John Bowlby maintained that babies need to attach to their mothers or at least a permanent mother substitute. He claimed that there would be a 'hierarchy of attachments with mother at the top'; in other words, mother is best. However, it is now recognised that a child is capable of multiple attachments, for example with father and other family and carers. Babies who attach to several adults can be just as deeply attached to each.

In 1964 a study of 60 Glasgow children, from birth to 18 months, was undertaken by Rudi Schaffer and Peggy Emerson. They concluded that when several adults took an interest in a baby, the baby could attach to them all. Schaffer and Emerson found that each attachment was much the same in quality. The infants responded in the same way to each attached adult. They seemed to use different adults for different things: if they were frightened they usually preferred their mother; if they wanted to play they usually preferred their father.

Schaffer and Emerson concluded that attachments are more likely to be formed with those people who are most sensitive to the baby's needs. They do not necessarily attach to those people who spend most time with them.

CHECK!

1 Explain, according to our present understanding, what causes bonds of attachment to develop.
2 What do babies do to attract and keep an adult's attention?
3 What response is necessary from the adult?

THINK!

1 What are the implications of Schaffer and Emerson's research for those who care for children in the absence of their primary carer?
2 If they are to develop a bond of attachment with the child what qualities should they display?

Conditions necessary for the formation of bonds of attachment

Certain conditions are thought necessary to the formation of bonds of attachment. These are summarised as follows:

- interaction needs to occur between the baby and carers who want to spend time and get involved with them
- relationships need to develop with a few people who will stay with the baby most of the time, not deserting them
- communication needs to develop with carers who respond sensitively to the baby
- loving physical affection is needed from carers.

In order to develop a bond of attachment, babies need to experience a warm, continuous, loving relationship with a small and relatively permanent group of carers who respond sensitively to them.

How the bond of attachment develops

A bond of attachment is established over a period of time. This period can be divided up into four main stages:

- during pregnancy
- at delivery
- immediately after delivery
- during the first six months.

Factors that may encourage the development of a bond of attachment include the responses of both infant and carers, and external or environmental factors, such as financial security. You will notice that some factors apply to more than one stage in the process. These are not necessarily repeated in the list.

For each factor encouraging the development of the bond of attachment list a factor that may hinder it.

FACTORS THAT ENCOURAGE THE DEVELOPMENT OF A BOND OF ATTACHMENT

During pregnancy

A positive bond is encouraged by:

- a planned, confirmed, wanted pregnancy, welcomed by partners and the wider family
- partners having a stable and mutually supportive relationship
- a normal healthy pregnancy; feeling fetal movements
- making full use of antenatal health care, which includes an understanding of the process of pregnancy and preparation for delivery
- security in material things such as finances and housing
- making physical preparations for the baby's arrival
- parents being emotionally stable and mature.

1 Why are each of the factors during pregnancy important to the development of a bond of attachment?
2 What life crises could occur that may hinder the development of the bond?

During delivery

A positive bond is encouraged by:

- a planned and expected delivery
- a natural delivery with little medical intervention, fulfilling parents' expectations, over which they felt they had control
- having health care staff in attendance who are known and caring, in a friendly, non-medical setting
- being supported by a partner or relative or friend
- having a healthy 'normal' baby of the desired gender whose appearance fulfils parents' expectations
- the baby being given immediately to parents and placed in contact with their skin or put to the breast
- the baby remaining undisturbed with the parents in the first few hours of life.

1 Why are the factors during delivery so important to the development of a bond of attachment?

The period shortly after birth

This can be a very sensitive period. Research has shown that bonding is encouraged by:

- the baby staying physically close to the parents, not separated for long periods of time
- the parents feeling well and emotionally stable, being emotionally mature, having experienced a strong bond of attachment with their own parent or carer.
- the mother sharing the parenting role with a chosen adult
- health care staff being supportive but not intrusive
- the baby remaining healthy and thriving, feeding, sleeping well
- the baby being welcomed by siblings and the wider family.

THINK!

1 Why are the factors occurring shortly after the birth important?
2 What illnesses in the mother and/or the child may show themselves at this stage?
3 What effect might these illnesses have physically and, particularly, emotionally?

The first 6 months of life

By the end of this stage infants will usually have established a bond of attachment. Their experiences during this period are crucial. Many of the factors already listed will continue to influence the development of the bond of attachment. However the interaction between carers and baby becomes more significant. This interaction often focuses on carers meeting the child's needs, but positive feedback from baby to carer will also strengthen the bond. For example the baby expresses needs by crying, smiling, babbling, clinging or raising her arms. The carer meets the baby's needs by feeding her, talking to her, cuddling her. Gradually the infant learns to trust that the carer will meet her needs and the bond is established.

The carer, for their part, may initiate positive interaction, for example talking to the baby. The baby responds positively by perhaps cooing or smiling The carer is then motivated to initiate further positive interaction and the cycle begins again. This leads to feelings of self-esteem and self worth on the part of the carer and strengthens the bond of attachment.

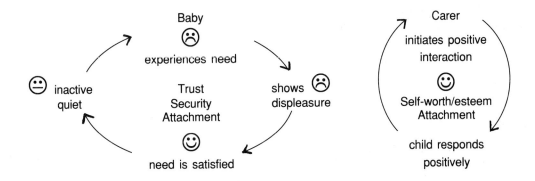

The baby expresses needs:	Both share:	Carers in turn:
crying	skin contact	talk to the baby
smiling	eye contact	smile at her
babbling	general interaction	feed her
scanning		change the nappies
sucking		cuddle
clinging		lift
raising arms		make the baby comfortable

Developing a bond of attachment: the first six months

We can see that meeting children's needs encourages a bond of attachment to develop. The success and the intensity of the attachment does not, however, depend on the amount of time the carer spends with the infant, but rather on the quality of that involvement. Infants can develop bonds of attachment with people who spend relatively short periods of time with them, for example an hour a day. This will happen if that time is spent in certain ways: these include the carer playing with the baby, cuddling them, providing them with individual attention, entering into 'conversations' with them, and generally creating a situation in which both of them are enjoying each other's company. The baby forms a stronger attachment with this person than with someone who cares for them physically for a longer period of time, but does not play with them.

This aspect of bonding has implications for those providing substitute care for a child, in the absence of their primary carers, either in residential or day-care settings.

CHILD CARE IN A KIBBUTZ

In Israel about four per cent of the population live in large agricultural communes called *kibbutzim*. There are farms, some light industry, and some shops and offices in each kibbutz. The people try to be self-sufficient, growing and making enough to keep everyone fully employed. Everything should be shared equally between all those who live in the kibbutz. Everyone works and receives the same wage and a share in the profits. The aim is for everyone to be regarded as equal in all respects, and there is no discrimination.

This way of life has important implications for child care. In order to return to work and start contributing again, the mothers of new born babies only stay with them for a few weeks. During this time intense bonding behaviour usually occurs, with cuddling, talking, playing and handling. The mother starts to go back to work, just for an hour or two a day. A trained nurse called a *metapelet* looks after the baby. Gradually the mother increases the number of hours she works and the metapelet increases her time with the baby.

By the end of the first year the mother has returned to full-time work and the child is living in the children's house with all the other youngsters. The children spend an hour or so in the evenings with their parents before returning to sleep in the children's house.

Children stay more closely attached to their parents who spend just an hour or two each day with them than they do with the metapelet who is with them all day. The parents have not abandoned the child; they just leave the routine of childminding to someone else.

████████ **THINK!**

1 Why is the process of intense bonding carried out by mothers in the first few weeks after birth so important?
2 What features of the process of handing over routine care to the metapelet are important in maintaining the bond of attachment?
3 Why do the children in the kibbutz remain more closely attached to their parents than to the metapelet?
4 What can you learn from this description of child care on a kibbutz about your role in caring for children in the absence of their primary carer?

████████ **DO!**

Talk to some parents of a young child about the number of people their child is attached to. Discuss with them how much time each adult spends with the child. Is there any difference in the way each of the adults interacts with the child?

Disability and the formation of bonds of attachment

Society often views and portrays disability in a negative way. Disability is not viewed as a difference to be celebrated but rather as a condition to be pitied. Consequently parents of disabled children may feel a sense of disappointment and failure when they discover their child has a disability. This may lead to difficulty or delay in the formation of a bond of attachment.

The formation of this bond may be encouraged in a different way by disabled carers and/or children. While recognising that all disabled people are individuals, it is important to think about the implications of particular disabilities on the bonding process.

Disabled children and carers have the same needs as other people but the methods of meeting these needs may vary according to the nature of the disability involved. Children and carers with sensory impairment, that is sight or hearing loss, will in particular need to have alternative or additional ways of responding to one another. Blind babies or carers may not be able to join in communication games that rely on visual clues such as facial expression or body posture. They will not recognise the carers' face by sight and respond to this. If sight loss has not been diagnosed, babies may be considered unresponsive by their carers. For example, when the carer of a blind baby enters the room, the baby 'freezes' so they can listen very hard. Some carers may interpret this as the baby not welcoming them. Strategies need to be worked out to encourage alternative patterns of interaction.

Carers and/or children with hearing loss will also need to use alternative methods

Early use of sign language develops deaf children's understanding and does not delay the acquisition of spoken language

of responding to one another. This is vital to the development of the bond which in turn affects all-round development.

Many of the difficulties disabled children and adults face are related to the responses of other people to them, rather than to the disability itself. For example, children with hearing loss often experience difficulty in developing an understanding of language. The development of language relies on communication between children and others. This communication must be accessible and meaningful to children. Recent research indicates that early use of sign language develops deaf children's understanding and does not delay the acquisition of spoken language.

Relatively few deaf children are exposed to sign language early enough. The exception to this is deaf children with deaf carers. Research by Susan Gregory and Susan Barlow (1989) highlighted the skills deaf parents show in interaction with their deaf children. This research confirmed subjective observations that deaf children with deaf carers tend to be more advanced in all-round development than other deaf children.

THINK!

1 How could carers encourage interaction between themselves and their blind baby?
2 How could you learn about the needs of children with a sight loss?
3 Why do deaf carers often develop a strong bond of attachment with deaf children?
4 What can child-care workers learn from deaf carers?

How we know if attachment has occurred

By around 6–8 months, most babies will be firmly attached to their primary caregivers, if the conditions have been fulfilled. Evidence for this can be observed in two ways. Firstly, a baby with a firm attachment bond at this age or stage will show stranger anxiety (fear of strangers); secondly, they will show separation anxiety, that is become upset when they are separated from the person to whom they are attached. This anxiety is considered more fully in Chapter 14, *Separation and loss*.

DEVELOPMENT OF THE BOND OF ATTACHMENT: BEHAVIOUR PATTERNS

Up 3–4 months
Except for breast-fed hungry babies, babies generally do not mind who is with them; they will often smile at strangers.

3–5 months
Babies start to decide who they feel safe with. They may 'freeze' if approached by a stranger.

6–7 months
Babies express their preference clearly. Stranger anxiety begins. This will be more severe if the baby is not being held by the person they have an attachment to and is in a strange place. The way the stranger approaches the baby is also significant. If the stranger approaches slowly, does not get too close, does not try to pick up the baby, and does not talk too loudly, the baby will show less fear.

6–18 months
Babies start to make additional attachments if other adults are willing, and fulfil the conditions necessary, that is, spend quality time with the infant.

2 years onwards
Stranger anxiety and separation anxiety slowly disappear in well attached children, so long as the separation is not for too long. Well attached children will be increasingly independent and willing to explore new situations. Less well attached children are less adventurous and less independent.

3–5 years
Children are becoming steadily less clingy to primary carers. Peer group relationships become important.

The importance of bonds of attachment

Bonds of attachment are important because they affect all aspects of children's development. A weak or damaged bond has far reaching implications for a child. Its effects may extend into the next generation.

In this section we will examine separately the importance of the bond of attachment to each aspect of children's development: physical, intellectual, linguistic, emotional and social. This separation into different areas of development is for clarity only: as has been stated before in this book, a child develops as a whole person and the areas of development are interrelated and interdependent.

PHYSICAL DEVELOPMENT

A strong bond of attachment helps to motivate carers to meet children's physical needs. In a young baby this can be a very demanding task. If a baby is responsive, the carers' self esteem will be increased, and the bond of attachment will provide the motivation to put the needs of the baby before their own, for example getting up in the night, sacrificing their own sleep to meet the baby's need for food.

Failure to meet children's physical needs may lead to neglect and failure to thrive.

THINK!

1 What are the physical needs of children?
2 In what ways could they be neglected?
3 What are the effects on children of neglecting their physical needs?

INTELLECTUAL DEVELOPMENT

Children with a strong bond of attachment will have the confidence to explore and make discoveries. Attachment and dependency are not the same thing. The researcher Mary Ainsworth concluded that 'the anxious, insecure child may appear more strongly attached to his mother than the secure child who can explore fairly freely in a strange situation, using his mother as a safe base.'

Children who have a strong bond of attachment are more secure and confident and are more likely to learn, because they feel free to leave their carers and explore.

During the first year of life children learn consequences and they learn cause and effect. For example they learn that being fed stops the discomfort of hunger; they learn that crying brings adult attention. Cognitive development is built on this foundation. Studies in the USA show that children in the care system (who are therefore more likely to have had erratic parenting and a weak bond of attachment) are four or five times more likely to have learning difficulties.

THINK!

1 How do children develop intellectually?
2 How may a weak bond of attachment affect intellectual development? Why is this so?

LINGUISTIC DEVELOPMENT

Bonds of attachment develop through interaction between carers and babies, and they also encourage further interaction. Long before babies can talk or understand words, carers and babies hold 'conversations'. These conversations are a mixture of words and gestures from the carer and noises and movement from the baby, patterned like adult conversation. Early signs of pre-speech are evident even in newborn babies. It seems that babies may be born with a natural drive towards communication. A bond of attachment will motivate carer and baby to engage in early conversations that encourage the development of language.

THINK!

1 Why are early 'conversations' important in the development of language?
2 Why does a bond of attachment encourage these conversations?
3 What are the implications for children and carers with sensory impairments? (See the section *Disability and the formation of bonds of attachment on page* 197.)

CHECK!

1 Re-read Chapter 8, *Language development*, and remind yourself of its importance to children's all-round development.

EMOTIONAL DEVELOPMENT

Coping with frustration

If babies have their emotional needs met through the attachment relationship they will be more able to cope with stress and frustration. This is true both in childhood and later in life.

THINK!

1 Why is it easier for children to cope with frustration if their own needs have been met?
2 What kinds of frustration do young children experience?

Developing independence

From her research Mary Ainsworth concludes that 'an infant whose mother has responded promptly to his cries in the past should develop both trust in her responsiveness and confidence in his increased ability to control what happens to him.' Ainsworth used the term 'sensitive mother' to refer to one who is quick to respond to her baby's needs. These babies she says feel loved and secure, which helps them become more independent later on. Babies whose needs are not dealt with sensitively may tend to become more demanding and clingy.

A poem *Food For Thought* ends with the following lines:

If children live with security, they learn to have faith.
If they live with approval, they learn to like themselves.
If they live with acceptance and friendship, they learn to find love in the world.

In terms of emotional development a child learns to be independent by experiencing dependence.

1 Explain the difference between attachment and dependency.
2 How do 'sensitive mothers' respond to their babies?

Developing a positive self-image

Another important result of a strong bond is the development of a positive self-image. Children learn to understand themselves through the responses and reactions of those close to them. They believe the messages that are repeatedly given to them. If these messages are largely positive, in other words reinforce the child's belief that they are worthwhile and worth attention from the adult, they will help to build self-esteem and a positive self-image.

1 How do children develop a positive self-image?

Responding to control and discipline

Children with a positive self-image, who think they are worthwhile valuable human beings, will be able to tolerate frustration more easily; they will also be easier to manage, control or discipline. Methods of control or discipline often rely on children wanting to be close or attached to their carer. The carer disciplines the child by distancing them physically and emotionally, for example with disapproving looks or perhaps sending the child to their room. They rely on children wanting to re-establish closeness. This process will only work with children who are attached and who modify their behaviour to re-establish closeness.

Children who feel worthwhile and valued will feel that they deserve good things to happen to them. If the carer then controls through positive re-inforcement, for example 'If you (pick up the toys), something good will happen (you will have a story read)', then children are more likely to believe them. They believe that they are worthy of a reward, and they trust the carer to give it to them. They then modify their behaviour to obtain the reward.

1 Why is it important for children to have a positive self-image?
2 Why are children with a positive self-image easier to control or discipline?

Coping with fears and worries

Children with a strong bond of attachment are better able to cope with fears and worries. Their experience of life leads them to feel safe and to trust that people will care for them and protect them from overwhelming fears and anxieties.

SOCIAL DEVELOPMENT

Making relationships

A strong bond of attachment develops children's feelings of trust in their carer and their sense of security. This makes children feel safe, but also encourages them to rely on other people. This is essential to the development of any relationship.

Later relationships will be built on the foundation of the attachment relationship. The child's experience of this will influence their desire and ability later to be part of others. Through the development of the bond of attachment children are learning how to take their part in a reciprocal, or give-and-take, relationship.

THINK!

1 Why does a sense of security encourage children to rely on others?
2 Why is the ability to rely on others essential to the development of a relationship?

The development of social emotions

Around the age of 18 months children with a good bond of attachment demonstrate social emotions. Toddlers can display some *empathy* or understanding of how other people feel in particular situations. They can demonstrate care for others, sympathy (feeling sorry for others), pride and embarrassment. Children whose own needs have been met by the attachment relationship are freer to care for others.

The development of conscience

Through experiencing embarrassment children can be made to feel shame and guilt. In the right balance these feelings are healthy; they lead on to the development of conscience, in other words the ability to know right from wrong. A conscience is important to the development of relationships. Without conscience children's behaviour may be entirely self-centred. Self-centred children have difficulty forming and maintaining relationships.

THINK!

1 Why do feelings of embarrassment, shame and guilt lead on to the development of conscience?
2 Why is the development of conscience important to the ability to make and maintain relationships?

A poor or weak bond of attachment

A poor or weak bond has far-reaching affects on the child. It influences all aspects of development, not only social and emotional, and its effects continue often into adulthood.

THINK!

Read through the section on the importance of bonds of attachment and from the information given work out for yourself the effects of a weak or poor bond on each aspect of children's development. Summarise your findings in a paragraph.

14 SEPARATION AND LOSS

This chapter includes:
- **Separation**
- **Maternal deprivation**
- **Substitute care**
- **Maternal deprivation reassessed**
- **Transitions**
- **Loss and grief**
- **The stages of grief**
- **The role of the adult**
- **The effects of grief on growth and development**
- **Grief and mourning in a multicultural society.**

Separation

In the previous chapter we established that the experience of a good bond of attachment is of great importance to children's all-round development.

We need to be aware not only of the possible effects on a child of a weak or poor bond, but also of the consequences of an interruption to any bond caused by the separation of the child from the carer. Situations that involve separation include:
- situations brought about by a change of full-time carers (short- and long-term)
- transitions that a child experiences when moving from one care situation to another on a daily basis
- situations experienced by children following the total loss of their carer, in particular a death.

Maternal deprivation

During the 1930s and 1940s John Bowlby, whose work has been mentioned in earlier chapters of Section 3, studied young people who persistently broke the law. In his book *Maternal Care and Mental Health*, he put their delinquency down to 'the prolonged deprivation of young children of maternal care'. He maintained that this 'had grave and far reaching effects on young children's character and future life.' This lack of maternal care came to be referred to as 'maternal deprivation'. This term will be referred to later, but is not now used. It can be defined as the loss by children of their mother's love.

During the 1950s and 1960s James and Joyce Robertson, colleagues of John Bowlby, undertook observations of children who went into hospital or residential nurseries. They were convinced that separating babies from their mothers was harmful. At this time this idea was contrary to medical opinion. The researchers used a cine-camera and filmed children during periods of separation both in hospitals and residential nurseries. (These films or videos are still available to hire or buy.) The Robertsons noted that during periods of separation, many of the children went through a similar sequence of behaviour. This process, which occurs if children are separated and do not receive adequate care, is referred to as the *distress syndrome*.

THE DISTRESS SYNDROME

The distress syndrome followed a pattern of behaviour shown by the children:
- it started with a period of distress or protest, shown by crying, screaming and other expressions of anger at being left
- this gave way to a period of despair when the children, apparently fearing their carer might not return, became listless, needed more rest, were dull, disinterested and refused to play
- finally there was a period of detachment: if the children became convinced that their carer would never return they appeared to try to separate themselves from any memory of the past. They were unable to make any deep relationships. Their behaviour lacked concentration; they flitted from one thing to another. Behaviour was also erratic; the children sometimes seemed dull and lifeless, sometimes highly active and excitable.

The Robertsons also noted the difficulty children experienced in linking up and relating to their mothers or carers when the separation ended. They followed the children up after separation and noted changes in their behaviour. They found that the separated children cried more than previously, had tantrums and did not show as much affection as before the separation. The Robertsons concluded that these separation experiences might have long-term effects.

IMPLICATIONS FOR CHILD-CARE PRACTICE

Bowlby's view that maternal deprivation can lead to delinquent behaviour and mental ill health has now been changed and modified, or added to, by others. His views, however, together with those of the Robertsons and other researchers, have resulted in far-reaching changes to child-care practice. Many professions concerned with children have changed their practices to avoid the unnecessary separation of children from their parents.

These changes include:
- new babies being kept beside their mothers on maternity wards
- parents of babies in special care baby units being encouraged to be involved in the care of their ill or tiny babies
- parents being encouraged to remain with their children in hospital, and the provision of facilities for them to stay overnight
- many social workers being taught to regard the separation of children from their primary carers as the worst possible solution to a family's problems
- the introduction of Child Benefit (previously called Family Allowance) to encourage a parent to stay at home and look after young children.

CHECK!

1 What is *maternal deprivation*?
2 What does the *distress syndrome* mean?

DO!

1 Describe the behaviour that you might observe in a 2-year-old child during each stage of the distress syndrome.
2 Try to watch one of the early film records (available on video) by James and Joyce Robertson. The film *John* is particularly relevant.

THINK!

1 Why might each of the changes to current child-care practice encourage children and their carers to develop and retain bonds of attachment?

Substitute care

The Robertsons' observations also highlighted the importance of the type of replacement or substitute care given to children during periods of separation. Substitute care is poor when it is organised in a way that fails to meet the emotional needs of children. Substitute care is unlikely to meet children's needs if children are:

- cared for by constantly changing caregivers, with limited time to provide individual attention
- given little opportunity to form an attachment with any one caregiver
- poorly prepared for separation or for being reunited
- not encouraged to keep in contact with the people they were attached to.

The research of the Robertsons and others has had an effect on the provision of substitute care for children. In the past children were often cared for in large institutions. The staff, who worked shifts, had responsibility for many children and were not encouraged to develop special relationships with individuals.

Today children who cannot remain with their parents are cared for, if possible, by members of their extended family or people they know. Those who are cared for by the local authority social services department are now placed in foster homes or small group homes. Residential nurseries are now rare.

The emphasis now is on substitute care that is as much like family care as possible. Substitute carers are encouraged to develop a bond with the children. Children in small children's homes will have a limited number of carers, one of whom will be their key worker or special carer. In addition, many children in the long-term care of the social services department may now be adopted. Disabled children, previously cared for in residential institutions, may also be placed with adopters.

Under The Children Act 1989 local authorities are encouraged to provide a range of services to enable 'children in need' to remain in their own homes and to be cared for by their own families. This avoids the emotional damage that can be caused by separation. These services include:

- day nurseries

- family centres
- family aids, people employed by the social services who go into homes to give practical help with child care and domestic tasks
- respite care, for disabled children; this provides short-term care which enables families to have a break, and hopefully prevents family breakdown
- liaison with voluntary agencies providing services to children and their families.

MATERNAL DEPRIVATION REASSESSED

Michael Rutter, in his book *Maternal Deprivation Reassessed*, concluded that children's needs can be met satisfactorily by substitute care, if it is organised in a way that is sensitive to their needs. Researchers now seem to agree that the 'maternal deprivation' observed by both Bowlby and the Robertsons happened not simply because the children missed their carers, but also because they missed their individual caring behaviour. If a caring environment provides this type of care, children are less likely to be so profoundly affected by separation. How such care can be provided will be considered in the following section, *Transitions*.

THINK!

1 In what ways can poorly organised care fail to meet the emotional needs of children?

Transitions

A transition, in the context of child-care, refers to the movement of a child from one care situation to another. This usually involves a change of physical environment and a change of carer(s), for example when a child goes to school. Young children need stability and security in their environment (see Chapter 13, *Bonding and attachment*); because of this they need help to cope with any transitions they may have to make. Transitions involve change and loss; any change is potentially threatening to children's feelings of security and trust.

When children have formed an attachment to a carer, they may experience feelings of loss if they are separated from that carer. We will now examine:
- situations arising from such separations
- how children can be prepared for separation
- the best ways to care for children during the separation
- how to help children when they are reunited with their carer(s).

SITUATIONS INVOLVING TRANSITION AND SEPARATION

Children may experience separation from their main carers in a variety of situations. These can be divided into two main types: residential care and day care.

Residential care
Residential care is care for children 'provided with accommodation', in the words of The Children Act (1989), or care for children received into the care of the local authority following a court order, or admitted to hospital. In these circumstances children are cared for during both the day and the night in foster homes, residential accommodation, or in hospitals.

Day care
Day care means care for children who are looked after for the whole or part of the day, but who return to their main carers at night. This includes those placed with child minders, in day nurseries, nursery schools and primary schools. Children looked after by nannies usually remain in their own home but in most cases do not have their parent(s) present for the whole time, so still experience some loss.

HOW TO HELP CHILDREN COPE WITH TRANSITIONS

The research that has been carried out into the effects of attachment and loss has had a direct effect on the way that children are both prepared for transition and cared for in residential or day care. The conclusions reached by research have also been included in *Principles and Regulations* in the Children Act (1989), suggesting the best ways to care for children in any setting.

Preparation for change
Children's reactions to separation can be affected by the way they are prepared. In the past there was little or no awareness of the value of preparation. Children were taken to school or hospital and left to cope with the experience. Good preparation is now accepted as beneficial to all children when moving to any setting. Preparation has become part of the policy of most institutions, including nurseries, schools, hospitals, child minders and long-term foster care.

Children can be prepared in many ways which can be built into the procedures of a day-care setting or an institution. (A procedure is a pre-set agreed way of doing something.) Those dealing with children at times of change need to understand, and be sensitive to, children's needs. The following guidelines for preparation can be applied to a variety of settings. They can be used, for example, when children start school or go into hospital.

Before a transition, prepare children by:
- talking to them and explaining honestly what is about to happen
- listening to and reassuring them
- reading books and watching relevant videos with them
- providing experiences for imaginative and expressive play; these help children to express their feelings
- arranging introductory visits for them and their carers, when information and experiences can be given both at their own and an adult's level
- making sure that any relevant personal details about a child, including their cultural background, are available to the substitute carer.

Reading relevant books can help to prepare a child for change

EFFECTIVE WAYS TO CARE FOR CHILDREN DURING SEPARATION

It is essential that professional carers have a thorough knowledge and understanding of child development. They also need to be aware of the particular stages of development that the children in their care have reached. As shown in the tables below, The Children Act (1989) recognises that younger children have a need for close contact with a recognisable carer. It therefore provides guidance for the ratios of children to carers: the younger the child the higher the ratio.

Age	Children–carer ratio
Under 2	3:1
Over 2 but under 3	4:1
Over 3 but under 5	8:1
Over 5 but under 8	8:1

The Children Act (1989): Suggested ratios for day nurseries

Age	Children–carer ratio
Under 5	3:1
Over 5 but under 8	6:1
Under 8 (of whom no more than three are under 5)	6:1

The Children Act (1989): Suggested ratios for child minders

When caring for children, you should remember the following points:
- children under 3 years benefit from a one to one relationship with a specific person
- the particular needs and background of children need to be known
- children's comfort objects should be readily available to them

- children should be provided with activities appropriate to their developmental age and stage, especially play that encourages the expression of feelings
- honest reassurance should be given
- children's parents or carers should have access whenever possible and appropriate
- children should have reminders of their parents or carers, such as photographs, and positive images of them should be promoted.

Children's comfort objects should be readily available to them

REUNITING CHILDREN WITH THEIR MAIN CARERS

Children who have been prepared for separation and cared for appropriately as outlined above will find it easier to be reunited with their carers and to readjust to their home environment. This can apply as much to children starting school as to children who are returning home from full-time care.

Children can be helped with being reunited if you remember to be:

- honest about when they will be reunited
- allow them to talk and express their feelings through play
- keep alive a positive image of their parents or carers during separation
- advise the parent(s) to expect and accept some disturbance in their child's feelings and possibly some *regressive* (going back to an earlier developmental stage) behaviour.

STARTING NURSERY OR SCHOOL

Most children go to school. Some may start by attending a nursery school, others start when they are the statutory school age of five. Whatever their age children may experience anxiety and stress when they start school. The possible sources of anxiety are:

- separation from their carer
- being among a large unfamiliar group of children who may already be established in friendship groups

Allow the child to talk and express their feelings through play

- the day may seem very long
- they may be unfamiliar with the predominant culture and language of the school
- the routines will be unfamiliar and they may have a fear of doing something wrong
- different activities such as PE, playtime, milk and dinner time can feel strange to them
- the scale and unfamiliarity of the buildings may be frightening
- being directed and having to concentrate for longer than they are used to.

The routines may be unfamiliar and they may have a fear of doing something wrong

Easing the transition from home to school

Possible sources of help for children when they start school are shown in the table opposite. These sources include the policies of the school, both towards admissions and to parents, the staff of the school and the child's parents or family.

Frequent transitions

Children whose admission to school is handled sensitively, with attention to the points above, usually learn to cope with attending school each day. Children can also be

```
┌─────────────────────────────────────────────────┐
│ School policies can include:                      │
│ ■ an appropriate admission programme              │
│ ■ an admission policy that staggers the           │
│   intake of children                              │
│ ■ a helpful and informative brochure,             │
│   provided in the home languages of               │
│   parents and children                            │
│ ■ appropriate classrooms and staff                │
│ ■ good liaison with parents                       │
│ ■ a welcoming environment.                        │
└─────────────────────────────────────────────────┘
                        │
              ┌──────────────────────┐
              │   Sources of help    │
              └──────────────────────┘
          ┌──────────┴──────────┐
┌──────────────────────────┐ ┌──────────────────────────┐
│ Staff (teachers, nursery  │ │ Parents and carers can    │
│ nurses, classroom         │ │ help by: encouraging      │
│ assistants, etc.) can     │ │ independence skills,      │
│ provide:                  │ │ e.g. dressing, washing,   │
│ ■ a relaxed classroom     │ │ eating                    │
│   routine                 │ │ ■ giving children some    │
│ ■ appropriate activities  │ │   experience of           │
│   and expectations        │ │   separation before they  │
│ ■ individual attention    │ │   start school            │
│ ■ observation and         │ │ ■ being there for the     │
│   monitoring of new       │ │   child when they need    │
│   children                │ │   reassurance             │
│ ■ an awareness of         │ │ ■ having a positive       │
│   cultural and language   │ │   attitude towards school │
│   differences             │ │ ■ reading books about     │
│ ■ a welcome to parents    │ │   starting school and     │
│   to participate.         │ │   encouraging realistic   │
│                           │ │   expectations            │
│                           │ │ ■ establishing routines   │
│                           │ │   (e.g. bedtime) that fit │
│                           │ │   in with school          │
│                           │ │ ■ providing the           │
│                           │ │   appropriate equipment   │
│                           │ │   (e.g. lunch box, PE     │
│                           │ │   kit).                   │
└──────────────────────────┘ └──────────────────────────┘
```

Sources of help for children starting school

helped to adjust to frequent hospital admissions if necessary. Some children also have to cope with movement between their family home and residential accommodation or foster care. This may be because of family difficulties; parents may be unable to care for them because they are experiencing problems. Sometimes, if a child has a disability, a period of respite care in a community children's home enables the child to receive training or assessment. It also gives their families a rest. If it is handled well a child can adjust to periodic changes of residence of this kind.

MULTIPLE TRANSITIONS

Some children, however, experience frequent moves. This may be because of constant and unpredictable family breakdowns. Such children become increasingly distrustful of adults. They become accustomed to change, but become increasingly unable to relate closely to any carers. Their emotional and social development is disturbed and this makes them difficult to care for. It is for this reason that frequent changes of environment for young children are to be avoided if at all possible. Social workers try to make long-term, permanent plans for children. These may involve placing children with adopters or long-term foster parents.

THINK!

1 Think of any transitions other than those described on page 209, both long- and short-term, that young children may have to cope with.
2 Can you think of any possible sources of anxiety for children other than those listed under *Starting nursery or school* on page 211?

DO!

1 Write down the ways that a young child could be prepared for a stay in hospital. Include the things that can be done at home, at school and by the hospital.
2 Describe how a young child's emotional needs can best be met during a stay in hospital.
3 Outline some play activities that it would be appropriate to provide for children who are experiencing stress when separated from their main carer(s).
4 Bearing in mind the points in the above table, design a school brochure that will help children and parents to cope with the transition to school.
5 Imagine you are working in an infant class. Think of some practical ways that you could help a new child to adjust to school life.
6 a) Identify the social and emotional needs of the following children if they have:
   - just started attending a nursery
   - just started attending a nursery where the dominant language is not the one used at home
   - attended nursery for some months, and their mother has just had a baby
   - just moved to a new infant school at the age of 6.
   b) Plan an activity that you could use to help each of these children.

Loss and grief

The term *grief* is usually reserved for feelings of deep sorrow at the loss, through death, of a loved person. The term also applies to the feelings and reactions of children to the long-term loss in other circumstances of a person with whom they have formed an attachment. This long-term loss may occur when a carer:
- separates or divorces from their partner and loses contact with the child
- is in prison for a long period
- is seriously ill and unable to communicate (for example, in a coma)
- goes away, including to another country, leaving the child behind.

If any of the above happens, the child may experience feelings of grief. Research has shown that grief felt by both children and adults follows a recognisable path or pattern. It is essential to have an awareness of this pattern when working with children who are experiencing grief. This awareness will enable you to:

- understand the child's feelings and behaviour
- be sensitive to the child's needs
- be able to provide and care for the child in the most appropriate way.

THE STAGES OF GRIEF

This section will concentrate on the child whose carer has died, but you need to remember that a child may feel *as if* a carer has died in any of the circumstances listed above.

The process of grief can be understood as a number of stages that people pass through. Each stage involves experiencing feelings and behaving in certain ways. One stage has to be worked through before a person can move on to the next. Although it is useful to look at stages in this way, it can make the process appear orderly and systematic. In practice the stages tend to merge into one another. Children (and adults) may return to the feelings of a previous stage at any time during the process of grieving.

The strength of feeling people have when they lose someone or something is directly linked to the strength of feeling they have for the person or to the value they place on the object. The length of time the feelings last varies with the importance of the loss. Children may work through the stages of grief for a person within a year. Adults may take considerably longer; three years can be quite normal. It is usually necessary for the dates of special anniversaries associated with the lost person, for example their birthday, to pass at least once before both children and adults can begin fully to adjust to the loss.

An experience of loss

The following description is of a woman who loses a treasured piece of jewellery. It shows the range of typical feelings and reactions that people often pass through when they lose something precious.

'When she saw that the ring was no longer on her finger she could not believe it. Where had it gone? Perhaps she hadn't put it on after all. She looked everywhere. She even searched in places she had not been to that day. Finally she had to admit that it was lost. She sat down and wept. The ring had belonged to her grandmother. How could she have been so careless? What would her grandfather say when she told him? It was her mother's fault for not taking it to the jewellers for her to get the size adjusted. She could think of nothing else. In the days that followed she often burst into tears. She did not feel like eating, and she slept badly. Her mother was very understanding. She let her talk and cry and get things sorted out in her mind. Gradually she began to forget about the loss for longer periods of time. She got on with other things. She knew however that there would always be a feeling of sadness and regret locked away inside her.'

If you can understand and empathise with the feelings of this woman, you will also be able to understand the stages of grief that a child (and an adult) goes through when they lose a person. These stages can be divided into early grief, acute grief and subsiding grief.

This chart summarises the possible feelings and behaviour of a child during stages of grief.

Stage of grief	Possible feelings of the child	Possible behaviour of the child
Early grief Immediately after the the death or loss	Shock, numbness, disbelief, denial, panic, alarm	Listlessness, or hyperactivity, dislike of being alone, prone to illness
Acute grief Follows the acceptance of the death	Extreme sadness, anger, guilt, shame, yearning, despair	Pining, searching, restlessness, crying, compulsive and irrational acts, lack of concentration, prone to illness
Subsiding grief When acute feelings have been worked through	Less absorbed by grief, calmer, less preoccupied, shows interest in other things, higher self-esteem	Shows interest in life, forms other attachments, involved in activities, better concentration

DEALING WITH A GRIEVING CHILD

People usually experience grief when they lose a person with whom they have an emotional bond. In any person's life the number of people with whom they have such a bond is quite limited. A child will probably only experience grief at the loss of a close carer.

Children are immature and very vulnerable at times of loss. They need special consideration and care. However, it is probable that the adults who are closest to them are also suffering loss. This means that the child's needs may not always be given the highest priority. It is very common in white British culture, unlike perhaps Asian families, for children to be excluded during the period of mourning. They may not be informed of a death until later, they may not be allowed to attend a funeral even if they want to, or they may be sent away to stay with people who are not directly involved. This exclusion is probably the result of adults believing it is better not to upset the child, and also feeling that they do not have the emotional energy to cope with the child's grief as well as their own. Whatever the reasons all available research shows that excluding a child at this time can create problems for the child. In the long term their unexpressed and unresolved feelings can return and complicate their adult mental health.

Adults who are not themselves involved in the grief of a child, for example child-care workers and teachers, can be of great help to a child. They can give the child uncomplicated attention and consideration. Despite this many adults find such involvement difficult. This may be because:

- they themselves have unresolved grief. Perhaps they were denied a period of mourning when they were young. Any contact with a grieving child can therefore activate painful memories
- they do not understand the process of grief, or the time that it takes, or the appropriate way to respond
- they have (along with many people) a fear of death, and unconsciously want to avoid any contact with it.

Avoidance is not helpful to a child. It should be a part of any child-care worker's training to examine their own feelings and attitudes, and to learn as much as possible about the process of grief.

THINK!

1 How do you feel when you lose something? Try to remember the range of feelings and behaviour that occur when you lose something that you value, for example, a bag, a purse or wallet, or a piece of jewellery.
2 For how many people would you experience grief at their loss (include possible future relationships)?

DO!

1 Re-read the description of a woman losing a treasured piece of jewellery. Identify the woman's feelings in the order in which they occur.

The role of the adult

The following chart examines the possible feelings and behaviour of a child during each stage of grief and outlines some practical ways that an adult can help the child at each stage.

Stages of grief and the role of the adult

Stage of grief	Feelings and behaviour	What must be done for the child and why	Role of the adult carer
Early grief	Shock	Give the child advance warning of the loss, if possible, to lessen the initial shock and disbelief	Tell the child if a carer is terminally ill (i.e. will not recover, death is the only possible end) Tell the child if the carers are about to separate or divorce
			Explain what long-term imprisonment will mean
	Denial and disbelief	Encourage the child to accept that the loss is real Be honest with the child	Keep the child at home; do not send them away Allow the child to see and share other people's sorrow Involve the child appropriately in a funeral
	Panic and alarm	Comfort the child; physical comfort is especially important	Provide a comfortable and quiet environment Hold and cuddle the child Give soft food that can be easily swallowed, e.g. soups Give favourite foods
Acute grief	Extreme feelings of sadness, anger, guilt and shame	Accept that the child will suffer pain Allow the child to express feelings; adults usually	Give the child time and attention Include the child in the feelings of adults who may

continued on following page

Stage of grief	Feelings and behaviour	What must be done for the child and why	Role of the adult carer
		want to protect children from suffering and distract them from sad feelings, but if a child does not express the feelings that arise from loss it can be damaging to long-term development.	also be grieving Help the child to be patient with their feelings Reassure the child that the hurt is inevitable Tell them that grieving takes time Reassure them that the pain will gradually ease
	Yearning and pining	Accept the child's need to do this Acknowledge that these feelings will probably come back to the child throughout life Recognise the child's desire to return and hold on to the past	Make allowances if the child regresses Recognise that the child is going back to a simpler and familiar stage of life Do not criticise or appear to be shocked Provide play therapy through which children can resolve some of their conflicting feelings
	Searching	Recognise that the child has to know that the lost person cannot be retrieved. Recognise that loss usually leads to a strong effort by the child to recover the person who is lost. Understand that this may lead to the child behaving restlessly and irrationally	Allow the child to search and feel they have tried to regain the carer Be honest and clear with the child; when parents separate it is vital that children are given a clear message. The child must not think that they have the power to reunite their parents.
	Disorganisation and despair	Adult support needed because: ■ they may find it difficult to concentrate ■ school performance may decline ■ they may have strong emotional responses to things ■ movement and speech may slow down	Make allowances for the disorganisation. Avoid being demanding, especially within an organised environment like a school Help the child to organise him or herself Listen to the child, give time and good attention Protect the child and share their feelings
Subsiding grief	Feelings are less acute, more normal for longer periods of time	Help to focus on the future as they gradually begin to adjust to the loss and become able to form attachments to other people	Encourage the child to participate in a range of activities. Promote the child's physical well being and self-esteem Make sure that the child can always trust the adult carer

The effects of grief on growth and development

Grief can be such a powerful experience that the developmental growth of a child may be affected in every area. For example a child may:

- not want to eat or run around
- be unable to concentrate or be too sad to play
- be self-absorbed and unwilling to communicate
- be feel insecure, lose trust in adults, have low self-esteem
- not want to be with friends or relatives.

DO!

1 Name the areas of development affected by the responses described above.

CHECK!

1 What are the main stages of grief in children?
2 Write in your own words the main ways that an adult can provide for a child who is experiencing grief.

Grief and mourning in a multicultural society

People have differing cultural practices for dealing with death and mourning. The mourning period is the time when people show conventional signs of grief, such as wearing black, or wearing white, weeping together, closing curtains. A knowledge of and respect for different customs and beliefs is vital when you are working with children whose cultural and religious background is different from yours. Without this knowledge a child-care worker might respond unsuitably, or offer words of comfort that are inappropriate and even offensive.

DO!

1 Find out the different beliefs and customs concerning death and mourning of the families of children with whom you work.

Key terms
You need to know what these words and phrases mean. Go back through the chapter and find out.

Maternal deprivation	Policies	Shock
The distress syndrome	Grief	Denial
Substitute care	Transitions	Yearning and pining
Provided with accommodation	Residential Care	Despair
Respite care	Procedures	Mourning period

---

15 THE STAGES OF SOCIAL AND EMOTIONAL DEVELOPMENT

Principles of development

In this section the stages of social and emotional development are outlined in isolation from physical and cognitive development. As has been stated before in this book, most people find it simpler and easier to understand children's developmental progress by examining one area of development at a time. There are, however, important things to remember when studying emotional and social development separately:

- development is a whole process; all areas of development are integrated and interact with each other; they mix together and are affected by each other
- their interaction results in an individual pattern of development which varies from one child to another
- development is usually made up of a period of rapid growth followed by a period of relative calm. During this period of calm the previous growth is consolidated. This means that it becomes a definite and practised part of the child's being. One developmental area may be relatively calm when there is more rapid growth in another
- children do not develop in isolation; they develop within family systems. Families have individual characteristics which all influence each child differently
- a child's family exists within a larger cultural system. The experience of this cultural environment has a profound effect on both the family and a child's behaviour
- the family and cultural environments interact with and affect children's developing skills, their awareness of themselves and their relationships with others.

Ages and stages of social and emotional development

The development described here follows the path of a newborn baby until the age of 8. The path moves from complete immaturity and dependence towards social and emotional maturity and the development of social skills and independence. The main aspects of development covered are:

- emotional: children's feelings about and for other people
- self-image and identity: children's feelings about, and views of, themselves
- social: children's relationships with other people
- social skills: the development of skills that lead to independence.

BIRTH

At birth and for the first month or so of life, a baby's behaviour is largely governed by in-built reflexes and reactions. These reflexes govern the way the infant listens, looks around, explores and relates to others. However, even at this stage carers become aware of characteristics that they see as individual to the child and that seem to be the product of nature. Newborn infants begin to learn from the moment of birth, but at this stage behaviour and communication with adults is limited. Babies cry to make their needs known and are peaceful when those needs are met.

Development
At this stage babies:
- are utterly dependent on others
- have rooting, sucking and swallowing reflexes
- sleep most of the time
- prefer to be left undisturbed
- cry when hungry, in pain or unattended to
- are usually content in close contact with carer; startle to noise, and turn to the light, providing it is not too bright.

The newborn is usually content in close contact with the carer

1 MONTH

Babies have been observed to smile spontaneously from birth; but when they are between 4 to 8 weeks old they begin to smile in response to happenings outside themselves. The baby learns to smile at a voice and a face; they are also attracted to the movement of a face.

Development
Around this age babies:
- sleep most of the time when not being handled or fed
- cry for their needs to be attended to; different cries are evident for hunger, pain, panic and discomfort

- will turn to the breast
- look briefly at a human face
- will quieten in response to a human voice and smile in response to the main carer's voice
- develop a social smile and respond with vocalisations to the sight and sound of a person (at around 6 weeks)
- grasp a finger if the hand is opened and the palm is touched.

2 MONTHS

From 2 months babies have less primitive reactions and gradually learn a range of responses and behaviour. These are the result both of physical maturation and of the baby beginning to explore the environment. At 2 months the baby is capable of having conversations with the carer. These are a mixture of gestures and noises, but follow the pattern of a conversation in that one person is quiet while the other speaks.

Development
Around this age babies:
- stop crying when they are picked up
- differentiate between objects, including beginning to tell one face from another; follow a human face when it moves
- sleep less during the day and more during the night
- smile and become more responsive to others
- explore using their five senses.

3 MONTHS

Physical maturation continues rapidly. Babies will take a lot of interest in their environment at this stage: they turn their heads to see what people are doing and in response to different sounds. They are beginning to learn a range of social skills rapidly from the people in their environment. The essential requirement for the baby in this early period is that someone takes the time to communicate and be with them. Babies appear to have a natural capacity to communicate, but this does not develop without contact and interaction with other people. They need to be handled and talked to. By 3 months babies have learned to respond with pleasure to friendly handling. An infant and carer gradually build up a complex pattern of responses.

Development
Around this age infants:
- respond to friendly handling and smile at most people; use sounds to interact socially and reach out to the human face
- become more oriented to their mother, and any other main carer if there is one; look at their carers' face when feeding
- begin to connect what they hear and what they see
- show pleasure, fear, excitement, contentment, unhappiness
- have an awareness of the feelings and emotions of others.

At 3 months babies respond to friendly handling and smile at most people

6 MONTHS

There has been very rapid development during the past months. Infants are awake for much longer periods; if they have been stimulated by the presence of other people during this period they will show great interest in their environment and be very happy in response to attention. They laugh, show excitement and delight. They also show likes and dislikes strongly.

Development
Around this age infants:
- show a marked preference for their main carer(s)
- begin to be more reserved with, or afraid of, strangers

At 6 months babies show a preference for a main carer and begin to be more reserved with strangers

- reach out for familiar people and show a desire to be picked up and held
- smile at their own image in a mirror
- may like to play peek-a-boo
- show eagerness, anger and pleasure by body movement, facial expression and vocally
- play alone with contentment
- stop crying when communicated with
- become more aware of themselves in relation to other people and things.
  They may have the following skills:
- increasing use of their hands to hold things; look at their hands and feet with interest
- drink from a cup that is held for them.

9 MONTHS

From this age strong attachments have been formed with the main carer(s), and infants have usually begun to move around independently. This requires new adaptations to be made by both infants and carers. Infants take great pleasure in playing with their carers and learn a great deal from this interaction. They can be a delight to be with. The development of infants who do not experience this positive interaction will of course be affected.

Development
Around this age infants:
- clearly distinguish familiar people and show a marked preference for them
- show a fear of strangers and need reassurance when in their company, often clinging to the known adult and hiding their face in them
- play peek-a-boo, copy hand clapping and pat a mirror image
- still cry for attention to their needs, but also their use their voice to attract people to themselves
- show some signs of willingness to wait for attention
- show pleasure and interest at familiar words

At 9 months babies show a fear of strangers, need reassurance, cling to the known adult and hide their face in them.

- understand 'No'
- begin to respond to their own name
- try to copy sounds
- offer objects to others but do not release them.
  They may have the following skills:
- put their hands around a cup or bottle when feeding.

12 MONTHS

By this age, many children have started to stand independently and walk. They therefore gain a very different view of the world around them. Their physical skills enable them both to pick up small objects, and to explore the environment. In a secure environment children can be very varied in their interaction with adults. Their development will be significantly affected if they are not spoken to or played with at this age.

Development
Around this age infants:
- like to be within sight and hearing of a familiar adult
- can distinguish between different members of the family and act socially with them
- will wave goodbye
- may be shy with strangers
- are capable of a variety of emotional responses including fear, anger, happiness and humour
- show rage when thwarted
- become increasingly aware of the emotions of others
- actively seek attention by vocalising rather than by crying
- copy actions or sounds of adults or children
- will obey simple instructions
- know their own name.

At 12 months infants like to be within sight and hearing of a familiar adult and will wave goodbye

They may have the following skills:

- assist with feeding by holding a spoon and may drink from a cup by themselves
- help with dressing by holding out their arms or legs.

15 MONTHS

By this age toddlers use their main carer as a safe base from which to explore the world. They are anxious and apprehensive about being physically separated from them, and tend to be very much 'under the feet' of their carers. They are very curious about their environment. Their explorations can lead to conflict with their carers.

Development
Around this age children:

- have a sense of 'Me' and 'Mine' and begin to express themselves defiantly
- begin to distinguish between 'You' and 'Me' but do not understand that others are individuals just like themselves
- can point to members of the family in answer to questions like 'Where's granny?'
- tend to show off
- are not dissuaded from undesirable behaviour by verbal reasoning, but react poorly to the sound of sharp discipline; (the most useful disciplinary technique in this period is to divert a child and change the environment)
- have an interest in strangers but are either fearful or very wary of them
- show interest in other children
- show jealousy of the attention given by adults to other children
- throw toys when angry
- are emotionally very unstable
- resist changes in routine or sudden transitions
- swing from dependence to independence.

   They may have the following skills:

- hold a cup and drink without assistance

At 15 months toddlers will hold a spoon and bring it to the mouth, probably spilling some food in the process

- hold a spoon and bring it to the mouth, spilling some food in the process
- help with dressing and undressing.

18 MONTHS

At this age children are very *egocentric* or self-centred (*ego*, self; *centric*, centred on). Children are also often defiant and resistant in this period. They have only recently discovered themselves as separate individuals. Their defiant behaviour can be seen as an attempt to protect themselves and their individuality.

Development
At this age children:
- are trying to establish themselves as members of the social group
- begin to *internalise* the values of the people around them, that is they begin to understand the things that their carers think are important and of value
- respond by stopping doing something when the word 'No' is used, but this usually needs to be reinforced; reinforcement means that the adult's response has to be repeated or even backed up by some form of punishment
- are still very dependent on a familiar carer; they also often return to a fear of strangers
- tend to follow their carer around, be sociable and imitate them by helping with small household tasks
- are conscious of their family group
- imitate and mimic others during their play; engage in solitary or parallel play but like to do this near a familiar adult or sibling
- show intense curiosity

Around 18 months children imitate others during solitary play

- show some social emotions, for example sympathy for someone who is hurt
- cannot tolerate frustration
- have intense mood swings, from dependence to independence, eagerness to irritation, co-operation to resistance.
  They may have the following skills:
- use a cup and spoon well and successfully get food into their mouth
- take off a piece of clothing and help with dressing
- although still in nappies, make their carers aware of their toileting needs through words or by restless behaviour.

2 YEARS

At this age children do not fully accept that their parent is a separate individual. Sometimes a child can be very self-contained; at other times they will be very dependent. Children by this stage are capable of a wide range of feelings and able to empathise with the feelings of those close to them. For example if their carer is upset, they are capable of trying to comfort them. By this stage children are able to use symbols in language and in thinking (see Chapter 8, *Language development*). These newly acquired language skills enable the children to achieve new levels of social development, just as their physical mobility already has.

Development
Around this age children:
- demand their carer's attention and want their needs to be met immediately they make demands
- will ask for food
- can respond to a reasonable demand to wait for attention or for the satisfaction of their needs
- sometimes have tantrums if crossed or frustrated, or if they have to share the attention of their carer with another person
- are loving and responsive

At 2 years children can lift up a mug and put it down again

- will try to be independent
- are possessive of their own toys and objects, and have little idea of sharing
- tend to play parallel to other children, engage in role play, but are beginning to play interactive games
- tend to be easily distracted by an adult if they are frustrated or angry
- join in when an adult sings or tells a simple story
- can point to parts of the body and other features when asked.
  They may have the following skills:
- feed themselves without spilling
- lift a cup up and put it down
- put some clothes on with supervision
- say when they need the toilet; become dry in the daytime.

2 YEARS 6 MONTHS

Children between the ages of 2 and 3 are still emotionally and socially very dependent on familiar adult carers; they are also capable of being very independent in some of their behaviour. During this period extremes of moods and behaviour are common. Children can change between aggressive and withdrawn behaviour, awkwardness and helpfulness very rapidly.

Development
Around this age children:
- develop their sense of self-identity: they know their name, their position in the family and their gender
- play with other children; among other things this tends to reinforce their developing concept of gender roles. They also learn that different toys are intended for girls and boys
- may engage in role play or make-believe
- behave impulsively, wanting to have anything they see and do anything that occurs to them

At 2 years 6 months children can dress with supervision

- throw tantrums when thwarted and are not so easy to distract
- are often in conflict with their carers, who have to limit their children's behaviour; this need to limit a child's impulses is necessary for future social development. It is also essential for the child's own survival.

  They may have the following skills:
- awareness of and ability to avoid certain hazards like stairs and hot stoves
- ability to use a spoon well, and possibly a fork or chop sticks
- get themselves a drink, through ability to pour from one container to another
- probably dress with supervision, unzip zips, unbuckle and buckle, and unbutton and button clothing
- are toilet trained during the day, and can be dry at night, especially if lifted.

3 YEARS

By this age children are usually happier and more contented than during their previous year. They have gained a certain amount of physical and emotional control. This may lead to more settled feelings and more balance in the way they express them. They are generally friendly and helpful in their manner to others.

Development

Around this age children:
- can feel secure when in a strange place away from their main carers; this is as long as they are with people with whom they became familiar when they were with their carer
- can wait for their needs to be met
- are less rebellious and use language rather than physical outbursts to express themselves
- still respond to distraction as a method of controlling their behaviour; they are, however, also ready to respond to reasoning and bargaining
- are beginning to learn the appropriate behaviour for a range of different social settings; for example they can understand when it is necessary to be quiet or when they can be noisy

At 3 years children can toilet themselves and wash their hands

- adopt the attitudes and moods of adults
- want the approval of loved adults
- can show affection for younger siblings
- have an ability to share things and to take turns
- enjoy make-believe play both alone and with other children
- project their own experiences onto dolls and toys
- may have imaginary fears and anxieties
- towards the end of this year show some insecurity, expressed as shyness, irritability and self-consciousness.
  They may have the following skills:
- ability to use a fork and spoon to eat (in some cultures it will be more appropriate to use hands to eat some food) and can be proficient with chop sticks
- toilet themselves during the day, and may be dry through the night; will wash their hands but may have difficulty drying them
- learning to dress without supervision.

4 YEARS

At this age children are constantly trying to understand and make sense of their experiences and of the world around them. Although they can be very sociable at this age they often return to a more stubborn phase. This may involve them using some physical as well as verbal aggression.

Development
By this age children:
- are very sociable with, and talkative to, both adults and children, and enjoy silly talk
- may have one particular friend
- are confident and assured
- may be afraid of the dark and have other fears
- have adopted the standards of behaviour of the adults to whom they are closest
- turn to adults for comfort when overtired, ill or hurt
- play with groups of children; groups tend to centre around an activity, then dissolve and reform
- can take turns but are not consistent about this
- are often very dramatic in their play; engage in elaborate and prolonged imaginative play
- are developing a strong sense of past and future
- are able to cope with delay in having their needs met
- show purpose and persistence and some control over their emotions
- can be dogmatic and argumentative; may blame others when they misbehave, and may even behave badly in order to arouse a reaction
- may swear and use bad language.
  They may have the following skills:
- feed themselves proficiently
- dress and undress, but may have difficulty with back buttons, ties and laces
- wash and dry hands and face and clean teeth.

By this age children can feel secure away from their main carers, are learning appropriate behaviour, are able to take turns and play in a group of children

5 YEARS

Children achieve a level of balance, self containment and independence by this age. They are usually friendly, willing to talk to anyone, and able to be polite.

Development
By this age children:
- enjoy brief separations from home and carers
- show good control of emotions on the whole
- are increasingly aware of a range of differences between themselves and other people, including gender and status differences
- are developing a sense of shame (an important development which affects the adult's ability to control the child)
- want the approval of adults
- argue with parents when they request something
- still respond to discipline based on bargaining
- are not so easily distracted from their own anger as when they were younger
- often show the stress of conflict in being overactive; may regain their balance by having 'time-out'
- prefer games of rivalry to team games
- enjoy co-operative group play, but these often need an adult to arbitrate
- boast, show off and threaten

- show a desire to excel and can be purposeful and persistent.
  They may have the following skills:
- use a knife and fork well
- are able to dress and undress; may be able to lace shoes and tie ties
- wash and dry face and hands, but need supervision to complete other washing.

At 5 years children can undress and dress

6–8 YEARS

By this age children have progressed a long way along the path to independence and maturity in the following ways:
- they have developed a wide range of appropriate emotional responses
- they are able to behave appropriately in a variety of social situations
- they have learned all the basic skills needed for independence in eating, hygiene and toileting routines.

Throughout these years children grow steadily more independent and truly sociable. They are generally self-confident and friendly; they are able to co-operate in quite sophisticated ways with adults and children.

Some particular developmental characteristics may occur during these years. At 6 years children:
- are often irritable and possessive about their own things
- may have spells of being rebellious and aggressive.
  At 7 years children:
- become very self-critical about their work
- may be miserable and sulky, and give up trying for short periods
- may be so enthusiastic for life that carers have to guard against them becoming overtired
- are more aware of gender characteristics; friendship groups are often separated by gender
- are under the influence of the peer group, which becomes increasingly important to

children over these years; peer group opinion is increasingly influential and will be used and quoted by children to carers as either their own ideas or to justify what they want to do. 'Hero' figures become influential and are used as role models by children at this stage.

Children's all-round development is increasingly sophisticated. This sophistication, coupled with skills of perseverance, opens up opportunity for success in many and varied activities of increasing complexity, for example sewing, painting, playing a musical instrument and so on.

Disabled children

It is often at this stage that the differences of disabled children become more apparent. The development of sophisticated skills is the norm for children at this age; because of this the carers of a child who has a disability may be faced more starkly with their child's difference. They may struggle between:

- a concern to see their child treated as 'normal'
- acceptance of their child's disability and a recognition of the need for special support.

8 YEARS

The saying 'Give me a child until he is seven and I will give you the man' sums up the fact that much of the child's personality is established by the end of this period. By the time they are 8 years old children's experiences in their families and in their social and cultural environments will have led to the establishment of:

- their personal identity
- their social and cultural identity
- their gender role
- their attitudes to life.

DO!

Go back through the chapter, pick out and write down the main stages of:
1 Emotional development (children's feelings about and for other people)
2 Social development (children's relationships with other people)
3 The growth of each of the social skills (the skills that lead to independence).

> **Key terms**
> You need to understand what these words and phrases mean. Go back through the chapter and find out.
> Immaturity
> Independence
> Social skills
> Egocentric

SECTION 4
Disabled children and their families

16 UNDERSTANDING DISABILITY

Introduction

Disability is generally seen as an undesirable condition experienced by other people that individuals hope will never happen to them. Disability in children is often regarded as a tragedy, eliciting pity for the 'victims' and their families. These and other attitudes, together with the environment (for example physical access to buildings) often cause unnecessary disability. Ignorance and fear can lead to separation, exclusion, prejudice and discrimination against disabled people.

The information given here aims to affect readers' attitudes as much as to increase their knowledge. Working with young children provides an ideal opportunity to influence attitudes. Children do not exclude or devalue each other until they are taught to do so by the unconscious or uninformed behaviour of adults.

The information given here cannot cover every aspect of disability. There are many condition- or impairment-specific organisations working with particular groups of disa-

Children do not exclude or devalue each other until they are taught to do so by the unconscious or uninformed behaviour of adults.

bled people which produce useful information and offer disability awareness training. To be authentic, such information and training should include those most closely involved: disabled people themselves.

For child-care practice to be truly inclusive, the needs of disabled children and their families must be recognised (see the section on access in Chapter 20, *Providing inclusive care and education*).

CHECK!

1 How is disability often seen by society?
2 What causes unnecessary disability?

The implications of history

During the Industrial Revolution in Britain there was a move away from small family-based cottage industry to employment in large factories. This served to discriminate against disabled people because they were no longer able to control their own surroundings nor their pace of work. Disabled people were forced into dependency and poverty, losing the status that comes from employment.

At about the same time the influence of the medical profession was increasing. Doctors sought to treat people and cure their impairments so that they could fit into society. If this was not possible, disabled people were hidden away in hospitals and long-stay institutions out of sight; there was little contact with the outside world.

Children with disabilities were hidden away in long-stay institutions

Models of disability

THE MEDICAL OR PERSONAL TRAGEDY MODEL

The result of the past is that society has become conditioned to treat disabled people according to a *medical model*. Society separates and excludes incurably disabled people as if they are somehow not quite human. Disability is viewed predominantly as a personal tragedy needing medical intervention. This encourages a negative view, focusing on what a person cannot do, rather than what they can. Disability is seen as a problem to be solved or cured rather than a difference to be accepted. It is all too easy, within this medical model, to see disabled people themselves as problem individuals who should adapt themselves to fit into society.

THE SOCIAL MODEL

Disabled people, however, are no longer prepared to accept the medical model of disability. Through organisations such as the Disability Movement they are campaigning for acceptance of a *social model* of disability. They want people to see *impairment* (the medically defined condition) as a challenge, and to change society to include disabled people whether or not they can be cured. This will involve responding to their true needs.

The social model views disability as a problem within society rather than within disabled people. It maintains that many of the difficulties disabled people face could be

A mobility problem is seen to be caused by the presence of steps rather than by an individual's inability to walk

eliminated by changes in people's attitudes and in the environment. According to the social model, a mobility problem, for example, is seen to be caused by the presence of steps rather than by an individual's inability to walk; a deaf person's difficulty with accessing information is seen to be caused by other people's lack of skill in British Sign Language rather than by an individual's hearing loss.

Disabled people have taken the social model a stage further and defined disability as a social creation, a problem created by the institutions, organisations and processes that make up society. This model of disability has led to disabled people coming together to campaign for their rights, for social change and to fight against institutional oppression. One example of this was *The Campaign for Accessible Transport*: mass attempts were organised for wheelchair users to get on buses and tubes in London. This direct action was intended to draw attention to public transport systems which serve only able-bodied people and discriminate against disabled people.

THINK!

1 Think of as many examples as you can of the ways institutions and organisations create problems for disabled people.
2 What are the implications of accepting a social model of disability:
   a) for society
   b) for you in your role?

CHECK!

1 Check that you understand the medical and social models of disability.

The importance of terminology

Terminology reflects and influences the way disability is viewed by society, including disabled people themselves. It also influences people's perceptions and attitudes, which subsequently affect the provision of resources and services.

Over the years disabled people have been referred to and labelled using many different terms, usually conferred on them by able-bodied professionals. These have included general classifications which de-humanise, like 'the infirmed' and 'the handi-capped', or even 'the disabled'.

In addition people have been referred to in such a way that they become their impairment: 'Jane is a spastic', 'John is an epileptic', 'Our Down's syndrome child', 'Paul is a wheelchair case'. Many of these terms are patronising and contemptuous of disabled people. Some terms are used as a form of abuse amongst able-bodied people, for example 'cripples', 'dummies', 'spazzies', 'idiots', 'mongols', 'invalids' and worse.

There are many different conditions or impairments which disabled people have (see Chapter 17, *Impairments and conditions*); when the condition or impairment is known, the correct name should be used for it. This is particularly true for disabled children, who are often denied accurate information about themselves.

Explaining terminology to young children, both able-bodied and disabled, provides an opportunity to teach basic information about such topics as bodies, health or illness. This is not a taboo topic to young children who need, and like, to know the truth. It provides an opportunity to dispel some of the myths and fears surrounding disability, and influence attitudes at a formative stage.

CHECK!

1 Why is it important to use the correct terminology to describe disabled people?

THINK!

1 How do the terms listed above reflect and influence the way disabled people are viewed by others?
2 How may these terms affect a disabled person's self image?
3 Why are some of these terms used as a form of abuse?

Definitions of terms

The following definitions seek to respect the views of disabled people and promote good practice in the use of terminology. They were devised by the Union of the Physically Impaired Against Segregation in 1976. They are widely accepted by the Disability Movement and those working on disability equality issues.

Impairment: lacking part or all of a limb, or having altered or reduced function in a limb, organ or mechanism of the body. Mike Oliver in his book (see Bibliography, page 284) defines impairment as 'individual limitation'.

Disability: the disadvantage or restriction of activity caused by contemporary social organisation which takes little or no account of people who have physical or mental impairments and thus excludes them from the mainstream of social activities. Oliver defines disability as 'socially imposed restriction'.

It is important to remember that disabled people are individuals with names. However, using the above definitions it is appropriate to refer to *disabled people* or *children*. This term enables individual disabled people to identify themselves as a group with a common struggle, to end oppression by a disabling society. The adjective 'disabled' is similar to the term 'black' in that it was a negative term but now represents the pride people feel in their identity. It follows from the above definitions that people may have physical impairments, sensory (hearing or visual) impairments, and/or learning impairments.

There may, however, be preference for other terms within these groups of disabled people. For example, some adults who have lost their hearing in later life, may refer to themselves as 'hard of hearing'. People born with a hearing loss may refer to themselves as 'deaf', 'partially hearing', or 'partially deaf'. Some people with learning impairments prefer to be referred to as 'having learning difficulties'.

CHECK!

1 Define *impairment* and *disability*.

Children with special needs

The term *special needs* is now in common usage, especially in educational settings in relation to children. The term is frequently used by child-care professionals to describe children whose development is atypical.

In the past these children may have been categorised as 'handicapped', or 'subnormal'. Individual children may have been labelled as 'physically handicapped', 'visually handicapped' or 'mentally subnormal'.

Those who advocate use of the term *special needs* suggest that these other labels are unsatisfactory because they:

- focus on weaknesses, not strengths
- do not indicate the practical effects of the difficulty and so the measures which may support the child
- suggest that all 'handicapped' or 'subnormal' children are the same and need the same kinds of support
- encourage people to focus on the condition and view children with particular difficulties in stereotypical ways; for example, children with Down's syndrome are seen as sweet, innocent and lovable; deaf children are assumed to be slow on the uptake
- imply a clear-cut division between 'handicapped' and 'subnormal' children and other children.

Supporters of the term 'special needs' seek to emphasise the similarities between children with special needs and children who are developing according to the norm. They hope that the change in terminology from 'handicap' to 'needs' will encourage the treatment of each child as a unique individual with their own personality, ideas, sense of humour and level of ability. However the term *special needs* still conforms to the medical model of disability.

Within the term *special needs* children can be considered to have:

- moderate to severe learning difficulties
- *sensory* impairment, that is hearing and/or visual impairment
- physical or *neurological* (linked to the function of the brain) impairment
- speech and language difficulties
- emotional or behavioural difficulties
- specific learning difficulties; this term is used to describe children's difficulties learning to read, write, spell or in doing mathematics. (Such children do not have difficulty learning other skills. The term *dyslexia* is used, though inaccurately, to refer to difficulty developing literacy skills.)

CHECK!

1 What area is covered by the term *special needs*?

1 What are the advantages and disadvantages of using the term *special needs*?

1 Find out how you can have your awareness raised about the implications of each of the above special needs. Any disability awareness programme should include disabled people's views!

Key terms

You need to know what these words and phrases mean. Go back through the chapter and find out.

Disability	Specific learning difficulties
Impairment	Emotional or behavioural difficulties
Condition	Social creation
Medical model	Institutional oppression
Social model	Discrimination
Moderate or severe learning difficulties	Taboo topic
Sensory impairments	Contemporary social organisation
Physical or neurological impairments	Individual limitation
Speech and language difficulties	Socially imposed restriction

---

CONDITIONS AND IMPAIRMENTS

Introduction

This chapter follows a medical model of disability, but it is also intended to give information which will help you to provide appropriate support and encourage the all-round development of children. It includes an outline of conditions and impairments. The information is brief, containing only the main points, and is designed to give an overview. The way a child is affected will vary, and it is important that the child-care worker responds to each child's individual needs.

Those working with children who have a specific condition or impairment will need to obtain more information. A useful source is the support agencies who will have helpful up-to-date information; their addresses are included. Support agencies usually rely on money from donations to support their work, so if you request information from them a contribution will be appreciated. You may find it helpful to refer to Chapter 6 in this book to refresh your memory about factors affecting development.

Conditions and impairments: an outline

Information about each condition or impairment is given under the following headings:
- Condition or impairment
- Causes
- Characteristics
- Diagnosis
- Treatment and progress
- Support agency.

ASTHMA

Causes
Asthma (reversible airways obstruction) is a condition in which the airways in the lungs become narrowed. Allergy to certain substances such as pollen, dust or pet hair cause the lining of the airways to swell. There may also be a spasm of the airways causing further narrowing and restricting the supply of air. Other factors such as infection, exercise, the weather or emotional upset may also precipitate attacks.

Characteristics

Breathing becomes difficult and the child wheezes and is breathless. Attacks vary in severity. In a severe attack breathing becomes very difficult and the child anxious and afraid. In between attacks breathing is normal. Severe asthma attacks are serious and can be fatal.

Diagnosis

Diagnosis is by observing the attacks. Skin tests may help identify the allergen.

Treatment and progress

The usual form of treatment is to give drugs called *bronchodilators* which help the airways to relax and dilate (widen). These are commonly given by inhaler so that the drug is breathed in and goes straight to the affected air passages. Drugs can also be given in tablet or linctus form. It is important to try to prevent attacks by avoiding allergens and situations which are known to be problematic.

Support agency

The Asthma Society
300 Upper Street, LONDON N1 2XX

AUTISM

Causes

A child with autism has difficulty in relating to other people and making sense of the social world. The primary cause is unknown. Autism occurs in all parts of the world and usually begins from birth.

Characteristics

An autistic child may:
- lack awareness of other people
- pay more attention to objects than people
- have a problem in using non-verbal and/or verbal communication
- not develop language
- lack imagination and the ability to play
- repeat activities and have unco-ordinated body movements
- have learning difficulties.

Some children may have an ability in which they excel, such as drawing.

Diagnosis

Diagnosis is by observation of the child's progress. Parents or carers often recognise that their child is behaving differently from an early age. They are frequently frustrated that no diagnosis is made. The things they notice may include lack of eye contact, difficulty with feeding, screaming, lack of motor co-ordination, resistance to change.

Treatment is centred around modifying the child's behaviour. Consistent one-to-one care requires patience and skill on the part of all the family members. Pre-school activities are important. Respite care and long-term provision is helpful to enable young people to gain some independence.

Support agency
The National Autistic Society
276 Willesden Lane, LONDON NW2 5RB

CEREBRAL PALSY

Causes
Cerebral palsy is a disorder of movement and posture; the part of the brain which controls movement and posture is damaged or fails to develop. There are many causes which may occur before, during or after birth. These include:
- rubella during pregnancy
- lack of oxygen to the brain
- Rhesus incompatibility (see Chapter 6)
- toxaemia of pregnancy (see Chapter 6)
- birth injury
- accidents or infections after birth.

Characteristics
The term *cerebral palsy* covers a wide range of impairment. There are three main types of impairment of movement:
- *spasticity*, where the movements are stiff, the muscles are tight and the limbs are held rigidly and turned in towards the body
- *athetosis*, when the limbs are floppy; movements are frequent and involuntary, especially when attempts are made to make the movements purposeful
- *ataxia*, lack of balance and poor co-ordination.
Cerebral palsy may affect and involve one or more limbs.

Diagnosis
Diagnosis is by observation of the child's progress associated with a history of possible brain damage.

Treatment and progress
No way has been found to repair the damage to the brain. Early assessment is very important. Therapy needs to be individual and works at maximising the child's potential; it may involve physiotherapy, speech therapy, occupational therapy or conductive education. Equipment can aid communication, mobility and independent living .

Support agency
The Spastics Society
12 Park Lane Crescent,
LONDON WIN 4EQ

CLEFT LIP AND/OR PALATE

Causes
A cleft lip or palate is a structural impairment of the top lip, palate or both. The development of the lip and/or the palate fails to take place in the early weeks of fetal life.

Characteristics
The development failure may occur in different ways:
- the lip only may be affected and will be divided into two or three sections by one or two clefts
- the palate only may be similarly affected
- the lip and the palate may both be divided.

Diagnosis
Diagnosis is by examination at or soon after the birth.

Treatment and progress
Treatment varies depending on the extent of the impairment; it can be lengthy and involve a series of operations to repair the gaps in the lip and palate. In general the lip is repaired first, the palate later. Feeding will need careful management and speech therapy may be required. Progress is individual and positive, with good results in many instances.

Support agency
Cleft Lip and Palate Association
1 Eastwood Gardens, Kenton, NEWCASTLE-UPON-TYNE NE3 3DQ

COELIAC DISEASE

Causes
Coeliac disease is a metabolic disorder involving sensitivity to *gluten* (a protein found in wheat, rye, barley and oats); there is difficulty in digesting food. There is thought to be a familial tendency to the disease. The lining of the small intestine is sensitive to gluten and the resulting damage reduces the ability to absorb nutrients from the food broken down by the digestive process.

Characteristics
The child exhibits the signs of malnutrition and does not gain weight and grow normally. The child may also be irritable, have, pale, bulky, foul-smelling stools and may vomit.

Diagnosis
Diagnosis in children is by observation of the failure to grow and gain weight satisfactorily, particularly after weaning onto foods containing gluten. A positive diagnosis can be made by biopsy and examination of tissue from the intestine.

Treatment and progress
A diet free of gluten must be followed. The intestine usually recovers and the child will begin to grow normally.

Support agency
The Coeliac Society
PO Box 220, HIGH WYCOMBE, Bucks HP11 2HY

CONGENITAL DISLOCATION OF THE HIP

Causes
Congenital means that the condition is present at birth. The hip joint consists of the head of the femur (the long bone in the thigh) and the socket in the pelvis (hip girdle). In this condition the hip joint is unstable because of failure to develop properly before birth; this may be associated with the position of the fetus in the uterus, but there may also be a genetic link.

Characteristics
When the hip is dislocated the head of the femur is displaced from the socket and one leg appears to be shorter than the other. If left untreated the development of walking will be affected.

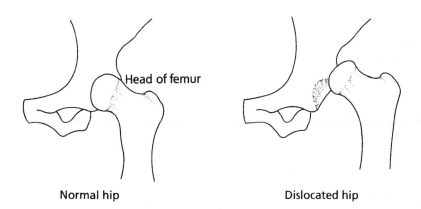

Normal hip   Dislocated hip

Congenital dislocation of the hip

Diagnosis
The baby's hips are tested soon after birth and then at regular intervals up to one year. The baby's legs are *abducted* (turned outwards) and the typical 'click' can be felt as the head of the femur slips back into the socket.

Treatment and progress
The treatment takes place in stages and is aimed at making the hip joint stable. The baby's legs are held in the abducted position by the use of splints or a 'frog plaster'. Progress is usually good and normal walking can usually be achieved.

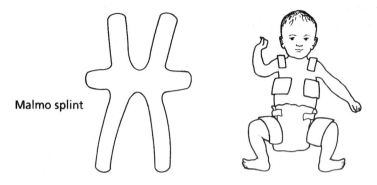

Treatment for congenital dislocation of the hip using a splint

Support agency
There is no national support agency but support will be available locally from health visitors and the hospital to which the child is referred.

CYSTIC FIBROSIS (CF)

Causes
Cystic fibrosis is a hereditary and life-threatening condition which affects the lungs and the digestive system. It is a recessively inherited condition. For the child to be affected both parents must carry the CF gene.

Characteristics
Mucus throughout the body is thick and sticky and the airways in the lungs become clogged. There are breathing difficulties, coughing and repeated chest infections. The pancreas fails to develop properly and mucus clogs the ducts, affecting the flow of enzymes into the digestive tract. Food is not digested and absorbed properly and the child will not gain weight satisfactorily.

Diagnosis
Family history and genetic counselling may mean that prenatal diagnosis is possible. After birth diagnosis is by observation of the baby's symptoms, followed by a sweat test and/or a blood test.

Treatment and progress
The treatment is aimed at:
- keeping the lungs free from infection, with antibiotic therapy
- respiratory education and therapy to expel mucus and keep the lungs clear
- pancreatic enzymes taken with every meal; a high-protein diet with vitamin and mineral supplements is prescribed.
Treatment is time-consuming, but children gradually become more independent and are able to manage and understand their condition.

Support agency
The Cystic Fibrosis Research Trust
Alexandra House, 5 Blythe Road, BROMLEY, Kent BR1 3RS

DIABETES

Cause
Diabetes occurs when the pancreas gland produces insufficient amounts of insulin, or none at all, resulting in high levels of sugar in the blood. Insulin controls the amount of sugar in the body and its absence results in abnormally high levels of sugar in the blood and urine. There are two types of diabetes:

- type 1, usually starting before 30 years of age and requiring insulin injections
- type 2, common in older people and controlled with diet and medication.

Characteristics
Early symptoms of diabetes are excessive thirst, frequent passing of urine; children may lose weight. Complications include visual impairment, kidney damage and problems with circulation. Untreated diabetes will lead to the insulin levels dropping; unconsciousness and coma quickly follow.

Diagnosis
Diagnosis is by observation of the child's symptoms, and by testing the blood and/or urine for sugar.

Treatment and progress
For children treatment is by injections of insulin together with a carefully controlled diet which restricts the amount of carbohydrate that can be eaten. Children quickly learn how to test their own blood and/or urine and keep a record of the results. They also learn how to give their own insulin. To keep healthy requires regular meals, regular insulin, regular exercise and regular medical supervision. Once the child and family have adjusted to the need for regular treatment and diet, a full and active life is possible.

Support agency
British Diabetic Association
10 Queen Anne Street, LONDON WIM OBD

DOWN'S SYNDROME

Cause
There is an abnormality usually on chromosome 21 (see the section on heredity in Chapter 6.

Characteristics
Down's syndrome may affect the child's appearance and development. The condition may be identified soon after birth by the presence of typical characteristics. Not all the

children will show all the characteristics to the same degree but they may include some of the following:

- almond-shaped eyes
- short hands and feet; the hands may have a single palmar crease
- small jaw, so that the tongue appears large
- poor muscle tone
- poorly developed, nose, sinuses and lungs, with increased susceptibility to infections.

There may be other impairments, such as heart disease.

Diagnosis
A prenatal test (amniocentesis) is available for high-risk groups. Diagnosis is also by observation of the characteristics after birth.

Treatment and progress
Treatment is given to respiratory tract infections and any other impairments which may affect the child. There is assessment and help with areas of development which may be affected. A stimulating environment and positive attitude help the children reach their full potential.

Support agency
Down's Syndrome Association
12 Clapham Common Southside, LONDON SW4 7AA

EPILEPSY

Cause
Epilepsy is a condition in which there are recurrent attacks of temporary disturbance of the brain function. It may be caused by severe injury, stroke or brain tumour. It may occur spontaneously or be triggered by stimuli such as flickering lights, fever or drugs. There may be a familial tendency towards the condition.

Characteristics
Epilepsy can take many different forms. The condition is different for each child and ranges from disturbances in consciousness that are scarcely noticeable, such as mild sensations and lapses of concentration, to severe seizures with convulsions and loss of consciousness.

Diagnosis
Diagnosis is by observation and history of seizures, by EEG (electroencephalogram) which measures the electrical activity of the brain. Tests are also undertaken to exclude other causes.

Treatment and progress
Anti-convulsant drugs are used to control the seizures. Care is important so that obvious dangers are avoided and to make sure that medication is taken regularly. The stigma of epilepsy has always been reinforced by fear and misconception, so the child will need

plenty of understanding and support. Most children with epilepsy go to mainstream schools.

Support agency
National Society for Epilepsy
Chalfont Centre, Chalfont St Peter, GERRARDS CROSS, Bucks SL9 0RJ

HAEMOPHILIA

Cause
Haemophilia is an inherited blood disorder where there is a defect in one of the clotting factors. It is inherited through the female line, but causes bleeding only in the male. (See the section on heredity in Chapter 6).

Characteristics
Bleeding will occur for much longer than normal after an injury; it may occur spontaneously into joints and elsewhere in the body, causing pain and swelling. Bruising is common.

Diagnosis
Diagnosis is by family history and by observation of the symptoms.

Treatment and progress
Haemophilia centres provide treatment and support. Treatment is given with injections of the appropriate clotting factor. Progress will depend on a balance being achieved between adequate protection and allowing the child to grow up into a well adjusted healthy adult.

Support agency
The Haemophilia Society
123 Westminster Bridge Road, LONDON SE1 7HR

HEARING IMPAIRMENT

Causes
Causes of hearing impairment include:
- heredity
- impairment of the cochlea nerve
- maternal rubella in pregnancy
- congenital defects
- head injury
- *otitis media* (infection of the middle ear)
- infections such as meningitis
- toxic action of drugs, e.g. streptomycin
- blockage of the ear canal by wax or other foreign bodies.

Characteristics

There is a wide range of impairment affecting a substantial proportion of people in Britain. Hearing impairment falls into two main categories:

■ *conductive deafness*, an interruption to the mechanical process of conducting sound through the eardrum and across the middle ear

■ *nerve deafness* which is damage to the *cochlea*, (part of the inner ear) the auditory nerve or the hearing centres in the brain.

The range of impairment is very wide, from slight hearing loss to profound deafness.

Diagnosis

Initially parents or carers often suspect a hearing difficulty. Diagnosis is by hearing tests; the first hearing test is usually at seven months, but testing is possible at any age if a hearing loss is suspected.

Treatment and progress

Conductive deafness can often be treated by removing blockages, treating infections, and some surgical treatments. Nerve deafness can rarely be treated but a cochlea implant has recently become available.

Early diagnosis is very important. Child-care workers need to be aware that most children will experience hearing loss at some time, usually caused by middle ear infections related to colds. Carers need to be aware and supportive.

There is more information about deafness in Chapter 20.

Support agency

The Royal National Institute for the Deaf
105, Gower St, LONDON WCIE 6AH

HYDROCEPHALUS

Cause

Hydrocephalus is an increase in the fluid surrounding the brain. The cause is not known but is often associated with spina bifida (see page 255).

Characteristics

Cerebro-spinal fluid (surrounding the brain and spinal cord) increases because it is unable to drain in the usual way. The head becomes larger and in a small baby the fontanelles and sutures may widen. Increasing pressure on the brain causes pain and brain damage.

Diagnosis

Diagnosis can be made prenatally by ultrasound scan. After birth early diagnosis is by measuring the head circumference.

Treatment and progress

The introduction of a valve (shunt) allows the cerebro-spinal fluid to drain satisfactorily. Early detection stops damage to the brain. The child should then be able to make progress, although frequent hospital visits and susceptibility to infection may be a problem.

Support agency
Association for Spina Bifida and Hydrocephalus
22 Upper Woburn Place, LONDON WC1 0EP

DUCHENNE MUSCULAR DYSTROPHY

Cause
Duchenne muscular dystrophy is an inherited life-threatening progressive condition involving destruction of muscle tissue. The condition only affects boys and is inherited through the female line.

Characteristics
Duchenne is the most common and most severe type of muscular dystrophy. At birth there is usually no sign of disability. Later clumsiness in walking, frequent falls and difficulty in running becomes evident. Muscle weakness is slowly progressive so that everyday activities become more difficult. As walking becomes impossible a wheelchair will be needed. Eventually the muscles of the hands, face, and respiration are affected and respiratory tract infections usually prove fatal.

Diagnosis
Diagnosis is by family history, supported by prenatal tests. There will also be observation of above characteristics after birth.

Treatment and progress
Parents or carers may often know that there is a problem early on. Treatment is aimed at maintaining mobility and independence for as long as possible. Parents or carers and families will need information and support. The child will need to be able to discuss his feelings and have long-term support to understand the progressive nature of his condition.

Support agency
Muscular Dystrophy Group of Great Britain
Nattrass House, 35 Macaulay Road, LONDON SW4 0QP

PHENYLKETONURIA (PKU)

Cause
PKU is a metabolic impairment which prevents the normal digestion of protein. It is recessively inherited. A child will develop PKU if both parents carry and pass on one altered PKU gene. There is an inherited defect in an enzyme, called phenylalanine hydroxylase. This means that the child cannot use the amino acid phenylalanine, which is part of protein, in the usual way.

Characteristics

If PKU is left untreated, the developing brain will be damaged by the high levels of phenylalanine which build up in the body. All areas of development may be affected.

Diagnosis

All babies are screened for PKU by a blood test which is done a few days after birth.

Treatment and progress

Early diagnosis means that babies with PKU can be given a diet in which the amount of phenylalanine is carefully controlled. The treatment is complex but with support the children can learn to manage their diet and be independent.

Support agency

The National Society for Phenylketonuria and Allied Disorders
26 Towngate Grove, MIRFIELD, West Yorkshire WF14 9JF

SICKLE CELL ANAEMIA

Causes

Sickle cell anaemia is an inherited condition of haemoglobin formation. If a child inherits sickle haemoglobin from one parent, they will have sickle cell trait, which is symptom free. If, however, a child inherits sickle haemoglobin from both parents they will have sickle cell anaemia.

Characteristics

Sickle cell anaemia causes bouts of anaemia, pain, jaundice and infection, called crises. Painful crises are caused by the red cells in the blood changing their shape from the normal round shape to a crescent or sickle shape. The sickle cells clump together and block the smaller blood vessels causing pain and swelling. The sickle cells are also removed more quickly from the bloodstream, causing anaemia.

Diagnosis

Diagnosis is by family history, a specific blood test and by observation of the symptoms.

Treatment and progress

Prompt recognition and treatment are important. Carers will aim to maintain good general health and diet and arrange for early treatment of infections, keeping the child warm and dry with plenty of rest. Blood transfusions may be needed. Support and understanding are needed particularly during crises. Co-operation between home, school and hospital will give the child the best opportunity to manage the condition and become independent.

Support agency

Organisation for Sickle Cell Research (OSCAR)
22 Pellatt Grove, LONDON N22 5PL

SPINA BIFIDA

Causes
An area of the spine fails to develop properly before birth. There is a gap in the bones of the spine leaving the contents of the spinal cord exposed. The fault can occur anywhere on the spine. The precise cause is not known but there are thought to be environmental and genetic factors that prevent the normal development of the bones of the spine.

Characteristics
There are three main forms of spina bifida:
1 *spina bifida occulta* in which the skin is intact; this rarely causes disability
2 *spina bifida cystica*, which has two types:
   - *meningocele*, in which there is a fluid-filled sac on the back, where the fluid and membranes of the spinal cord protrude through the gap in the bones of the spine
   - *mylomeningocele*, in which the sac contains spinal fluid and the nerves of the spinal cord. This is the most severe form. As a result there is some degree of paralysis below the lesion.

Diagnosis
Diagnosis is by prenatal blood tests, ultrasound scan and amniocentesis.

Treatment and progress
Treatment is by closure of the lesion and prevention of infection. There will also be treatment of associated hydrocephalus (see page 252). Ongoing support is needed to enable the child to take part in all the usual activities for their age such as playgroup, nursery or mainstream school.

Support agency
Association for Spina Bifida and Hydrocephalus
22 Upper Woburn Place LONDON WC1H 0EP

VISUAL IMPAIRMENT

Causes
The causes of congenital blindness include infections in pregnancy such as rubella and syphilis, optic nerve atrophy or tumour. Causes after birth include cataract, glaucoma and infections such as measles and the herpes virus. There are some hereditary conditions such as retinitis pigmentosa.

Characteristics
There are three main categories of visual impairment:
- blind
- partially sighted and entitled to use the services appropriate to blind people
- partially sighted.

The experience of visual loss is very different for those who become blind and can use their experience of sight, from those who are born blind.

Diagnosis
The condition is usually detected early as parents or carers recognise the lack of response to visual stimuli and eye contact. Later, vision tests may confirm earlier problems.

Treatment and progress
Early diagnosis is followed with support, practical information and time for families to adjust. Spectacles and contact lenses are valuable aids for some partially sighted children. Carers will need to encourage exploration and independence. The Royal National Institute for the Blind has a full range of support services, including education advice services, specialist schools and a wide range of supporting aids, books in braille, Moon and talking books. Progress towards independence will vary with individual children.

There is more information about visual impairment in Chapter 20.

Support agency
Royal National Institute for the Blind
224 Great Portland Street, LONDON W1N 6AA

THINK!

1 Next time you make a trip to town on the bus, to any public place, take notice of how well or badly the needs of people with sensory or physical impairments are met.

DO!

1 Make a list of all the things you might have to check out or do if a child with a condition which affected their physical mobility was joining your nursery.
2 Choose one of the conditions or impairments explained in this chapter. Imagine that you have to explain this to the children in your infant class. How would you do this? What four strategies could you use?

Key terms
You need to know what these words and phrases mean. Go back through the chapter and find out.

Dilate	Anti-convulsant
Allergen	Progressive
Conductive education	Co-ordination
Recessive inheritance	Congenital
Metabolic impairment	Abducted

18 THE NEEDS OF DISABLED CHILDREN AND THEIR FAMILIES

> **This chapter includes:**
> - **Understanding the needs of disabled children**
> - **Meeting disabled children's needs**
> - **Empowerment**
> - **Diagnosis**
> - **The needs of parents and carers**
> - **The needs of siblings**
> - **Disabled parents and carers.**

Understanding the needs of disabled children

Understanding the needs of disabled children requires a thorough knowledge of child development. The earlier chapters of this book provide detailed information on each aspect of children's development: physical, intellectual/linguistic, and emotional/social. All of this is relevant to the development of disabled children and their needs should be considered alongside those of all children. You need to remember this in your work with disabled children.

This book emphasises the fact that development does not correlate with age. Children may reach stages or milestones of development at different ages. Individual children also proceed at different rates through the different stages of the developmental areas (physical, intellectual/linguistic, emotional/social).

Disabled children are often made to feel that they are younger than they are because they have not reached so called 'normal' milestones in all aspects of their development. If, for example, a disabled child needs to wear nappies at 5 years or ride a three-wheeler at 10 years, they may well be treated as younger than they are.

Special needs of disabled children

Another danger for disabled children, is that their special needs override their ordinary needs. Following the medical model of disability the implication is that there is something wrong, and that the child's efforts should be directed to specific therapeutic goals. This attitude may be encouraged through special programmes such as Conductive Education. These programmes are undoubtedly beneficial to the child, but their focus on physical development can lead to neglect of social and other needs (see the *Learning and therapy programmes* section in Chapter 21).

Disabled children may need physiotherapy, speech therapy or special learning programmes but these should not always override their ordinary needs. All children need periods of self-directed play. Disabled children need adults who will facilitate, rather than always direct, play activities.

CHECK!

1 Why are disabled children often made to feel younger than they are?
2 Name two special education programmes for disabled children.

THINK!

1 Why is it important to have a thorough knowledge of child development in order to understand the needs of disabled children?
2 What are the advantages and disadvantages of special programmes such as Portage and Conductive Education?
3 Why do all children need periods of self-directed play?
4 How can adults facilitate self-directed play for young disabled children in group settings? You will find further information in Chapter 20, *Inclusive care and education.*

Meeting disabled children's needs

Each disabled child is an individual with unique gifts and needs. In order to meet their needs, some knowledge of the causes and medical implications of their specific impairment or condition, may be helpful (see Chapter 17, *Conditions and impairments*).

This knowledge will be most helpful when combined with a positive attitude and a willingness to learn how to maximise individual children's potential. You can support your knowledge by further reading or talking to professionals, but remember that the full-time carer of each child may often be the best source of information and guidance.

In order to meet the needs of disabled children attitudes and assumptions about disability need to be examined. Disability Equality Training, led by an experienced DET trainer, and involving disabled people themselves, is one of the best ways of doing this.

CHECK!

1 Who is normally the best source of information and guidance about individual disabled children?
2 What is one of the best ways of examining attitudes and assumptions about disability?

Empowerment

Like all children, disabled children need to be enabled (*empowered*) to take part in the world effectively, but this needs to be on their own terms, rather than having to conform to the expectations of non-disabled people. This may be encouraged by:

- responding to disabled children's expressed needs and initiatives. Disabled children may not find self-expression or communication easy. They need adults who will listen, wait and recognise the smallest indications that a choice has been made, or a need expressed. Adults may need to make guesses, try many alternatives and keep looking to see if they have judged correctly
- praising and rewarding effort rather than achievement. Children, especially disabled children, should not be compared to one another. It is better to compare their success and achievement to their own previous attempts.
- responding positively to the things over which children have control, rather than to innate ability or attributes. Adults often praise young children for achievements over which the child has little control, for example their size, speed, or their cleverness and physical skill: 'Oh, she smiled at three days', 'He's eating solids already!', 'She never cries', 'He started reading before he went to school'. This serves to devalue children who are small, slow, inept, and so on. Comments like 'Oh, that was a kind thing to do!' and 'You have worked really hard today' help to give value to the things over which children do have control.

CHECK!

1 How can disabled children be empowered?

THINK!

1 Consider any condition or impairment. What do you think are the main needs of children with this condition/impairment?
2 Read some books or articles or leaflets about people with this condition/impairment. What do they suggest are the main needs of children with this condition/impairment?

DO!

1 Ask a disabled person about their childhood. Find out what they felt their needs were.
2 Were these needs met? If not, why not?
3 Are the needs they express the same as those you thought yourself or read about?

Diagnosis

When a child is born with a specific condition or impairment, or one is later diagnosed, parents or carers will react in their own individual way. Society predominantly views disability as a tragedy, and it is possible to recognise in many parents or carers a pattern of response similar to that experienced following other 'tragedies', such as bereavement (see Chapter 14, *Separation and loss*).

This pattern of response is divided into four stages. Individuals may progress through these stages at different rates:

1 Shock and disbelief: 'This can't be happening to us.'
2 A period of mourning and isolation: 'We were grief stricken. We felt we were being punished. We didn't want to be with anyone who did not know about our child.'
3 A period of adaptation: 'We felt it was a challenge. We wanted information, help and understanding, and not to feel alone.'
4 Adjustment: 'We are learning to cope, and enjoy our child. When we could face up to telling friends and relatives things became easier.'

As with bereavement and loss in other circumstances, some people do not move through the stages of grief but may remain stuck at one particular stage.

CHECK!

1 Describe the pattern of response that may be demonstrated by parents or carers when their child's disability is diagnosed.

THINK!

1 What are the needs of parents or carers at the time their child's disability is diagnosed?

The needs of parents and carers

In common with all parents or carers, those of disabled children need to find pleasure in their child, and to feel confident and pleased with themselves as parents. In order to accomplish this they are likely to need:

- information about their child's condition/impairment, the social model of disability, the services available, new ideas, etc.
- emotional support, and help in finding pleasure in their child
- practical help, for example child sitting, respite care, environmental aids and adaptations, domestic help, financial support
- contact with other parents or carers of disabled children, and opportunities to work together to obtain the services they need.
- reassurance by service providers (of education and care), that their child is wanted and can be coped with
- contact with disabled adults for advice, support, information, etc.
- training in self-advocacy (putting forward their view point and getting what is needed for themselves and their family)
- time to be themselves and meet their own needs and the needs of other family members
- recognition that usually they are the ones who know their child best.

1 What are the needs of disabled children's parents or carers?

The needs of siblings

It is impossible to generalise about the effects on siblings of having a disabled child in the family. Much will depend on factors such as the nature of the condition or impairment, the number of children in the family, their birth order and so on. The need of brothers and sisters may be similar to the overriding need of parents or carers, that is to find pleasure in having a disabled sibling. In addition they may have the following needs:

- encouragement to express their feelings openly and honestly
- information with meaningful terms at a level they can understand
- preparation for the possible negative attitudes and behaviour of other people
- reassurance of their own value and worth, and that of their disabled sibling
- individual attention
- involvement in the care of the disabled child, without too much responsibility.

While it is relatively easy to outline possible disadvantages, it is possible for siblings to benefit from growing up alongside a disabled child.

CHECK!

1 What needs may disabled children's siblings have?

THINK!

1 What are the advantages and disadvantages of having a sibling with:
   a) cerebral palsy   b) a hearing loss   c) cystic fibrosis?
2 How would you explain the following to a five-year-old-child:
   a) brain damage   b) spinal injury   c) cerebral palsy   d) epilepsy?

Disabled parents and carers

Many disabled people are themselves parents or carers. Often they are not recognised by society as capable of being responsible caring adults, with much to give. Their own understanding and experience of the possible effects of specific conditions/impairments may not be used by those around them.

In professional and non-professional roles disabled adults may be willing to support the carers of disabled children. They may also be willing to act as role models for disabled children.

It is possible for young disabled children to grow up with little or no contact with disabled adults. This has implications for the process of identification and the

Many disabled people are themselves parents or carers

development of self-image (see Chapter 12, *Development of self-image and self-concept*).

Disabled parents and carers are sometimes thought to disadvantage their own children. This has, on occasions, led to their children being accommodated away from home by a local authority. Often alternative measures such as help with domestic chores, environmental aids and adaptations or financial support could be used to overcome the difficulties.

Disabled adults sometimes find themselves excluded from the services provided for their children. Inclusive care and education will consider their needs alongside other service users. The emphasis on parents and carers as partners with professionals, should include disabled carers as well.

CHECK!

1 What can disabled parents or carers offer to disabled children?

DO!

1 Draw up a checklist to ensure the inclusion of disabled adults in your workplace.

THINK!

1 Why is it important for disabled children to have contact with disabled adults?
2 How could this be achieved in practice?

Key terms

You need to know what these words and phrases mean. Go back through the chapter and find out.

Correlate with

Milestones of development

Specific therapeutic goals

Self-directed play

Facilitate

Medical implications

Specific conditions or impairments

Maximise potential

Empowerment

Innate ability/attributes

Devalue

Diagnosis

Service providers

Self-advocacy

Role models

Identification

Self image

Inclusive care

19 THE LEGAL FRAMEWORK

> **This chapter includes:**
> - **Introduction**
> - **The Education Act (1981)**
> - **Statutory assessment procedures**
> - **Statements of special educational needs**
> - **The Education Reform Act (1988)**
> - **The Children Act (1989)**

Introduction

Legislation concerning the care and education of disabled children is regularly changed and updated. This section aims to explain the underlying principles contained in current legislation. You will need, however, to refer to the legislation in full for more detail, and update yourself regularly on recent changes.

The Education Act (1981)

The Education Act (1981) is the main piece of legislation regarding special education in England and Wales. There is a separate but similar act covering Scotland. The driving force behind the act was the Warnock Committee Report on special education, published in 1978.

The 1981 act introduces the concept of 'special educational needs'. This replaces the categories used previously such as maladjusted, educationally subnormal, epileptic and so on. It aims to shift the focus to individual children rather than their impairments. Children with special needs include those whose learning difficulties call for special educational provision to be made. The act states that children have learning difficulties if:

- they have significantly greater difficulty in learning than the majority of children of their age; or
- they have a disability which prevents or hinders them from making use of educational facilities of a kind generally provided in school, for children of their age, within the local authority concerned.

CHECK!

1 What is the main piece of legislation concerning special needs in England and Wales?

2 What concept was introduced by this legislation?

THINK!

1 What is meant by the term *special educational needs*?
2 Why was this term introduced?

Statutory assessment procedures

The Education Act (1981) states that local education authorities have a statutory duty to:

- ensure that special educational provision is made for pupils who have special educational needs
- identify and assess children with special educational needs in order to determine the educational provision that will meet their needs
- respond to parents' requests for their child's assessment, as long as the request is reasonable (parents have the right of appeal to the secretary of state)
- involve parents in the assessment process.

A subsequent circular, *1/83, Assessments and Statements of Special Educational Needs* advises that assessments should follow the five stages laid down in the Warnock Report. The assessments should not be an end in themselves, but part of a continuous process involving regular reviews, to reflect the changing needs of the children as they get older.

The assessments should include:

- direct representations from parents (verbal or written)
- evidence submitted either by the parent or at the request of the parent
- written educational, medical and psychological advice
- information relating to the health and welfare of the child from the district health or social services authorities.

CHECK!

1 According to the Education Act (1981), what statutory duties do local education authorities have concerning assessments of disabled children?
2 What should be included in assessments and statements of special educational needs?

THINK!

1 Why is it important to make regular assessments of the educational needs of disabled children?

Statements of special educational needs

As a result of the statutory assessment procedures a local education authority may issue a child who has special needs with a statement. This is a formal document describing the child's special needs and recording how and where these needs should be met. Every statement is in five parts:

Part 1 Introductory page, including factual information such as name, address, age, etc.

Part 2 The child's special educational needs as identified by the professionals involved in the assessment.

Part 3 The educational provision considered necessary to meet the child's special educational needs, specifying any facilities, teaching arrangements, curriculum and equipment needed for the pupil.

Part 4 The type of school or establishment (for example hospital) thought appropriate for the child.

Part 5 Any additional non-educational provision considered necessary to enable the child to benefit from the proposed educational provision, for example hearing aids from the health authority, or a family provided by social services.

Initially the statement is in draft form. It is sent to the parents, with an explanation of their right to appeal. If the parent disagrees with any of the content they have 15 days in which to put their views to the local education authority. Ultimately the parents have right of appeal to the secretary of state, whose decision is binding on the parents and the local authority.

The confidentiality of the statements is crucial. In most circumstances no disclosure from the statement can be made without the parents' consent. The statement is usually kept in the administrative offices of the local authority.

CHECK!

1 What is included in each of the five sections of a statement?
2 Where are the statements kept?

THINK!

1 What is the purpose of a statement of a child's educational needs?
2 Why do only some disabled children have a statement of educational need?
3 What can parents do if they do not agree with any part of the statement?

The Education Reform Act (1988)

The 1988 Act requires all maintained schools, including special schools, to provide the National Curriculum. For a child with a statement it is not necessary to modify or exempt the child from the requirements of the National Curriculum, but it is possible if modification is in the child's best interests. The 1988 Act encourages *inclusion* rather than *exclusion* in the National Curriculum of children with special needs.

The Children Act (1989)

The Children Act (1989) brings together most public and private laws relating to children. It includes the functions of social services departments in relation to disabled children. Disabled children are treated in the act in the same way as all other children.

The act defines a category of 'children in need' for whom the social services department should provide services. Disabled children are included in this category. The Children Act defines disability as follows:

'A child is disabled if he is blind, deaf or dumb or suffers from mental disorder of any kind or is substantially and permanently handicapped by illness, injury or congenital deformity or such other disability as may be prescribed.'

DUTIES OF LOCAL AUTHORITIES

The act places a general duty on the local authority to provide an appropriate range and level of services to safeguard and promote the welfare of children in need. This is to be done in a way that promotes the upbringing of such children within their own families.

UNDERLYING PRINCIPLES

The Children Act outlines the following principles for work with disabled children:
- the welfare of the child should be safeguarded and promoted by those providing services
- a primary aim should be to promote access for all children to the same range of services
- the need to remember that disabled children are *children* first, not disabled people
- the importance in children's lives of parents and families
- partnership between parents and local authorities and other agencies
- the views of children and parents should be sought and taken into account.

SERVICES

In order to encourage families to care for disabled children at home, local authorities are encouraged to provide the following services, either directly or through voluntary organisations:

- domiciliary services, for example the Portage Home Teaching scheme and befriending schemes
- guidance and counselling or social work
- respite care (see the section on respite care in Chapter 20, *Inclusive Care and Education*); this would be provided in co-operation with district health authorities, and may be in health service settings, or in settings run by voluntary organisations
- day-care services, including family centres and child minding services; wherever possible these would be in day-care settings available to all children rather than in separate or segregated settings
- services from occupational therapists, rehabilitation workers, technical officers, specialist social workers and provision of environmental aids and adaptations
- information on a range of services provided by other agencies
- *advocacy* (speaking on behalf of or in favour of disabled people) and representation for children and parents
- help with transport costs to visit children living away from home
- holiday play schemes
- toy libraries
- support groups
- loans of equipment or play materials.

Other services for the disabled child and their family may include:

- identifying a need in their area and publicising services available
- working together with local education authorities and district health authorities
- compiling a register of children with disabilities in their area
- assessing, reassessing and reviewing children in need and planning for their long-term future
- planning services in partnership with parents and disabled children themselves.

ACCOMMODATION AWAY FROM HOME

Disabled children may be accommodated away from home in foster care or residential settings. The act provides new safeguards for them:

- their cases must be reviewed
- consideration must be given to their welfare
- they and their parents must be consulted before decisions are taken.

The act requires local authorities to ensure that the accommodation they provide or that provided by education or health authorities for disabled children is suitable to the child's needs.

This will mean in practice that disabled children should have access to all the accommodation and the same rights to privacy as their non-disabled counterparts. Homes that accommodate disabled children must provide the necessary equipment, facilities and adaptations. The aim should be to integrate children in every aspect of life in the home. Health and safety aspects concerning disabled children must be considered.

CHECK!

1 What elements are brought together in the Children Act (1989)?
2 How does the act define children in need?
3 What are the underlying principles of the act?
4 What services does the act encourage local authorities to provide?
5 What new safeguards are offered to disabled children accommodated away from home?
6 What are local education authorities required to provide when children are accommodated away from home?

THINK!

1 Why is it important for disabled children to be cared for by their own families?
2 Why are disabled children treated in the same way as all others in the act?

DO!

1 Find out how disabled children have been looked after in residential settings in the past.
2 Find out the range of services provided by your own local authority for disabled children and their families.
3 Where did you obtain the information? How easy was it to obtain?

Key terms
You need to know what these words and phrases mean. Go back through the chapter and find out.

Legislation	Safeguard/promote welfare of child
Special educational needs	Promote access
Statements	Domiciliary services
Statutory duties	Segregated settings
Statutory assessment procedures	Advocacy
Educational provision	Environmental aids and adaptations
Draft form	Accommodation away from home
National curriculum	Residential settings
Children in need	Integrate

20 PROVIDING INCLUSIVE CARE AND EDUCATION

Introduction

Recent legislation encourages the involvement of disabled children in 'mainstream' settings, both in education and care. It is therefore now more likely that disabled children will be in such mainstream settings as nursery classes, schools, day nurseries, family centres or residential establishments. Consideration of the needs of all children will be necessary if these settings are to be truly inclusive.

Recent legislation encourages the involvement of disabled children in mainstream settings

If settings adopt the social model of disability they will want to consider their provision to ensure that the environment, attitudes, and practices do not disable children with specific conditions or impairments.

1 What do you understand by the terms *inclusive education* or *inclusive care?*
2 Why is inclusive education or care now so essential?

Access

For an establishment to include disabled children certain aspects need to be considered. Detailed information and training on inclusion of disabled children is available from condition- or impairment-specific voluntary organisations and self-help groups, but outlines of general principles for good practice are listed below. Establishments including disabled children need to provide:

- equipment that all children can use; much equipment produced for disabled people is inclusive: ramps, lifts, adjustable tables, automatic doors, long-handled taps, touch-sensitive controls, large print and grab rails can be used by all children
- a range of options such as tapes, braille and print versions of documents
- a range of seat and table sizes and shapes
- empty floor space that is kept uncluttered
- flexible, adjustable equipment, for example a sand tray that comes off the stand, high chairs with removable trays
- sturdy versions of 'ordinary' toys, and furniture
- a range of scissors, knives and other implements
- soft play areas for activities such as crawling, jumping, climbing
- extra adult supervision to facilitate integration
- some equipment for individual children to facilitate integration; there should be discussions with the child and full-time carers about what to buy before expensive purchases are made
- spacious toilet facilities designed for wheelchair users that can then be used by all children
- private age-appropriate toilet or changing area
- disability awareness and equality training for all staff.

CHECK!

1 What must establishments consider in order to include disabled children in mainstream settings?

Access for children with sensory impairments

Children with impaired sight

The following aspects need to be considered in order to include blind and partially sighted children. Establishments will need to provide:

- opportunities to explore the environment and people using touch, smell, hearing and any residual sight

- the opportunity for children to orientate themselves physically (this may involve visiting the setting when few people are present)
- stability and order, a place for everything and everything in its place; the child will need to be informed and shown any changes
- plenty of light
- a hazard-free environment, or an indication of hazardous things such as steps or sharp corners
- information about other children's needs, for example a child with a hearing loss who may not respond to them
- some specific items such as books in braille, toys or board games which are especially designed to be inclusive.

Children with impaired hearing

The following points need to be considered by an establishment including deaf and hearing-impaired children:

- hearing impairment is largely invisible; even a mild hearing loss is significant in a noisy crowded room
- a child with impaired hearing cannot tell you what they missed!
- hearing aids are not a replacement for hearing and may be of little use to some children
- deaf children's greatest special need is access to language and communication; complete access can only come about through universal use of language and communication accessible to deaf children. This will often mean British Sign Language, which will need to be used by everyone in the setting
- deaf children need to communicate with other children as well as adults
- deaf children have a range of intellectual ability as all children do; if we deny them access to language we create a learning difficulty for them.

CHECK!

1 What must establishments consider in order to include both deaf and blind children in mainstream settings?

THINK!

1 Look again at the list of access provision. Why is each point important to enable the inclusion of disabled children? Can you add anything to the list?

DO!

1 Consider your own work place and write a list of physical changes that would need to be made to include:
   a) a blind child
   b) a child in a wheelchair.
2 What other aspects would need to be considered?

Principles of good practice

LANGUAGE

As with issues of race and gender, the setting should have a clear policy about the use of language to describe disabled children (see *The importance of terminology*, page 239). This policy should be clearly explained to all users of the setting.

IMAGES

Everything learned about images of other marginalised or minority groups applies to disabled children. In the past nearly all images of disabled people were produced by non-disabled people, often on behalf of charities. Their aim was to evoke sympathy, pity, fear and guilt. This was justified as necessary to raise money for disabled people.

It is very difficult to find positive images of disabled children. Children's books have few disabled characters. The books available often focus entirely on the impairment, with titles such as *Mary Has a Hearing Loss* or *I Have Cerebral Palsy*. Rarely are disabled people portrayed as ordinary people.

TOYS

Toys which include the daily stuff of disabled children's lives such as wheelchairs, hearing aids, splints or glasses are rare, but invaluable. It may be possible, with permission, to use actual equipment belonging to disabled children.

ACTIVITIES

Organised directed activities should always seek to be inclusive. The needs of disabled children in the group should be considered at the planning stage. If a child cannot do something in the same way as most children, they may be consulted about what they could do instead.

In educational settings teachers will aim to use *differentiation* in the tasks set. Differentiation occurs when individual or groups of children are given different tasks related to the aim of the lesson, at a level that provides a manageable challenge to them. This will involve careful planning if disabled children are not to be segregated from the class. Special needs support assistants may be involved in this process at the planning and implementation stage.

ROLE MODELS

The involvement of disabled adults, of all ages and at all levels in care and education settings can provide positive role models for disabled children. Disabled adults can also help to raise the level of disability awareness in the setting.

The involvement of disabled adults can provide positive role models for disabled children

CHECK!

1 What are the principles of good practice which should be applied when including disabled children in mainstream settings?
2 What points should be considered when providing toys and activities for disabled children?
3 How can the involvement of disabled adults benefit in any educational setting?

THINK!

1 Think of four measures that could be taken to ensure the full involvement of:
   a) a 2-year-old-child with Down's syndrome in a private day nursery
   b) a 6-year-old-child with muscular dystrophy in an infant class,
   c) a 4-year-old-child with diabetes in a nursery class.

DO!

1 Visit your local library and look at a range of children's books. Note any that include disabled people. What roles do these people fulfil? What messages do these books give about disabled people?
2 Make up a simple story (suitable, say, for a 6-year-old) including a disabled person, but which does not focus on their condition or impairment. The story could include disabled people involved in everyday activities alongside able-bodied people.

Residential care

Recent legislation confirms that the best place for a disabled child to be brought up is within their own family. For many reasons, however, this may not be possible. Some disabled children need medical care and for this reason are accommodated in health service institutions. Some attend residential special schools where they may be weekly or termly boarders.

Disabled children in residential care are particularly vulnerable. There have been many incidents, some recorded in the biographies of disabled people, of long term mistreatment in residential institutions. The Children Act (1989) aims to provide safeguards concerning the welfare of disabled children accommodated away from home.

If a child has to be accommodated away from home, their residential homes must be registered and regulated. Social services departments are empowered to enter a care home in order to find out if children's welfare is being satisfactorily safeguarded and promoted.

Generally speaking children should not be accommodated long-term in National Health Service hospital settings. The intention of the Children Act is that disabled children in residential care, including independent special schools, should not be forgotten and that social services departments should assess the quality of child care offered.

CHECK!

1 Which is the best place for a disabled child to be brought up?

THINK!

1 Why are disabled children in residential accommodation particularly vulnerable ?
2 Why is it generally undesirable for disabled children to spend long periods of time in hospital settings?

Foster placements

There has been an increase in the number of successful foster placements for disabled children over the last ten years. Some national voluntary organisations provide specialist fostering programmes for disabled children.

Foster carers have to be willing to be involved in their disabled child's educational learning programmes where appropriate, in assessments and reviews, and be willing to encourage the disabled child to make friends in the community.

CHECK!

1 What must foster carers of disabled children be willing to undertake?

Respite care

Caring for a disabled child, though often rewarding, can be exhausting. If the best place for a disabled child to be brought up is within their own family, the family is likely to need support and encouragement to enable them to go on caring. Respite care provides one way of offering such support and encouragement.

There are four main types of respite care:

- residential care
- family-based care
- care in a child's own home
- holiday schemes.

These services are offered by different agencies, both statutory and voluntary, and groups of parents who have banded together for the purpose. The service may be provided by a voluntary organisation while the cost is met by social services. Each service offers parents or carers time off and have advantages and disadvantages. Rarely are all available to the parents or carers of disabled children; occasionally none is available.

RESIDENTIAL CARE

The disabled child goes to stay in approved accommodation for an agreed period of time. This accommodation is usually provided by an institution such as a hospital ward, a children's home or a boarding school.

The disadvantage is that it is usually institutionalised care, a complete contrast to family life at home. The advantages include the possibility of it becoming familiar to the child and does not depend on any one person offering the service.

FAMILY-BASED CARE

The family of a disabled child is linked to another family (or single person), who are willing to take the disabled child into their home, for periods of time. Such schemes are usually managed by Social Services or a voluntary organisation.

CARE IN A CHILD'S OWN HOME

This type of care is a specialised child-sitting service. It may be an extension of a home-help service except that the 'family aid' cares for the child rather than the home.

HOLIDAY SCHEMES

There are holiday schemes for disabled children. Some provide for children only,

others for the whole family. They are organised by a number of voluntary societies and take a number of different forms, for example adventure holidays, foreign trips. Often parents or carers have to pay for this service.

CHECK!

1 Describe the four types of respite care.

THINK!

1 Think of the advantages and disadvantages of the four types of respite care.

Key terms

You need to know what these words and phrases mean. Go back through the chapter and find out.

Mainstream settings	Segregated
Inclusive care or education	Role models
Conditions or impairments	Disability awareness
Self-help groups	Residential special schools
Facilitate	Institution, institutionalised
Orientate	Vulnerable
British Sign Language	Accommodation away from home
Marginalised/minority groups	Learning programmes
Evoke sympathy	Respite care
Positive images	Voluntary organisations
Differentiation in tasks	Statutory organisations

---

21 THE ROLE OF PROFESSIONALS

> **This chapter includes:**
> - **Health service professionals**
> - **Education service professionals**
> - **Social service professionals**
> - **Social security**
> - **Voluntary organistions**
> - **Learning and therapy programmes.**

Health service professionals

PAEDIATRICIANS

Paediatricians are doctors specialising in the diagnosis and medical care of children. They may be the first health service professional to become involved with a disabled child in the maternity unit, the children's ward or out-patient department.

HEALTH VISITORS

Every child under the age of 5 has a health visitor. Health visitors are qualified nurses with additional training. They work in the community and usually undertake the routine developmental checks. The health visitor is often the health-care professional most closely involved with the family at home. They are able to provide a link to, and between, other professionals and services.

PHYSIOTHERAPISTS

Physiotherapists assess children's motor development and skills and how well they can move and balance. They may work in schools as well as hospital clinics. They may demonstrate exercises and activities that parents and other carers will carry out themselves.

OCCUPATIONAL THERAPISTS

Occupational therapists seek to encourage independent life skills such as dressing, eating and moving around independently. For this reason they may assess a child's fine motor skills. They can advise about any special equipment that may be helpful and arrange for it to be supplied. This may be out in the community as well as in hospital clinics.

SPEECH THERAPISTS

Speech therapists seek to develop all aspects of children's expressive and receptive communication skills and language development. As well as assessing speech, they also assess tongue and mouth movements and their effects on eating and swallowing. Speech therapists will work out programmes of activities and exercises to help children to acquire language, understand concepts and use speech. Parents or carers may be involved in carrying these programmes out. Speech therapists may be based in schools, hospital clinics or in the community.

CLINICAL PSYCHOLOGISTS

Clinical psychologists are mainly concerned with children's emotional, social and intellectual development. Their assessment of children covers all aspects of their circumstances. They will have discussions with their families and other carers as well as making direct observations of children's behaviour.

SCHOOL NURSES

School nurses often check children's weight, height, eyesight and hearing in school. They may pick up difficulties in any of these areas. They may be based full time in special schools where they supervise the routine medical care of disabled children.

PLAY THERAPISTS

Play therapists use play to help children handle particular feelings or experiences that may be hindering their development. The therapists need to have been trained for and supported in this task, as they are likely to be dealing with powerful emotions.

PLAY WORKERS

Play workers are usually trained nursery nurses, employed in some hospitals to play with children, both those visiting clinics and those admitted to the wards. They represent a non-threatening adult in a setting that may provoke anxiety for children. They may be involved in raising awareness and preparing children for a possible stay in hospital.

Education service professionals

EDUCATIONAL PSYCHOLOGISTS

Educational psychologists advise the local education authority about the education of individual children. They will be involved in the educational assessment of disabled children, including the assessment for the statement of special educational needs. They may advise the professionals who are working directly with a disabled child about learning and behaviour modification programmes. These programmes are set and recorded methods of altering children's behaviour, usually relying on rewards for acceptable behaviour.

SPECIAL NEEDS SUPPORT TEACHERS

Special needs support teachers, sometimes called specialist teachers, or support teachers, are teachers who often have additional training and experience; they are often *peripatetic* and visit disabled children in different schools and pre-school children at home. They may specialise in one particular impairment, for example hearing loss or visual impairment. They are involved in the direct teaching of individual children, as well as in advising staff and parents of ways to maximise children's learning potential.

SPECIAL NEEDS SUPPORT ASSISTANTS

Special needs support assistants have many different labels, for example special assistants, education care officers, classroom assistants or special needs nursery nurses. They may be qualified nursery nurses or child-care workers or they may have no formal child-care training. They may adopt a variety of different roles depending on the school or nursery and the children they are employed to support. Some work with individual statemented children, others with groups of children with a variety of special needs. The main focus of their work may be to provide medical or learning support. They may be involved in observing and monitoring children, liaising with other professionals and working under their direction. They may have regular contact with parents and carers.

SPECIAL NEEDS ADVISERS

Special needs advisers focus on the curriculum, teaching methods, materials, schemes and equipment used in schools. They have a role as inspectors to ensure provision of the National Curriculum.

EDUCATION WELFARE OFFICERS

Education welfare officers undertake welfare duties on behalf of children and their parents or carers. They will be involved with children whose attendance is irregular. They may arrange transport for disabled children to school.

Social service professionals

SOCIAL WORKERS

Social workers may be based in hospitals or in local area offices. Their work with disabled children will include any statutory child protection duties. They may advise on the availability of all services in the area: health, education, welfare benefits or care, or they may put families in touch with appropriate agencies. They may advocate on behalf of disabled children, for example enabling them to obtain the services to which they are entitled. Social workers may be involved in assessment for referral to day care, respite care and other domiciliary care, including family aids (home helps), etc.

SPECIALIST SOCIAL WORKERS AND TECHNICAL OFFICERS

Specialist social workers and technical officers may have additional training and experience to work with people with particular conditions or impairments, for example deaf or blind people.

NURSERY OFFICERS

Nursery officers will work in day nurseries and family centres. They may also visit family homes to liaise between home and nursery.

FAMILY AIDS

Family aids will provide practical support for families in their own home. The helpers may be involved in domestic duties, child care and other family needs.

RESIDENTIAL CHILD CARE OFFICERS

Residential child care officers may work in long- or short-stay residential accommodation for disabled children. The officer may be a key worker for a disabled child accommodated away from home by the local authority.

SOCIAL SECURITY

The main role of social security is the provision of welfare benefits. There is a range of benefits available to disabled children and their families. These are subject to change. The Citizens' Advice Bureau provides up-to-date advice and information about welfare benefits.

VOLUNTARY ORGANISATIONS

Collectively voluntary organisations provide every conceivable type of support for disabled children and their families. Some are national organisations and others local. It is beyond the scope of this book to provide information about the services they offer, but information is available from local libraries. In recent years there has been an increase in the role and extent of involvement by voluntary organisations in the lives of disabled children. Many of these organisations work in a highly professional and pioneering way. Much of the innovative work with and on behalf of disabled people is done through voluntary organisations and self-help groups.

Learning and therapy programmes

PORTAGE

The Portage Guide to Early Education was originally developed in a rural area centred on the town of Portage in Wisconsin, USA and the schemes devised are used with children with moderate and severe learning difficulties, behaviour problems and developmental delay. Weekly home visits of one to two hours are made by a Portage Home Visitor. Home visitors come from a range of professionals. Most approaches have found that a short training programme is all that is initially required. The purpose of each visit is to help the parent or carer to select and set short-term goals, expected to be achieved in one or two weeks, and to devise an appropriate way for the carer to teach these. As well as short-term goals, each Portage Home Visitor will set, with the parent or carer, long-term goals for the child to work towards, so that the weekly visits and short-term goals can be seen as steps in a general progression towards the desired objective.

Workers are trained to use a developmental checklist which covers development from birth to 6 years in the areas of socialisation and language, cognitive, self-help and motor skills. One of the aims of Portage is that parents and carers will become sufficiently skilled to enable the role of the Portage Home Visitor to change to consultant and supporter. The Portage method aims to enable parents and carers to become independent of the Home Visitor eventually, and to become the main worker with the child. Unfortunately, because of limited financial resources, some local authorities may see Portage as a relatively cheap solution to the needs of disabled children and their families, rather than as a service to offer alongside other services.

BOBATH TECHNIQUE

The Bobath technique is a form of physiotherapy developed by Professor Bobath and his wife, aimed at enabling the best possible posture and mobility for children with cerebral palsy. It is important that skills are transferred from the therapist to the parents or carers and from them to anyone caring for the child. Treatment begins with an initial assessment at the Bobath Centre in London.

DOMAN-DELACATO THERAPY (PATTERNING)

Doman-Delacato therapy claims that it is possible to treat the brain itself. Undamaged portions of the brain are taught to take over the function of the damaged part. The basic assumption behind the therapy is that mobility can be achieved through movement. This movement cannot occur spontaneously and must be initiated from the outside by other people. Movement must be frequent, intense and repetitive. Teams of volunteers put the child through a set of movements for between three and eight hours a day. Not surprisingly the child often protests at this and Doman-Delacato is consequently a controversial therapy.

CONDUCTIVE EDUCATION

According to Dr Mari Hari, a leading proponent, conductive education is 'a method of enabling "the motor impaired" to function in society without requiring special apparatus such as wheelchairs, ramps or other artificial aids.' It is based on the theory that under the right conditions the central nervous system will restructure itself.

Conductors, or therapists, use *orthofunction,* a teaching method that involves the whole person physically and mentally and 'instils in children the ability to function as members of society, and to participate in normal social settings appropriate to their age'. Conductive education offers a positive approach to a clear set of goals. It has produced results beyond the expectations of professionals and parents of children with cerebral palsy and spina bifida. It should be remembered, however, that the treatment places emphasis on adapting individuals rather than environments. It follows a medical, not a social, model of disability.

CHECK!

1 Check that you understand the roles of the professionals involved with disabled children in the health, education and social services.
2 What is the function of the Department of Social Security?
3 What are the roles and functions of voluntary organisations who are concerned with disabled children and their families?
4 Give brief explanations of the following learning and therapy programmes: Portage, Bobath technique, Doman-Delacato therapy, conductive education.

THINK!

1 What are the advantages and disadvantages of the learning and therapy programmes described above?

Key terms

You need to understand what these words and phrases mean. Go back through the chapter and find out.

Diagnosis	Statutory protection duties
Developmental checks	Advocate
Motor development	Domiciliary care
Independent life skills	Family aid
Non-threatening adult	Welfare benefits
Behaviour modification	Pioneering
Learning and therapy programmes	Innovative
Maximise learning potential	Self-help groups
Statemented children	Portage
Observe/monitor/liaise/record/refer	Bobath technique
Curriculum	Doman-Delacato therapy
Welfare duties	Conductive education

Bibliography and further reading

John Bowlby, *Maternal Care and Mental Health*, World Health Organization, Geneva, 1951

L and J Braga, Learning *and Growing: A Guide to Child Development*, Spectrum Books, Prentice Hall Inc, Englewood Cliffs, New Jersey, 1975

Cliff Cunningham and Hilton Davis, *Working with Parents*, Open University Press, 1985

G C Davenport, *An Introduction to Child Development*, Unwin Hyman Ltd, 15–17 Broadwick St, London, 1988

Vera Fahlberg, *Child Development*, British Agencies for Adoption, 1982

Barbara Furneaux, *Special Parents*, Open University Press, 1988

S Gregory and S Barlow, *Interaction between Deaf Babies and their Deaf and Hearing Mothers*, in B Wolls, *Language Development and Sign Language*, Monograph 1, International Sign Linguistics Association, 1989

ed. Michael Haralambous, *Sociology: A New Approach*, Causeway Press Ltd, 1983

Claudia Jewett, *Helping Children Cope with Separation and Loss*, Batsford, 1984

Jill Krementz, *How it Feels when a Parent Dies*, Victor Gollancz, 1986

C Lee, *The Growth and Development of Children*, Longman, 1969

Micheline Mason, *Inclusion: The Way Forward*, in *Starting Points: 15 Practical Guides for Early Years Workers*, Voluntary Organisations Liaison Council for Under 5s, 1993

Stephen Moore, *Sociology Alive!*, Stanley Thornes, 1993

Jenny Morris, *Pride Against Prejudice*, The Women's Press, 1991

M K Pringle, *The Needs of Children (3rd Edition)*, Unwin Hyman Ltd, 15–17 Broadwick St, London, 1975

C I Sandstrom, *The Psychology of Childhood and Adolescence, (2nd Edition)*, Penguin Books Ltd, Harmondsworth, Middlesex, 1968

Richard Woolfson, *Children with Special Needs*, Faber and Faber Ltd, 1991

John Swain, Vic Finkelstein, Sally French and Mike Oliver, *Disabling Barriers – Enabling Environments*, Open University Sage Publications, 1981

The Children Act (1989) Guidance and Regulations: Volume 6: Children with Disabilities, HMSO, 1989

Signposts To Special Needs, National Children's Bureau, NES Arnold

INDEX

reinforcement 123
reproductive organs
  female 12
  male 12
residential care 209, 274, 275, 276
residential care officers 281
respite care 175
responsibility 158
retinitis pigmentosa 102, 255
rewards 160, 259
rhesus factor 99
rhesus incompatibility 245
Robertsons 205, 207
role play 35, 161, 180
role model 273
rooting reflex 28
Royal National Institute for the Deaf 252
Royal National Institute for the Blind 256
rubella 95, 245, 251, 255
Rutter, Michael 208

schema 139
schizophrenia 102
school nurse 279
scrotum 12
security 156
self advocacy 260
self image 166, 174, 180, 184, 186, 195, 262
semen 14
seminal vesicle 12
sensory impairment 175, 176, 271
sensory motor 140 141
separation 205, 210
sequence of development 75
services 268
sex-linked inheritance 93, 94
shunt 252
siblings 261
sickle cell anaemia 254
Skinner, B.F. 111, 123
skull 3, 5
smoking 9, 10, 97

social security 281
social role 167
social worker 280
social status 170, 172
social model 238, 270
socialisation 148, 160, 162, 164
solitary play 227
spasticity 245
Spastics Society 245
special needs 241, 257, 264
Special Care Baby Unit (SCUBU) 18
speech therapist 279
sperm 12, 14, 90
spina bifida 102, 255
spinal cord 16
stages of development 220
standing 39, 41
startle (moro) reflex 29
statement of special educational needs 265, 266
statutory duty 265
stereotyping 168, 171, 185
stimulus 26
stranger anxiety 177, 199, 223
subconscious 109
substitute care 207
sucking reflex 28
supine 26, 30, 32, 36, 38
support teacher 280
support assistant 280
support agencies 243–6
symbolic thought 108
symbolic play 134
symmetrical 26
syphilis 96

talking with children 127
tantrums 228, 230
term (pregnancy) 98
terminology 239
testes 12, 104
tetanus 104
thalassaemia 102
thalidomide 97
therapy programmes 282
thymic hormone 104

thymus 104
thyroid 103, 104
thyroxine 103, 104
toilet training 77
tonsils 105
toxaemia 96, 97, 245
toxoplasmosis 96
transitions 109, 168, 208, 212, 213
trial and error learning 137

ultra sound scan 17
umbilical cord 15, 16
urethra 12
urine 12
uterus 12, 13, 15

vagina 12
vas deferens 12
vascular 13
ventouse 101
ventral suspension 26, 77
  neonate 27
  1 month 30
  3 months 33
vernix 18
villi 15
visual impairment 255–6
voluntary organisations 271, 281
Vygotsky, Lev Semyonovich 10, 123, 143

walking 23
walking reflex 29
Warnock report 261
whooping cough 104
World Health Organisation (WHO) 102
writing 116

x chromosome 90, 91, 93

y chromosome 90, 91, 93

zone of proximal development 10, 143